Brave Love 365

Daily Inspiration, Validation, and Support for Survivors of Narcissistic Abuse and Toxic Relationships

Erika Nelson, MAC

Trigger Warning: This book discusses sensitive topics including sexual, emotional, mental, and physical abuse, childhood abuse and neglect, self-harm, and suicide.

It is recommended that you have a support system in place while working through the contents of this book, including a medical or mental health professional, if necessary.

This book is for educational purposes only. It is not intended as a substitute for the professional advice or treatment of a licensed mental health professional or medical doctor. It is not intended to provide medical or mental health advice, counseling, or treatment of any kind, nor is it to be used for diagnostic purposes. Reading this book does not constitute a client/counselor therapeutic relationship with the author of this book as defined by law or ethics. This book does not render financial, legal, or other professional advice or services. If expert advice is needed, the services of a competent professional should be sought. Neither the author nor the publisher shall be liable or responsible for any damages arising from the use of this book.

This book is a work of nonfiction. Nonetheless, people and situations appearing in these pages are composites of a number of individuals and their experiences. Any resemblance to persons living or dead is entirely coincidental and unintentional. At the time of initial publication, the URLs displayed in this book link or refer to existing websites on the internet. Inward Press, LLC is not responsible for changes that occur after publication.

Copyright © 2022 Erika Nelson.

Editing: Jenn Kosh and Anna Frolik

Design: Anna Frolik

Published in the United States **by Inward Press**, LLC. erikanelson.com

For information regarding permissions, write to: erika@erikanelson.com.

All rights reserved. No portion of this book may be reproduced, stored in a retrieval system, distributed, or transmitted in any form or by any means, including photocopying, recording, or other electronic or mechanical methods, without prior written permission of the publisher, except in the case of brief quotations embodied in articles and reviews.

ISBN: 979-8-9863625-0-2 (paperback)

ISBN: 979-8-9863625-1-9 (hardcover)

ISBN: 979-8-9863625-2-6 (ebook)

This book is dedicated to all the courageous people who are in the process of forging a relationship with themselves—as you find your voice, realize your value, own your inherent power, shine your light, and change the world by refusing to shrink to make others comfortable.

This book is also dedicated to my beautiful mother, Judith Ann Olson, who is supporting me and cheering me on from above, and who I wish could have had this book when she needed it most.

The Invitation

On a blustery fall day that held a deep chill, the wind churned Lake Michigan into wild waves and ushered the last of the vibrant autumn leaves to the ground. Feeling as gray as the fast-moving clouds blowing through, I sank back into my therapist's couch, devastated and empty, after willingly turning my life upside down. I'd left a relationship with the person I had loved with all my heart—even more than I'd loved myself.

I soon learned that was a big part of the problem.

Intuitively, I knew that leaving was a matter of saving my life although I couldn't yet articulate or fully understand why. While it broke my heart to walk away, some part of me knew that I'd already been abandoned at every level that mattered even though my partner had still been physically present.

As I heard the words *narcissist* and *narcissistic abuse* leave my therapist's mouth, I listened with rapt attention. She brought to light the abusive nature of the actions and words my ex-partner had chosen, things that I'd just accepted, never really understanding their impact on me.

I was left with a sense of bewilderment. I had two bachelor's degrees, a master's degree in counseling, and I was a therapist myself. *How had I missed this?*

In hindsight, that moment proved to be a graphic reference point for the subtle nature and societal lack of awareness of narcissistic abuse.

After that session, I watched many YouTube videos posted by other therapists and survivors. Hearing words that described the things I'd been through released me from a solitary prison of confusion, anxiety, and pain. I'd been set free!

I discovered that other people had experienced narcissistic abuse too, and I felt relieved to know that I wasn't alone or crazy. Best of all, I discovered that the problems in the relationship weren't all my fault, nor were they due to my "inadequacies" as I'd been conditioned to believe.

However, even though I now understood what narcissistic abuse was, as a testament to its insidious and addictive nature, I walked back into the relationship for several months, a decision that resulted in further abuse.

After pulling myself out of the relationship again, my head and life spinning, I vowed to write a book informed by my experiences to help other survivors of narcissistic abuse and toxic relationships understand what I had missed along the way—and offer them support and validation in the process of freeing themselves.

First, I began my own healing journey. As I forged a relationship with myself and reviewed my life, I came to realize that I'd been a victim of narcissistic abuse since childhood, beginning with one of my parents. After leaving my childhood home, I always had a narcissist in my life holding that familiar, dysfunctional space.

The intensity and nature of the narcissistic abuse I'd experienced with my ex-partner reopened all my wounds from the abuse and neglect I'd endured in the past, giving me the opportunity to heal what I'd so carefully stored away and avoided but which continued to live deep inside of me.

I did things with the narcissist that went against my character and values. I neglected the people and things in my life that were important to me.

After the relationship ended, I sobbed, screamed, sang, danced, and breathed the pain of the past out of my cells, committed to healing while prioritizing my self-care.

I've experienced miracles on this journey, the greatest of which is peace, something I hadn't known in my life until I began the healing process.

In the fall of 2021, after much inner work and healing, I intuitively felt pulled to put my work as a trauma therapist aside and write the book that had been forming within me. The day after my work with clients was complete, the entire outline for this book poured out of me in a matter of hours.

Writing each entry wasn't nearly as simple, however. Much emotional and even physical pain arose as I delved into my personal experiences as well as those of other survivors who shared their stories with me, capturing in words the true essence of the experience we lived through during narcissistic abuse.

Though my professional credentials are important in offering insights into how to recognize and heal from narcissistic abuse in intimate relationships, I have also walked the road you're walking. I hold great understanding of and compassion for your journey of recovery.

While narcissistic abuse can happen with anyone—your parents, spouse, siblings, a friend, boss, colleague, spiritual teacher, or even a counselor, this book addresses intimate partner narcissistic abuse. The information that follows can be applied to other relationships and types of abuse as well.

In addition, the information in this book can offer support to those who have been in toxic relationships whether their partner met the criteria of being a narcissist or not. Abuse is abuse no matter what label we put on those who hurt us.

Brave Love 365 is a nurturing companion on your healing journey. Whether you are newly out of your abusive relationship or further along in the healing process, this book offers validation for your feelings, thoughts, and experiences.

It also offers inspiration and an invitation to delve deeper into the spiritual truths within you. It asks questions to guide you gently inward while encouraging you to connect with yourself and with God and the Unseen Support around you. It creates space for you to initiate a conversation with your soul, where your wisdom, remedies, and answers lie within you. The support that this book offers can help you propel yourself into a creative, soul-inspired life filled with peace and joy.

In addition, it offers educational information and reference points from other survivors' experiences to help you become more familiar with narcissistic abuse and its red flags, diminishing your susceptibility to it in the future.

There is no right or wrong way to use this book.

Honoring yourself *exactly where you're at* is the most important focus in the process of doing this work. If you're just getting started on your journey of healing from narcissistic abuse, you may receive the greatest benefit by starting on January 1st, regardless of the actual date.

Some of you may appreciate the continuity and predictability of reading the entry that corresponds with each consecutive day's date, or you may use the index at the back to find a topic that fits your needs.

You may also find value in using this book as a tool to assist in developing and trusting your intuition. By tuning into your inner guidance, you can go to the page number of the daily entry you're drawn to read and receive its messages.

Brave Love 365 will not provide you with "the answers." Instead, it will give you much to consider as you access the answers that lie within you.

It also doesn't define the right or wrong way to get through the healing process after narcissistic abuse *because there isn't one*. Nor is there a correct or incorrect way to feel, think, or be, as we are each on our own journey, honoring our individual path.

A creative tool you may consider incorporating into your use of this book is a journal. Putting your thoughts and feelings on paper can be a powerful way to help you engage more deeply with the questions and the prompts offered within these pages.

Daily entries invite you to explore yourself and your life. Your exploration may involve a quick thought about the subject, an hour spent journaling, a day of contemplation, a conversation with your counselor, or any other way that works for you. You get to decide how deep you're ready to go with your focus on honoring your needs in the process.

Brave Love 365 can be a useful tool on your healing journey for many years to come, allowing you to circle back around and delve deeper into subjects you weren't ready to explore your first time through. You can also revisit topics that you processed earlier, providing a reference point of how far you've come.

So what is Brave Love, you might be wondering?

It's a daring love that's born within us as we come to recognize the truth of who we are. As we show up for ourselves over time, lovingly and compassionately being present to all that is happening within us while prioritizing our self-care, we find ourselves shaking off the expectations of others and rejecting the false ideas we've taken on about ourselves. We become fiercely committed to creating space for ourselves to fully exist in our life.

As we cultivate this love for ourselves, we become one with our Source, whose love fills us up completely. Approaching life from this place of wholeness, we find that the judgments of others have little impact on us. We cultivate the courage to inhabit ourselves so completely that our knowledge of ourselves and our inherent value is nearly unshakable. Connected with our soul's wisdom, we no longer settle for less than we deserve, living our lives according to our highest good.

When we live from a place of Brave Love, our light inspires others to do the same.

In this book and in my life, my goal is to hold the focus and energy of love in every situation.

Why is that?

Because I want a different world than the one we currently inhabit—for myself and my children. I want to participate in creating a world in which we're empowered and connected by our similarities instead of being divided by the discrimination, separation, and polarization that we've always had and which have escalated greatly.

To live with integrity, I cannot lose sight of the fact that the narcissist is also a human being who was created by Source. I work to hold as much love in my heart as I can for those so completely disconnected from themselves and Source, respecting to the best of my ability the knowledge of our true soul connection. I do this without abandoning myself or forgetting their destructive, impactful behaviors and while maintaining firm boundaries and No Contact with the narcissists that I've had in my life. I will call out their behaviors that disempower, loudly, if necessary, to empower those affected by them. But I will not "trash" narcissists or anyone else.

Some may believe that I'm protecting narcissists or minimizing the effects of their destruction with this focus on love. Some may even assume that I've never seen the shattered lives that narcissists leave behind. In truth, I have experienced the death of someone I loved dearly, who was no longer able to carry their own pain and inner challenges along with the narcissist's pressure and judgment. They chose to end their life, something that changed mine forever. I do know the searing pain and rippling effects that the narcissist's horrific and sometimes deadly behavior causes...and still I choose love, accompanied by strong, safe, solid boundaries.

It's my hope that this book holds a space of connection for you day by day. Many people have walked this journey before you, and many are walking it with you at this very moment. Let the collective energy of our healing and the reclamation of our authentic value and power support you as you pull yourself out of the past and into a new life.

It's also my hope that this book serves as encouragement to help you develop a strong sense of self-love and a consistent, stable self-care focus and routine so that you will never again allow another human being to treat you in a way that injures you.

Above all, perhaps the most important goal of this book is to support you in having love, compassion, and understanding for yourself as you go through this process of discovery and recovery.

I see your courage and invite you in as you embark upon this sacred healing journey.

Erika

January 1

The Basics

Our relationship is over. We're broken and unsure if we'll even make it through this. Now is the time to focus on the basics:

Food. Some of us are too overwhelmed to even think about food. For others, food is the only source of comfort available during this unbearable time. Either way, we must be gentle with ourselves, knowing we'll do our best to give our body the fuel it needs.

Sleep. If we're unable to sleep, we can try a warm drink before bed, soothing music, a guided meditation, relaxation exercise, or even a gentle walk. We can also try keeping our bedroom temperature cooler and making it as dark as possible. Some of us may feel like we could sleep all day. We're exhausted at every level, and we may need extra sleep right now.

Safety. If our safety is in jeopardy, whether because of the narcissist or our own desire to harm ourselves, *it's essential to reach out for support.* We can contact our local law enforcement agency, our local domestic abuse organization or crisis center, a friend or family member we trust, or one of the resources at the back of this book. There is confidential support available from non-judgmental people who are ready to help us remain safe, no matter what our situation is.

Today, I will focus on meeting my basic needs. I will be kind to myself, knowing that I'm doing my best to get through this.

January 2

Support Team

After the narcissistic abuse relationship ends, we may feel emotionally overwhelmed and physically drained, unsure of which way to turn after our life is upended. One of the most powerful steps we can take is to create a solid support system around ourselves. This team of supportive people could include:

Family and Friends. We can ask for support from the family members and friends we feel safe with, even if we distanced ourselves from them while we were with the narcissist.

Counselor/Psychologist. We can reach out for professional support. It's helpful to find those who are familiar with narcissistic abuse and are trained in working with trauma. They can hold a safe space for us while we explore our experiences with the narcissist.

Community Resources. It's helpful to locate our available community resources. These may include economic support, public health, family services, legal support, child protection, behavioral health, domestic violence support, and crisis services.

Telephone Hotlines and Text Support. These services, many of which are provided by professionals, can be helpful when we prefer anonymous support or when we aren't sure which step to take next.

Though we may feel isolated and fearful that no one will understand what we're going through, support is available, and we can lovingly create a team around ourselves.

Today, I will think about the sources of support that feel right to me. I will take at least one step toward creating my team.

January 3

Awareness of Narcissistic Abuse

Remember how it felt when we heard the term *narcissistic abuse* for the first time? When we realized there were words for the indescribable torment and pain we'd gone through? Many of us felt set free when we discovered there was a name for it and that everything wasn't actually our fault.

It's said that if a frog is thrown into a pot of boiling water, it will immediately jump out, knowing that conditions are unsafe. If that frog is instead placed in a pot of water that is slowly warmed up to a boil, unaware of what's happening, it won't leave the pot. This is a perfect metaphor for understanding how we—smart, successful, loving, empathic people—were swept up into a narcissistic abuse relationship and accepted things we never would have prior to the narcissist's skillful manipulation that drew us in.

Awareness of narcissistic abuse allows us to begin taking steps toward our freedom and empowerment and gives us the ability to find the right tools to help us heal. We've been through a devastating form of abuse, and it's important to remember that there is support available to us.

Today, I will be patient, compassionate, and gentle with myself as I embark on or continue my healing journey after narcissistic abuse. I will remember that I only need to take things one step at a time, and that it's perfectly fine for me to rest when I need to.

January 4

Discretion

The information we learn about narcissistic abuse can be incredibly freeing for many of us. Often, we want to go back and share it with the narcissist for the following reasons:

1. To *prove* that what they did was horrible and destructive.
2. Because we're so relieved that there's a name for the hell we lived through—and that everything wasn't actually our fault.
3. Because we want to clobber them with the truth as a payback for abusing us.
4. Because we hope they will get help and we can be together again.
5. All of the above.

Going back to the narcissist and telling them that they are a personality disordered individual may not have the outcome we intended.

They may react strongly, jeopardizing our safety. They may use it against us and play the victim in situations such as a court proceeding where much is at stake. It's best to continue moving forward, letting the truth of the situation empower us without involving them. Our changed behavior will speak for itself.

Today, I will honor the wounded children within me that want to hit the narcissist with the truth. I will release those feelings of anger and helplessness in a way that's safe and works for me. I will use the new information to launch myself forward into the authentic life of my dreams.

January 5

Empowering Choices

After our relationship with the narcissist ends, there are many empowering choices we can make to help ourselves get back on our feet, moving forward once again.

We can set boundaries and make our life a safe space in which to heal, cutting off contact with the narcissist by blocking their phone number or changing our own. We can also block them in our social media and email accounts.

We can eat the foods we desire and wear the clothing we feel comfortable in.

We can reconnect with the people we've distanced ourselves from, who were somehow not good enough for the narcissist. We can spend time with the people we care about and expand our support system.

We can move forward with the new job or career that got put aside while we were with the narcissist.

We can do the things that we enjoy doing, reclaiming our autonomy and supporting our authentic self.

Today, I will consider the choices I could make that would empower and support me in moving myself and my life forward.

January 6

Narcissistic Supply

Narcissistic supply is the energy that the narcissist extracts from others and which they use to regulate their fragile self-esteem. Any reaction from the people who are their sources of narcissistic supply, positive or negative, feeds the narcissist and lets them know they exist.

Narcissists believe that who they are isn't enough to allow them to be accepted and get their needs met. To survive, they create a false persona and exile their true self, which leaves them disconnected from Source and the living energy that fuels us all. Afterwards, they often feel resentful and entitled, believing that others should meet their needs and become their source.

In the beginning, the narcissist showered us with their energy and attention, drawing us in deeper until they knew their source of narcissistic supply was secure. Then, they gave less and increased the opportunities to extract our energy through their triggering and devaluation of us. The abusive cycle continued until we were depleted, and they moved on to their next source of supply.

We worked diligently to meet the narcissist's needs in hopes that they would meet ours. Now, we no longer have to carry the burden of another's needs on our shoulders, as they are responsible for meeting their own needs. We are much more than just a "needs meeter."

Today, I will examine my life to see if there are other relationships in which I'm still living out the pattern of being a "needs meeter."

January 7

Narcissistic Abuse Cycle

The narcissistic abuse cycle began with the **idealization phase**. The narcissist created fantasies about our potential while pretending to already love everything about us. We were so enamored with them that we missed their subtle attempts to change us as they tried to realize their fantasies.

When the narcissist knew we were hooked, the **devaluation phase** began. The desire to change us was no longer subtle, and we were criticized and diminished when we didn't meet their expectations. Our pain and hurt made the narcissist feel powerful and provided them with the narcissistic supply they needed. After devaluing us, they offered us crumbs of affection to ensure we didn't leave. We believed the person we fell in love with still existed, so we tried to improve ourselves and give the relationship more time.

Finally, we moved into the **discard phase**. The narcissist abandoned us without a thought, seeking a new source of narcissistic supply. Even if we left the narcissist, they'd likely already discarded us and lacked the integrity to own up to it, afraid of looking bad, and feeling relief when we left. Afterwards, they may have used their hoovering tactic to suck us back in, sometimes all the way, other times just far enough so we were there if they ever lacked narcissistic supply.

Today, I will be proud of myself for my hard work of learning, growing, and healing. I know that education and awareness lead to empowerment and freedom.

January 8

Aftershock

Although we were often overwhelmed with grief when the narcissistic abuse relationship ended, many of us had felt stuck for so long that we couldn't wait to hit the ground running again in our own life.

Unfortunately, this is often when the exhaustion and depletion from narcissistic abuse finally hits us. We experience aftershock—an unexpected, unwelcome, and sometimes disabling phenomenon.

Once separated from the narcissist, our brain began to crave the chemicals it was showered with during the highs and lows of the narcissistic abuse cycle, which formed the toxic trauma bond between us and our abuser. The lack of those chemicals made us yearn for the narcissist. In truth, what we craved were the chemicals.

Aftershock is normal, and it's important to seek support from others at this tender time. Healing options can include 12-Step programs like Al-Anon or Co-Dependents Anonymous, the National Domestic Violence Hotline (www.thehotline.org), local community resources, and mental health professionals familiar with narcissistic abuse.

We can gain strength from the energy of all the survivors of narcissistic abuse who have gone before us and who learned to manage the chemical cravings, exhaustion, and other disruptive symptoms of aftershock.

Today, if I find myself experiencing the painful effects of aftershock, I will focus on getting my physical needs met first, prioritizing safety, sleep, and nourishment. Then I'll take the healing process one moment at a time, remembering that it won't always feel this bad.

January 9

Our True Source

Initially, the narcissist led us to believe that they would fulfill all our unmet needs, present and past, and be everything we'd ever desired.

Then, they broke us down mentally, physically, and emotionally, isolating us from our support system with their abusive behavior and making us dependent upon them. As we spiraled deeper into their abusive vortex, in essence, they became our source. We clung to the very person who was pulling us apart.

Our true Source created us, supports us, and knows how to heal us. It is within our connection to Source's love and grace that we are soothed and restored, remembering who we truly are.

After the narcissistic abuse relationship ended, many of us felt like we'd completely lost our spiritual connection and support. Though the flame of Source's energy within us may dim, it can never be extinguished.

When we quiet ourselves, bringing our focus within to where the connection with Source lies, we will find a love that fills us up completely and supports us in meeting our own needs. To sense and connect with Source's energy, we can hold a hand over our heart, feeling our heartbeat while sensing the awesome power and intelligence making that possible.

Today, I will take time to be still, listening for the thunder in the silence as I connect with my Source.

January 10

Excruciating Pain

The pain we endure while in a narcissistic relationship is incomprehensible to someone who hasn't experienced it, and the pain that comes after it can be even worse. It's the pain of all the wounds from the relationship, as well as the traumas of our past, triggered by the abuse. At times, we wonder if we'll survive it.

Narcissists blast through our defenses, getting into the places inside of us that we've never allowed anyone to enter before, leaving us completely vulnerable. It's important to be gentle and compassionate with ourselves while working to survive this pain and taking steps to heal.

First, we need to ensure that our basic needs are met. Once they are, we must take what we're going through seriously. We can reach out for professional support, work with a healing method that feels safe and aligned, or talk to a trusted friend or family member. We do not have to do this alone.

Declaring our willingness to heal initiates a process within us. As we become willing to face what's inside of us, the steps of our healing journey are revealed one at a time.

Today, I will ask Source to give me strength at this vulnerable time and to heal all that has been uncovered within me. I will remember that my life is meant to be about much more than chaos and pain, and that I have new, inspiring experiences ahead of me.

January 11

Suicide and Self-Harm

Before experiencing narcissistic abuse, many of us coped with mental health challenges due to past trauma. Narcissistic abuse resurrected our old wounds and created new ones. We often lacked the tools to deal with the strong emotions arising within us in a healthy, safe manner.

As our internal pain became unbearable, some of us tried to externalize it in a tangible way through self-harm. Perhaps we cut or burned ourselves, drank to excess, used harmful substances, over- or under-ate, or engaged in unsafe sexual behavior. We often felt our injuries or out-of-control behavior offered proof of the depth of our pain to ourselves and to others whose acknowledgement and support we needed.

Others chose to end their lives, unable to find a way out of the painful abuse that clouded their vision, sapped their strength, and told them lies about themselves.

Things can and will get better. With support, we can find a safe, loving way to keep going. There are healing resources available in the back of this book. We are not alone.

Today, I will remember that there are people who love me so much they would literally move mountains to help me get through this. Some of them I may not even know yet. I will trust that there are good things waiting for me, and I won't judge myself for my challenging thoughts or feelings because I know I'm doing the best I can.

January 12

Trauma Bond

A trauma bond is the relentless connection we have with our abuser. It lives in our brain and is caused by the addictive cocktail of chemicals released during the wild highs and lows of narcissistic abuse. The pain is as addictive as the exhilarating relief we feel when the narcissist begins to dole out crumbs of affection afterwards.

When we try to free ourselves from the narcissist, we may feel like an addict coming off hard drugs, feeling lost and empty when we imagine a life without them. The highs are so high that we stay, working hard to recreate them.

Some indicators of the presence of a trauma bond are:

- Knowing it's bad between us and our partner but being unable to leave—excusing and defending their behavior to others.
- Withholding details about the abuse from others to protect the narcissist, believing that people will only see the bad in them when we know the good.
- Trying to love them enough to help them return to being who they were in the beginning.
- Even after the relationship ends, they are still "in our heads" and interrupting our lives, leaving us unable to stop thinking about and yearning for them.

Today, I will assess whether the trauma bond is still alive in my brain. I will have patience with myself and will lovingly accept myself right where I'm at, no matter how long it takes me to fully break the trauma bond.

January 13

No Contact

Cutting ties with the narcissist and refusing to have any contact with them is referred to as "going No Contact." Establishing No Contact is a non-negotiable step we must take to heal from narcissistic abuse and find peace. The narcissist is an expert at whisking us back into their vortex—and their bed—before we even realize what's happening.

The following steps will support our efforts:

- Block the narcissist's phone number and remove their contact information from our phone, or change our own phone number.
- Block them and their harem on social media.
- Create an "I WILL NOT CALL" list that includes all the instances of the narcissist's hurt and betrayal we can think of. If we're on the verge of breaking No Contact, we can read this list to remind us why we established it in the first place.
- Refrain from driving by the narcissist's home or engaging with them if they drive by ours.
- Switch coffee shops, decline social events, or whatever measures are necessary to maintain No Contact.
- Continue our inner work.

If we break No Contact, it's important to be gentle with ourselves and remember that letting go is a process. In an instant, we can reestablish No Contact, get back on our feet, and keep moving forward.

Today, I will work on my I WILL NOT CALL list and remember that maintaining No Contact is the most precious gift I can give myself at this time.

January 14

The Narcissist's Vortex

The motion of a vortex creates suction whether it's a swirling body of air, water, fire, or energy.

The narcissist's insatiable needs create a magnetic vortex around them. With their seductive words and actions and our lack of a firm foundation beneath us, they easily swept us up into their wildly swirling, delusional reality.

The narcissist's vortex was also able to suck us in after the relationship ended. With the psychic connection between us still firmly in place, they could extract our energy without even being present with us. Every time we drove by their house or looked them up on social media, we reconnected ourselves to their vortex, feeding them our precious energy.

One survivor shared the moment they recognized the narcissist's vortex: "After being out of the relationship and working hard to heal, my wounds were still bigger than my developing foundation, and I decided to give the relationship another try. I was more aware this time but still susceptible. When I decided to step fully back into the relationship, I instantly felt the vortex creep in. The narcissist's needs were like a heavy blanket wrapped tightly around me, suffocating me and extracting my life force. I was swirling again. It was a feeling I couldn't deny. I ended the relationship and felt my freedom and life force return instantly."

Today, I will check my foundation. With my inner wisdom, I will determine what is needed to further strengthen it.

January 15

Our Precious Inner Children

There is a wealth of information available about our inner child. I propose to you a slightly different angle on that concept, focusing instead on our inner *children*.

Many of us endured traumatic, overwhelming experiences as children that we weren't mentally or emotionally able to process. If we lacked supportive adults to help us work through them, parts of us "got stuck" at that age holding the trauma, unable to integrate into our growing system of self.

As a result, our inner child may be represented in different ages and stages within us. We may have a frightened three-year-old, a perfectionistic five-year-old, and a wild teenager inside, all needing our support.

When present experiences trigger the traumas that our inner children hold, their reactions can project loudly into our consciousness, drowning out our soul's voice as they attempt to make their needs known.

Having an unexpected outburst of anger that we later regret, waking up completely overwhelmed with life, or suddenly feeling like a failure can be examples of our inner children's presence, holding the memories that act as the keys to freeing ourselves from our past.

Today, I will consider whether strong feelings within me are coming from my inner children. If they are, I will use the opportunity to connect with them and create space for them to voice their feelings and needs, providing them with the love, reassurance, and care they need.

January 16

Susceptibility

We were smart, successful people, yet we fell prey to the narcissist's manipulation. Does that mean we were weak? Or just plain stupid?

Absolutely not! There were powerful reasons it happened.

Initially, we were like a trophy to the narcissist. Later, the stronger we were, the further we fell as they toyed with us and broke us down. Our decline made them feel powerful and increased their self-esteem.

There were also other influential factors that assisted the narcissist's efforts to manipulate and control us:

- Wounds we held inside from past trauma left us yearning to have our needs met, something we hadn't learned to do for ourselves yet. The narcissist promised to meet them.
- We were attracted to what was familiar to us—abuse and neglect.
- We easily trusted and chose to see the good in the narcissist, overlooking or excusing their dark side.
- We had high levels of empathy and compassion, and we wanted to help the narcissist heal.
- We were honest, and they used our honesty against us.
- We had trouble setting boundaries, giving the narcissist free reign in our lives.
- We were resilient from past abuse, making us strong and able to take more abuse.

Today, I will explore why I was susceptible to the narcissist's manipulation. I will identify, with love and compassion, which inner children within me needed what the narcissist appeared to offer, and I will work to meet those needs.

January 17

Triangulation

Triangulation is a form of manipulation used by narcissists: They insert a third person between us and them—physically, mentally, or emotionally—threatening us with exclusion or abandonment and triggering our insecurity. At the root of the narcissist's behavior is their own insecurity.

Our narcissistic partner may have flirted with other people in front of us or used their past partners against us, mentioning flirtatious texts or photos they received from them, which they somehow always made sure we saw.

Their actions served to create drama in our relationship, which left us off balance, questioning our worth. The narcissist often remained in close contact with the third person, creating a situation in which we had to continually fight for them, leaving us feeling insecure in the relationship.

The ability to elicit a reaction from us gave the narcissist a sense of power—after they had undermined ours—gaining the upper hand in our relationship. Our insecurity made us easier to manipulate into doing things we wouldn't have done otherwise.

The frustration and betrayal we felt as we repeatedly tried to make the narcissist understand that their behavior was inappropriate and hurtful drained us and provided them with a great deal of narcissistic supply. Sometimes they even defended the third person, further betraying us.

Today, I will look at the ways that the narcissist, or anyone else, used triangulation to manipulate me. I will use this information to empower myself so I don't fall prey to it again.

January 18

Grounding

Grounding ourselves by using our breath and awareness to bring us back to the present moment can be especially helpful in our healing from narcissistic abuse. Each time we bring ourselves back to the present, we calm our body and mind, reminding ourselves that we're safe in this very moment, and that we're not in a traumatic moment from our past.

There are many ways we can use our breath and senses to ground ourselves and return to a space of inner calmness and truth. Here are some examples:

- Walk barefoot on the ground to reconnect with Earth's calming, nurturing energy.
- Breathe deeply and observe how our breath feels entering and leaving our body.
- Scan our body from head to toe, observing with curiosity what is happening inside. Are there areas of tension or heaviness? Are there colors or thoughts connected to the sensations?
- Count backwards slowly from 100.
- Repeat a calming affirmation: "Everything is okay." "I'm safe." "This feeling won't last forever."
- Sing a favorite song.
- Run cool water over our hands.
- Do something intellectual. Think of items in a category, such as different kinds of cars or movies we've enjoyed, or solve a math problem.

Today, I will check in with myself to see if I feel grounded and whether or not I need to commit or recommit to a grounding practice that supports me in being right here, right now.

January 19

Relapse

After our relationship ended, we implemented No Contact. Then, the narcissist showed up at our front door, feigning concern about us and promising to love us forever. We fell back in.

Relapse is a normal part of recovery from narcissistic abuse. We're bound to the narcissist by a trauma bond in our brain until we heal the wounds that support it. We go back as many times as it takes until we're done. Even though a relapse will affect our life and our loved ones, it's important to remember that we're doing our best.

One survivor shared the story of their last relapse: *"I lost myself for a month, spinning crazily around the narcissist's vortex. When my illusions shattered once again, all the pent-up rage from the past abuse poured out of me in loud, angry words, directed right at my beautiful child. I felt intense shame, and I knew, right then and there, that I would never go back to the narcissist and risk that happening again. I was done."*

When we love and support ourselves after a relapse, we are miles ahead of where we'd be if we beat ourselves up. When we do, shame can easily overtake us, forcing us to deal with the shame of the present as well as that of the past.

Today, I will have great compassion with myself about any relapses I've had. If shame comes up, I will do my best not to get lost in it.

January 20

Willingness

There is incredible support and beauty in the flow of our healing work with Source. When we do our part, taking responsibility for ourselves and our life, we can hand the rest over to our Higher Power, and we will be shown, one step at a time, what we can do to heal.

Perhaps we have an idea of what we'd like to see change, but we don't know where to start. We don't have to know. All that's required is a connection to Source and our willingness to do what's necessary. Then we'll be shown the way.

For those of us stuck in a trauma bond with the narcissist, it can feel like there's no way out. How do we start healing when we can't even function? How do we get the narcissist out of our head, once and for all?

If we're willing to do the hard work to make it happen, we can declare that willingness to Source. Then, as we trust in the process, believing that we will free ourselves, the first step will appear.

Are we ready to create a life that reflects our authentic self? We can speak it into existence. When we do, the Universe sets in motion a process to assist us in making it so.

Today, I'll let Source know of my willingness. I will stay tuned and spend time in quiet stillness, listening for my next step and feeling the love and support of my Source.

January 21

Refusing to Engage

Sometimes, narcissists walk out of our lives and never look back, captivated by their new source of narcissistic supply. Other times, they attempt to draw us back in, hoping to avoid expending the energy it takes to love bomb and groom a new source.

To maintain our self-care, we can refuse to engage with the narcissist. The following are steps we can take to support that decision:

- We can choose to bypass the places we know the narcissist frequents.
- If someone comes to us with a "message" or "gift" from the narcissist, we can make it clear to them that we're not interested.
- We can decline invitations to events that we know the narcissist will be attending.
- If we have unexpected contact with the narcissist, we can refuse to speak to them or even make eye contact as we now have autonomy over our body, mind, and voice, and can decide what is needed to keep us safe and healthy.

Refusing to engage with the narcissist does not mean we're weak, arrogant, or living in fear. It is evidence of our love and commitment to ourselves and is the key to our forward movement and deep healing.

Today, I will remember that by refusing to engage with the narcissist, I am refusing chaos and abuse. Instead, I'm taking the steps to bring a sense of peace and wholeness into my life.

January 22

Truths and Values

Our truths and values are our road map to life, determining our wants and needs, boundaries in relationships, and the direction we want our lives to take.

If we didn't have room to exist as a child in a toxic family, or as an adult in a dysfunctional relationship, we may have no idea what our truths and values are since we've never considered them. When we're in survival mode, our truths and values take a back seat. Our focus moves to the things and people outside of ourselves that will determine whether we are safe, loved, hurt, or abandoned.

We can give ourselves the time and space to connect within, letting our soul whisper in our ear. As we discover what's true for us and what we value, we have all the information we need to create boundaries and make choices that lead to a beautiful life. Our soul's truth was always there, patiently waiting to direct our lives. Instead of floating through life according to others' whims, we can now chart and travel our own course.

Today, I will spend some time looking at what I value. To get clues about this, I can start by looking at what goes against my values. I will pay attention to what is important to me and to the truths about myself that I've overlooked for far too long.

January 23

Harem

The people that narcissists keep around as sources of narcissistic supply are referred to as their harem, which consists of former lovers and those who are starstruck with the narcissist's facade. The narcissist often used their harem members against us, glorifying them and diminishing us via triangulation, which left us devastated and the narcissist emboldened and empowered.

Because of the bad feelings they created between us and the people in their harem, we often felt more wounded by their harem members than we did by the narcissist's abuse. The narcissist counted on that, knowing we'd project our hurt and anger onto other people instead of risking their abandonment by putting our feelings right where they belonged—square on the narcissist's shoulders. Their use of triangulation also guaranteed that we wouldn't talk to their harem members, compare notes, and discover the narcissist's lies.

Though we have gentle hearts, some of us may be unable to let go of our anger or bad feelings toward the harem members. We can give ourselves grace because those feelings can sometimes be part of the PTSD that many victims develop after narcissistic abuse.

When we're ready, it can be helpful to understand that the harem members may be as wounded inside as we are, and like us, they're being manipulated by the narcissist.

Today, if I can't get past my anger and hurt toward the narcissist's harem members, I will support myself right where I'm at, knowing that I'm just not there yet.

January 24

Ambient Narcissistic Abuse

Angst is a feeling of agony, anxiety, or uneasiness that causes unimaginable distress. This feeling is very familiar to victims of ambient narcissistic abuse, which is a mysterious, agonizing process that defies words. This "invisible" type of abuse is so subtle and insidious that it seems impossible to identify or put words to it as it tears us apart and drains us of our inner resources. However, those who have experienced it will immediately recognize the limited descriptions we can offer.

We may have tried to address our feelings with our abuser, but as we reviewed the overwhelming, confusing situation for the hundredth time, we weren't sure what to say.

"Is the narcissist really doing anything bad?" we asked ourselves. We internalized our desperate assessment of the situation, thinking it must be something within us driving us crazy, a view that the narcissist was quick to reinforce.

There is a name for it. *It really was happening.* While the narcissist tried to convince us that we were broken, there was a destructive, insidious process going on "in the background."

Today, I will validate all the feelings I had while immersed in ambient narcissistic abuse. I will go inside and listen to everything my wounded inner children have to say, believing them and knowing that their feelings are valid. I will release any pent-up feelings I have about how I was treated, allowing them to move through me as I set myself free.

January 25

Modified Contact

Some of us must continue to communicate with the narcissist after the relationship ends because we share custody and placement of our children.

It's possible to do so without handing over our precious energy or falling prey to their manipulation tactics designed to seduce and control us or keep us afraid and disempowered. When we can't maintain No Contact, we can implement Modified Contact, maintaining strict boundaries around when and how we will engage with the narcissist.

We can investigate alternate ways to communicate with them, excluding the use of our cell phone and texting, which allows them the freedom to contact us at any time, and which keeps us always on guard. One option is email, which also comes to our phone but gives us control over when we open and read their messages. We can also communicate via a neutral third party or through parenting apps that not only facilitate communication, but document it. (See Resources.)

During our children's custody exchanges, we can set clear, firm boundaries. These could include not allowing the narcissist to enter our home and not discussing anything with them at the time of exchange, offering only a polite greeting. As our children get older, there is often no need for any contact during exchanges.

Today, if I must continue to communicate with the narcissist, I will determine the boundaries that are healthy for me and my children and investigate available communication options which support my sobriety and continued healing.

January 26

Making Changes

Some of us have tried making positive changes in our lives with little success. As an example, some of us struggle to reach a healthy weight.

In this example, our inner children may be fighting our efforts to change, perhaps feeling unworthy of being fit and feeling good, or unwilling to release the protection they feel the weight provides. When our inner children are supported and their needs are met, they often feel safer and will stop working against us.

We can also impede the process of change by not accepting ourselves. Judging ourselves harshly for being overweight and disliking our body can sabotage our best efforts to lose weight. Instead, imagine if we attempted this goal from a place of love and self-acceptance, creating an entirely different foundation on which to implement change.

Before making difficult changes, we can quiet ourselves and listen closely to what's happening within us. We may need to explore our thoughts and feelings or offer our inner children reassurance, information, love, and compassion to quell their fears. Especially those who don't want us to succeed. Then, our soul has more room to work in our lives.

Today, I will contemplate a change that I desire to make, paying attention to all that arises within me. I will look at any resistance with curiosity instead of judgment, and I will lovingly meet my inner children's needs. I will accept everything that I see as a perfect starting point for change.

January 27

Living Above Our Lives

One day, during an especially difficult time in my life, I was sitting by the water on a windy day, watching a seagull soar high overhead on the shifts of air. The bird seemed to float effortlessly in its own flow. I felt Jesus' energy close, and I heard, *"Live above your life."*

These words of wisdom have provided comfort ever since, always a great reminder to pull myself up and out of the human fray and return to the calm stillness of my own heart. From there, I can soar high above my life while being surrounded by Jesus' love and support, gaining a completely different perspective.

Today, I will remember to live above my life, seeing the bigger picture, especially when the human experience becomes challenging. I will also remember that I am always connected to my Source.

January 28

Revenge

Many of us have felt the desire to get sweet revenge on the narcissist after enduring horrendous abuse and being discarded without a thought as we watched them move immediately on to their next conquest. Our desire to hurt them as deeply as they hurt us is completely understandable, though potentially dangerous—and self-destructive.

First, we cannot "win" against a narcissist. Whatever hurt we send their way could come back to us, multiplied exponentially. They have weapons in their arsenal that could wound us in ways we never imagined possible until we get hit with them. We don't have the capacity to fight the way they do because we aren't disconnected from ourselves as they are.

Second, when we contemplate revenge, we continue to be engaged in the narcissist's vortex and are still feeding them narcissistic supply. Revenge is providing them what they crave...a big energetic reaction from us. The best "revenge" is to disengage completely from the narcissist.

When we want revenge, we can honor that feeling and take a moment to explore within. In truth, we are likely reeling from the raw, unfelt pain within us. When we acknowledge and release our feelings, the desire for revenge will often fade.

Today, I will remember that the highest and best use of my precious time, energy, and creativity is on myself. I will also remember that feeling and healing are my tickets to freedom and a beautiful life after narcissistic abuse.

January 29

Tethers

One summer, I grew a watermelon plant in a raised bed garden. The soil contained bits of wood not yet decayed, and the ground around the bed was covered in wood mulch. I watched as the delicate tendrils of the plant searched for something to attach to. They wrapped themselves around tiny, broken twigs, doing the best they could to secure themselves with what they had as they tethered themselves to the loose objects.

In our young lives, our first and most important tethers were forming, but many of us lacked stable caregivers to attach to. Similarly, in toxic relationships, we have tethered our tender selves to people that we believed or convinced ourselves were stable and solid—a costly illusion at times.

There was also an invasive vine that grew in my yard. It had completely taken over a formerly beautiful lilac bush. I cut the vines away, surprised to see how tightly their tethers wound around the branches, cutting deep into the surface of the bark.

As the vines fell to the ground, I felt the same freedom that comes when we cast off those people that wrap their tethers too tightly around us, overtaking us and overriding our true essence.

Today, I will pay attention to who and what I am tethered to, detaching from all that's not secure or healthy. I will look for solid, grounded people and things to tether to, especially my Source.

January 30

The Narcissist's Truths

If we separate narcissists from their aberrant thoughts and beliefs as well as their appalling behavior, at their core they have a true self that is connected to Source, just like we do. Many also have deep inner wounds like us. Instead of addressing those wounds and working to heal them, narcissists disown the part of themselves that holds those inner wounds...their true self. Their life is consumed by efforts to conceal themselves, manipulate people to believe their false self, and extract energy from them to survive.

Though it can be an important step in our healing process to see the truth of who the narcissist is at their core, it's much more important, especially during our recovery from narcissistic abuse, to see the truth of the narcissist's false self and recognize the danger that they present to our health and safety. Some people don't survive narcissistic abuse, and some that do are severely impacted for the rest of their lives unless they find effective support to heal.

When we're working to maintain No Contact and regain our health, it's critical to remember the devastating truth of how we were treated by the narcissist.

Today, I acknowledge the narcissist's soul truth and know with complete certainty that the narcissist is on their own journey, of which I cannot safely be a part.

January 31

Dissociation

How did we miss the red flags flying by our eyes in the beginning of the narcissistic relationship? Dissociation.

Our need for the "love" and "acceptance" the narcissist provided was great. Too great for us to acknowledge what we were actually receiving. Instead of walking away, we continued to take the crumbs that the narcissist so freely offered during the love bombing stage of the narcissistic abuse cycle, dismissing our soul's inner warnings and nudges.

Dissociation is a survival mechanism we learn as children that helps us get through overwhelming situations that are too much to process. It's especially common during and after trauma.

We may find ourselves "spacing out," unable to focus in the present moment. Or we may become obsessive, unable to stop ruminating about something in our mind. That can be our way of "checking out" if what's happening in the present is too intense or triggers something from the past.

Dissociation can become severe. During their abusive relationship, one survivor reported seeing a car barreling at them as they pulled out into an alleyway. They were frozen, unable to move. This distressing event led them to uncover a crushing, traumatic memory from childhood that the narcissistic abuse had triggered.

Today, I will begin paying attention to whether I use dissociation to cope with overwhelming feelings of the present or past. If so, I will reach out for support when I'm ready to work through the inner wounds making dissociation necessary.

February 1

Idealization (Love Bombing)

Idealization is the first stage in the narcissistic abuse cycle, during which the narcissist asks the right questions to uncover our weaknesses and wounds from the past.

They shape-shift, appearing to be the opposite of everything that's ever hurt us, our dream come true. They love bomb us, showering us with affection and devotion, the likes of which we've never experienced before—all the while testing our boundaries to identify how far we'll go to meet their needs. We gladly go along with almost anything because the "love" we are experiencing feels sublime.

From one perspective, love bombing is the ultimate betrayal. The narcissist manipulates us with their "love" until we're extremely vulnerable. Then they drastically change their behavior, leaving us desperately trying to recreate those beautiful moments we experienced at the beginning of the relationship.

From another perspective, perhaps the narcissist gave us a glimpse of something we'd never experienced before: feeling loved and accepted. We can take the feelings we had in those magical moments and recreate them for ourselves. As we love and refuse to abandon ourselves, we bring back that magic. Only now it's real and sustainable.

We can create special moments of self-connection in our life, doing creative things we enjoy, such as cooking, art, or music, or lighting candles and letting our thoughts and feelings flow into our journals.

Today, I will do something wonderful for myself that will bring authentic beauty and magic into my life.

February 2

Physical Effects of the Love Bombing Stage

During the love bombing stage, we were swept away by the unending "love" and affection the narcissist showered upon us. As we relished each moment, other things were happening:

- We became sleep deprived and exhausted from long, passionate nights together.
- For those who are highly sensitive empaths, we abandoned our own needs to please the narcissist, neglecting important self-care activities such as taking time alone to recharge and connect with how we felt, or respecting our sensitivities to things like light, crowds, and noise.
- Perhaps we overused alcohol or began doing drugs, something that was not in our nature, causing us to become overstimulated, depleted, and further disconnected from ourselves.
- The narcissist may have contacted us incessantly, keeping us on edge and pulling us away from our jobs, our children, and ourselves.
- We experienced high levels of stress as we constantly tried to find equilibrium in a situation that was rife with chaos.

This process of breaking us down and isolating us through the use of love bombing made it easier for the narcissist to control us. As time went on, we realized this lifestyle was unsustainable, yet we were paralyzed by the fear that meeting our own needs would result in losing the "love" of the narcissist.

Today, I will explore the physical effects that the love bombing stage had on me. I will look at what I can do today to support my body's healing efforts.

February 3

The Devaluation Phase

During the initial stage of the narcissistic abuse cycle, the idealization phase, the narcissist showered us with "love," easily slipping into our lives. They became everything we desired, cementing us to them.

We entered the next stage, the devaluation phase, unguarded, trusting the narcissist completely, after sharing our fears and dreams with them and receiving more "love" in return than we'd ever known. We believed we'd found our forever love.

One day, we noticed things had changed. The narcissist spoke to us in a different tone and was often less affectionate toward us, our deep connection somehow broken. We chalked it up to the normal progression of a relationship and kept going. The mask of their false persona was slipping, giving us a glimpse under the facade.

As the abuse intensified, the narcissist became cruel and disrespectful, using the intimate details we'd shared about ourselves against us. Our reactions were a great source of narcissistic supply for the narcissist. Having isolated us from our support system made it easier for them to manipulate us and left us ever more dependent upon them. Occasionally, they returned to the idealization phase, throwing out just enough crumbs of affection to prevent us from walking away and abandoning them.

Today, I will contemplate what I experienced during the idealization and devaluation phases, noticing whether having a better understanding of the narcissistic abuse cycle offers me a different perspective on my relationship with the narcissist.

February 4

The Discard Phase

After the narcissist's overwhelming love in the idealization phase and their mind-bending transformation in the devaluation phase, the final stage of the narcissistic abuse cycle is the discard phase. In this phase, the narcissist ends the relationship, either by leaving us or by escalating the abuse so profoundly that our very survival depends upon us leaving them.

Sometimes, the narcissist's discard is temporary. They pull away just long enough to gain a sense of power and control over us, observing how their abandonment devastates us. This process provides them with an abundance of narcissistic supply.

Other times, their discard is permanent: They lose interest in us when we're no longer a quality source of narcissistic supply because they've drained us of our vital energy and inner resources, when they're bored with us and looking for a new conquest, or when we set boundaries and practice self-care, making their efforts to gain supply too difficult.

After the discard, the narcissist may attempt to hoover us back in all the way or just far enough to ensure that we're there if they're ever running low on narcissistic supply.

Understanding the narcissistic abuse cycle may offer us a different perspective on our experience, seeing the predictable sequence of events it followed, and knowing we're not alone, that many others before us have made it through and went on to heal themselves and their lives.

Today, I will remember that the narcissist's ending of the relationship was my new beginning.

February 5

Support

After narcissistic abuse, we walk through territory that many don't understand. It's impossible to comprehend the debilitating abuse we've been through without experiencing it firsthand. Well-meaning people say things that can hurt, adding to our feelings of abandonment and betrayal. Many of us have heard things like:

- Why are you so angry?
- Are you sure you're okay?
- You need to stop thinking about them.
- Forgive your ex. It's the right thing to do.
- At least you had good times with them.
- I went through that, too. You just have to let them go.

That isn't support. It's judgment and misunderstanding when we need presence and acceptance. We may feel resentful or ashamed, as if we're doing it wrong or we should be further along. We can honor those feelings and know that we are exactly where we're meant to be, doing the best we can in a messy, difficult situation.

Our friends and loved ones are doing the best they can, too, having no way to truly understand our experience. If we need to set boundaries or create distance with them while we're in the tender stages of our healing journey, it's okay to do so, supporting ourselves in whatever way is necessary to get through this difficult time.

For today, I will honor my feelings and care for myself during this painful time. I will reach out to the resources that feel right and offer true support, remembering that Source is always present, loving, and understanding.

February 6

Narcissistic Rage

Because of the insecurity and self-loathing within them, narcissists are sensitive to any slight or setback that impacts their feelings of superiority. These perceived threats may expose their self-created persona and the reality that supports it—a charade they work tirelessly to maintain.

Narcissists are highly skilled at using rage to control us, the intensity of which appeared in different forms: an angry outburst, cutting sarcasm, cold and calculated words, passive-aggressive behavior, neglect, or dead silence.

We may not have realized the magnitude of the rage being directed at us or the degree to which it impacted us, especially those of us who are empaths with highly sensitive systems. We were fortunate if we had someone outside of the narcissist's influence experience a rage episode and then reflect their perceptions and feelings back to us.

After walking on eggshells around their narcissistic rage long enough, exhausted and depleted, we did what was necessary to keep the peace. We learned to silence ourselves and our needs, and we stopped holding them accountable for their abusive behavior.

Today, I will sit with the feelings that weren't safe to express during the narcissistic relationship. I will find a supportive way to help their energy move through me, whether by taking a walk in nature, having a good scream while alone in the car, or dancing wildly or gently to just the right song.

February 7

Are They Really a Narcissist?

We've read the memes and listened to the videos on social media, and we've studied the blog posts from narcissistic abuse experts. We think our former partner was a narcissist, but we're not certain. Were we narcissistically abused? We hold our breath, unsure if we "qualify" for that label.

From one perspective, labels mean nothing. If we were abused, it doesn't matter whether society classifies our abuser as narcissistic, alcoholic, depressed, anxious, bipolar, psychopathic, sociopathic, or just plain toxic. What matters is that we acknowledge it really was *that bad*, our lives were greatly affected, and we received painful wounds as a result.

If we were abused, we are abuse victims. If we need permission to own that, here it is.

> We. Were. Victimized.

Once we can own and acknowledge that, we can begin our healing process.

From another perspective, it can be validating to learn more about narcissistic abuse from professionals who have written books, done research, and made videos on the harmful effects of narcissistic abuse on us and our lives. Gradually, we find the words to describe the mind-bending things we've experienced, and we discover that we aren't crazy or alone. Many others have been through it, too.

Today, I will honor my inner knowing even if no one else understands or agrees, free now to put the focus on myself and my healing.

February 8

Room to Exist

One of the most painful, infuriating things I faced while healing a lifetime of trauma was that I didn't have room to exist as a child. I was at the mercy of my parents' addictions and dysfunction, making it unsafe and impossible for me to explore who I was while waiting for the next inevitable crisis. I was trapped and suffocated by my parents' needs.

This was also true in my relationship with the narcissist, as I once again lived out the patterns from my childhood.

Narcissists feel threatened if we "exist too much," becoming too strong, bright, or successful. Because their survival depends upon them being in the spotlight and holding the power, they use abuse tactics to diminish us to a size they're comfortable with.

Consider the moments when we wanted to speak up because something didn't feel right, but we shut down instead, putting our needs aside. *What do we wish we'd have said or done instead?* Taking time to answer this question in our journal or in a conversation with a supportive friend or therapist may be deeply healing.

Today, I will accept any feelings that surface about not having had room to exist. I will explore what my needs and wants are and create space in my life to fulfill them. I will include the things that spark my soul and make me come alive as I make room in my life to fully exist as my authentic self.

February 9

Fixing the Narcissist

When we first met the narcissist, they seemed like the answer to every prayer, hope, and dream we had. As time went on, things changed, leaving us confused and devastated, wondering what happened to the magic we experienced initially.

We hoped that if we were patient and loving enough, they would once again become the person we cherished. The crumbs of love they doled out gave us hope. We looked for every opportunity to better ourselves, and we waited as the abuse cycle escalated.

We cannot fix or change the narcissist to be who they once were, as the person we knew in the beginning was a persona that the narcissist presented. Maintaining that persona was not sustainable for them.

Most narcissists don't choose to change anything about themselves, believing that they're fine and it's the people around them who have issues. There is no cure for narcissism, but treatment is available, namely psychotherapy (talk therapy). Those who seek treatment to receive help, instead of to manipulate the therapist, are sometimes able to better adapt to life and relate to those around them more realistically.

Today, I will remember that while I am powerless to fix the narcissist, I am empowered by my own choices. I can grieve the loss of the good times and feelings I experienced during some parts of the relationship while acknowledging the costs of the abuse and knowing that the person I fell in love with doesn't exist.

February 10

Doing Nothing

There is a concept in Taoist philosophy that defines the concept of "not doing." Wu Wei means effortless action or non-doing. Not acting can be a form of moving forward. It doesn't display laziness, but rather wisdom and restraint.

How many of us have rushed forward out of impulse, broken No Contact, and reached out to the narcissist? How many of us are now rolling our eyes as we read this, remembering the consequences of doing so? I know I am, with understanding and love for the wounded inner children who took that action. Sitting with the desire to contact the narcissist can make us extremely uncomfortable. We often act to avoid the feelings arising within us.

Sometimes, purposely doing nothing can feel like a relief, removing the ever-present pressure we feel to act. It can provide much-needed rest, especially if we are used to driving ourselves to be and do more.

The time after the narcissistic relationship ends is like a tornado, with inner chaos swirling around inside of us, caused by the abuse we experienced and the corresponding aftershock symptoms arising. This is a great time to practice doing nothing—sitting with things and not making any fast moves or unnecessary decisions.

Today, I will consider the process of non-doing, taking time to consciously sit with something before I act on it. I'll count my effort as a success even if it's only 30 seconds, knowing that tomorrow I might master one minute.

February 11

Isolation

Our support system is an important aspect of our self-care. The narcissist may have tried to win their favor initially, but as the relationship progressed, they often shamed us for needing any support at all, as if we were weak by being unable to shoulder life all by ourselves. Some insisted that their support alone should be sufficient, something that isolated us and gave them more control over us.

A red flag that we may have missed was when the narcissist began to point out things about our support people that they disapproved of and shared all the reasons they felt those people weren't worthy of us. After a while, many of us found ourselves devoid of a support system entirely as we fell deeper into the narcissist's control and skewed version of reality.

In truth, seeking support indicates wisdom and strength, and the support we need will always be there. All we have to do is reach out. If it seems we're lacking support, then perhaps it's a moment we need to handle alone—to see how strong we really are.

Today, I will be grateful for the support system I have. If I find myself without one, I will explore who I'd like to have on my support team and reach out to that person or organization now. I will also remember that Source's support is always with me—I am never alone and always loved and cared for.

February 12

Inner Wounds

The trauma wounds that we hold inside of us from the past are the very things that make us susceptible to narcissistic abuse. Narcissists are attracted to our weaknesses and vulnerabilities like sharks to blood. They observe carefully as we communicate, looking and listening for our empathic qualities, deep insecurities, lack of boundaries, or anything else that they can use to disempower us, ensuring the effectiveness of their abusive tactics. Using that information, they behave in a way that brings us face-to-face with our deepest, unresolved wounds.

Many of us have come to realize that the narcissistic abuse mirrored the abuse we experienced in our childhood. Unconsciously, we may have been drawn to the familiarity of toxic relationships while hoping for a different outcome—the love and devotion we deserved as a child and have yearned for since.

On the other side of our deepest, unresolved wounds is a treasure—our authentic self. As we connect with the wounds, we acknowledge our past hurts, leading to integration and healing.

Today, I will close my eyes, take a deep breath, and wrap my arms around myself, acknowledging that as a child I was worthy of love just as I am now. I will acknowledge my courage and strength to hold the pain of these inner wounds for as long as I had to, until it was safe for me to face them and heal.

February 13

Apologizing

We may have done things during or after the narcissistic relationship that were out of character for us. Perhaps we said hurtful things to the narcissist, vented our frustrations about them to others, looked through their phone, got physically aggressive with them, or threw all of their worldly belongings out onto the front lawn.

Rest assured, many of us have done things we later came to regret.

It's important to remember that we were being severely traumatized by someone possessing disordered personality traits. Although it may be in our nature to be kind to others and take responsibility for our less than stellar moments, it's important to understand that if we apologize to the narcissist, we're handing them fuel for more abuse. A narcissist will use our apology as proof to their new source of narcissistic supply or even to our friends and loved ones that we are the crazy one and they are the victim.

Once we review the entire situation and look at why we reacted as we did, we may decide that an acknowledgement of our behavior is more fitting than an apology.

Today, instead of apologizing to the narcissist, I will acknowledge my behavior to myself, a trusted friend, or to Source while I maintain No Contact with the narcissist. I will explore the reasons why I did hurtful things while showing myself great compassion for how I dealt with an impossible situation.

February 14

Love

Love can be fiery and passionate or quiet and gentle. It's the honest expression of our soul's truth, present when we're vulnerable and daring enough to claim it. When we embrace our precious selves, love rises within us.

After experiencing past abuse and neglect, we may have misinterpreted the abusive behaviors of the narcissist as love. However, we eventually came to understand that there was always a price to pay for the "love" of a narcissist.

When they controlled who we were, how we dressed, or what we did, we initially believed that they loved us so much they wanted the best for us. When they showed jealousy or wanted us all to themselves, we misinterpreted it as the ultimate show of love...until their "love" became a prison.

The narcissist's behaviors were the opposite of love. In a healthy relationship, both partners can fully exist as who they are in their own unique flow, the blending of two sovereign souls in a sacred dance.

Love breaks down our walls, inviting us to embrace the long-hidden and carefully protected places within us.

Loving ourselves is not selfish. It is empowering and stabilizing, the door to a beautiful life beyond our wildest imaginings and our greatest gift to ourselves and the world.

For today, I will work to recognize love, giving it to myself and others with the heart and spirit of a radiant child and the wisdom and discernment of a wise adult.

February 15

Our Family of Inner Children

Our family of inner children that dwells within us consists of the versions of us that got "stuck" at certain ages or stages due to trauma or overwhelming circumstances.

People have different ways of identifying and distinguishing between their inner children:

Some describe them by their ages. A three-year-old with confidence and style galore, or a five-year-old who can intuitively sense the things their adults try to hide.

Some identify them by archetypes. The warrior, dreamer, caregiver, comedian, peacemaker, storyteller, silent one, saboteur.

Some give them names. We can give our inner children real names, expressive names that we create, or those that intuitively come to us. *Zoe can read people. Petal the Flower is tender and vulnerable. Bob knows how to get things done.*

Much like a normal family, our inner children can be in conflict with one another.

An inner teenager who wants to be free and explore the world may conflict with a younger, overwhelmed inner child who wants to keep our life small, or a protector child that is fierce in their mission to keep us safe.

Our inner children can also support each other in an inner family led by a safe, loving adult(s) of their choosing, offering them a sense of stability and belonging they may not have experienced before.

Today, I will try on different ways of identifying my inner children, distinguishing and cherishing each precious past version of me as they make themselves known.

February 16

PTSD and C-PTSD

Post Traumatic Stress Disorder (PTSD) is a mental health condition that can develop after we experience or witness a traumatic event that threatens the life or safety of ourselves or someone else. It can also occur in someone who learns of a traumatic event that happened to a family member or friend.

Traumatic events can include war and combat, a major accident, sexual violence, a natural disaster, or serious injury. The event, too intense for our system to fully process, can cause upsetting symptoms that last long after the actual occurrence.

In her book *The Complex PTSD Workbook*, Arielle Schwartz, PhD, defines complex PTSD (C-PTSD) as *"another kind of post-traumatic stress which occurs as a result of long-term exposure to traumatic stress, rather than in response to a single incident."*

C-PTSD can occur when we're trapped in an abusive or neglectful environment—a child in a dysfunctional family of origin or an adult in the grip of narcissistic abuse. In these settings, we may endure continued traumatic stress and repeated traumatic events, causing PTSD, C-PTSD, or the exacerbation of pre-existing symptoms.

Many symptoms of PTSD and C-PTSD are similar and may include the following: anxiety, feelings of helplessness or hopelessness, nightmares, intrusive distressing memories, flashbacks, hypervigilance, dissociation or "zoning out," and the avoidance of trauma triggers.

Today, I will learn more about PTSD/C-PTSD and seek professional help if I feel the information applies to me and I desire more support in my healing.

February 17

Professional Support

We show strength when we reach out for professional support. Healing from narcissistic abuse may be one of the most difficult things we'll ever undertake. It's important to look for counselors and psychologists who are trained in working with trauma and familiar with narcissistic abuse.

We can search our local area listings or use the website www.PsychologyToday.com. We can also visit websites of professional organizations such as the American Counseling Association (www.counseling.org), Brainspotting International (www.Brainspotting.com), or the EMDR Institute, Inc. (www.emdr.com) to look for licensed professionals.*

Looking at practitioners' photos or exploring their websites can be a good way to find those who might be a fit. We can also reach out to them to inquire about their training in, or experience of, working with narcissistic abuse victims.

There have been victims of narcissistic abuse who were misdiagnosed with anxiety or depression and did not receive the help they needed. There are also those who were retraumatized by therapists who were uneducated about trauma bonds and the depth and destruction of narcissistic abuse.

It can be very healing to find a therapist who understands the narcissist's manipulation, validates our experiences, and helps us see the truth of the abusive nature of the relationship.

Today, I will acknowledge that reaching out for professional support shows strength, and I will explore that option if it seems like a helpful step for me at this time.

* The author is not sponsored by any of these platforms, but is offering them as optional, helpful resources for you to explore.

February 18

Healing Tools

There are evidence-based tools available to assist us in healing the effects of narcissistic abuse and addressing our inner wounds that made us susceptible to it.

Brainspotting and Eye Movement Desensitization and Reprocessing (EMDR) are powerful, brain-based psychotherapy techniques that can help us process traumas and wounds from the past. Brainspotting utilizes eye fixation on a point in our field of vision that corresponds with the location of a traumatic or negative experience held in our brain. EMDR uses rapid eye movements, instead of eye fixation, in the processing and resolution of trauma.

Emotional Freedom Technique (Tapping) is a technique that involves tapping on our energy meridian points with our fingers, which sends signals to the parts of our brain responsible for our stress response. The goal is to restore our body's energy balance, manage stress, and relieve symptoms that a negative experience or emotion may have caused. It's a simple, quick healing tool that has proven to be effective for many people.

Other effective evidence-based, trauma-focused counseling modalities include Cognitive Behavioral Therapy, Somatic Experiencing Therapy, Cognitive Processing Therapy, Prolonged Exposure, and Internal Family Systems. All have been found to be effective tools in processing and healing trauma—like that which caused our susceptibility to narcissistic abuse.

Today, I will explore healing resources to find what resonates with me and meets my healing needs at this time, checking with my healthcare provider to ensure the method I choose is safe for me.

February 19

Re-Engaging in Life

Re-entering life again after being in the isolation of an abusive relationship can be overwhelming. Although we realized the narcissist was abusing us, to our inner children it might have felt like they were providing protection and acting as a buffer between us and the rest of the world. After the relationship ended, they may have felt suddenly exposed and vulnerable without the narcissist by our side.

One survivor shared, "When I was in a relationship with a narcissist, I had a barrier between me and my dysfunctional family. It gave me the excuse to break ties with them. It was me and my partner versus them, and now I had the "courage" to say no to the family drama, refusing to participate. After the narcissistic relationship ended, it took me several months to emerge from my cocoon and get back into the world."

We can listen to the feelings in our body and to what our inner children have to say. By honoring them, we gain their trust, preparing them to re-engage in life.

Today, I will be gentle with myself as I move through life. If I am overwhelmed and newly alone, I won't push myself past the point that I'm ready or able to go, as I know gentleness and compassion will bring the greatest healing in the long run. When I am ready, I will open myself to all of the wonderful experiences awaiting me in my new life.

February 20

Refusing the Bait

When we'd had enough of the narcissist's games and started to pull back, or we walked away from the relationship, the narcissist may have done what they could to keep us engaged.

What was the carrot they dangled to try and get us back? Did they offer to seek counseling or promise to do things differently? Did they threaten us with a lawsuit or the loss of our children to get us to engage? Did they remind us of the "sacred love and connection" between us? Or did they feign concern, threatening to come check on us because they hadn't heard from us?

When we're ready—after we've committed to ourselves, learned to meet our own needs, and healed enough of the wounds from our past—we will find the courage and strength to disengage from the narcissist completely. Sometimes, disengaging from them is a matter of saving our own lives, even when it doesn't seem like we have the strength to do so. Continuing to maintain No Contact with the narcissist is the most important step in refusing the bait.

Today, I will explore what maneuvers, if any, the narcissist has used in their attempts to get me to re-engage with them, looking at how and why their actions affected me. By identifying my vulnerabilities, I can work to heal them and meet those needs for myself, so I will no longer be susceptible to abuse.

February 21

We Are Enough!

Do any of these statements sound familiar?

> You'd look so beautiful with more make-up.
> You should work in this job/that career.
> Breast implants would make you sexy.
> If you lost weight, you'd be stunning.
> You could get that mole removed.
> Those shoes/clothes aren't you.
> You need to use better posture.
> You should cut/color your hair.

These are often red flags which indicate that we're with a narcissist who expects us to meet their idealized version of us (beautiful, smart, thin, rich, successful,...). Then they can feel good about themselves thanks to the external validation they receive by being with us. The better we look, the better they feel.

Narcissists have a need to control us. They want to pose us, dress us, and show us how to act and be, according to what they think is best.

In a healthy relationship, no one is expected to change. It's about coming together, respecting one another, and deciding if we are compatible exactly as we are.

Today, I will remember that there is only one me and I was created by a wondrous Source who loves me unconditionally. I know that I am perfect in every way, exactly as I am. There may be things I'd like to change about myself, but there is nothing I need to change to make me acceptable to anyone else. I am me, and that's more than enough!

February 22

Gentleness

Many of us who were narcissistically abused never had the devotion from our caregivers that we so needed and deserved. We got used to working hard for crumbs of affection, attention, and approval, uncertain when, or if, we would receive any.

Though we may not have had anyone to support us in challenging times, we can now support ourselves, becoming the caregiver that we wanted and deserved, committed to loving and caring for ourselves.

There is never a reason to be hard on ourselves. Instead, we can choose to act from a place of gentleness and acceptance even as we hold ourselves accountable. We've tried the ways of shaming, being tough, and driving ourselves forward, with limited success and leading to inner depletion. Gentleness is not weakness. It's wholeness—and the way to true healing.

We must look inside for our own way, timing, and progress, because comparing ourselves to anyone else is like comparing apples and zebras. We cannot expect ourselves to do things like other people because we're all unique. Only we know what we truly need and what we're ready for.

Today, I will remember that there is always a loving way to get through anything, even though it may feel strange at first. I know that I'm doing my best, and I will be gentle and patient as I continue to move forward at a pace that works for me.

February 23

Gray Rock

When walking along the beach looking for treasures, we often pass right by the boring gray rocks in favor of the more interesting colorful ones. Being uninteresting and getting passed by is exactly the purpose of "gray rock," a self-care technique we can use when we must communicate with narcissists or toxic people.

The narcissist's goal is to obtain narcissistic supply by eliciting a positive or negative emotional reaction from us. The less drama we provide, the less value we have to them.

When using "gray rock," we become incredibly boring, saying as little as possible with the least emotion we can. We don't argue with the narcissist, instead keeping the conversation about business and staying with the facts of the matter.

We can avoid eye contact, use a shrug or nod to respond, stick with short replies like *uh-huh* or *okay*, and end the interaction as soon as possible. If we tell the narcissist what we're doing, they may use it against us. Instead, we want them to get bored with us on their own.

"Gray rock" is not a tactic to use with an abuser who is stalking us or being physically aggressive, as "gray rock" may further escalate the situation. Instead, it's best to take appropriate measures to ensure our safety.

Today, if it's safe to do so, I will practice using "gray rock" if I must communicate with a narcissist or anyone who is manipulative or abusive to me.

February 24

Intermittent Reinforcement

Intermittent reinforcement is a powerful tool of manipulation that the narcissist used to control us. It involves the delivery of a reward, such as a crumb of attention or affection, at irregular and unpredictable intervals. In research experiments, this type of reinforcement has been shown to generate the greatest response from subjects in maintaining a desired behavior pattern.

Intermittent reinforcement is most effectively used after continuous reinforcement, in which a reward is given at constant and predictable intervals, establishing the desired pattern of behavior.

During the love bombing stage of the narcissistic abuse cycle, the narcissist gave us continuous reinforcement—attention, affection, time, and energy—which they doled out until they knew we were addicted to and dependent upon them.

Confident we weren't going to abandon them, the narcissist stopped working as hard, giving us crumbs of "love" and acceptance less frequently and at unpredictable intervals—in other words, intermittent reinforcement.

Craving the attention and affection we received in the beginning, we worked hard at the desired behaviors to please the narcissist and avoid abandonment. During the devaluation phase, we worked even harder to regain their "love" that we so desperately craved.

This process strengthened the addictive trauma bond in our brain created by the ups and downs—intermittent reinforcement—of the abuse cycle, which we came to believe was love.

Today, I will consider what forms of continuous and intermittent reinforcement the narcissist used in their manipulation, and I will notice how my body and mind responded to them.

February 25

Loss

We all experience change and loss in our lives, a certainty that no one can escape. After our abusive relationship ended, we lost a lot, including the illusion of a perfect partner, our family unit, a sense of "normal" life, our identity, our hopes and dreams with the one we loved, and perhaps even the security of our own home.

In addition, we lost the chaos, unmeetable expectations, pressure, and judgment from the narcissist that defined our lives. Even though those things hurt as they were happening, they may have seemed "comfortable"—because that's what we were used to.

As we heal the wounds that made us susceptible to narcissistic abuse, great changes happen within us. Our relationships with others change. Some will end, some will adjust, and we will attract new relationships into our lives that nourish and support us.

Today, I accept that loss is a part of life. I will be present with the feelings that come up and allow them to flow through me, grateful to have the freedom and space to experience them fully. If I feel alone or lost, I will remember that my life is changing—and that there are new adventures and people ahead to fill the holes of what was lost.

February 26

Safety

Someone with narcissistic traits or narcissistic personality disorder can put us in mental, emotional, and physical danger. People have died from the effects of narcissistic abuse, whether by their own hand or those of the narcissist.

After the narcissistic relationship ended, many of us were swept back up into the narcissist's vortex. Because of the trauma bond in our brain and the narcissist's expert manipulation, we craved the very person who was harming us. It's important to remember that each time we go back, the abuse intensifies.

If we feel unsafe, we must reach out for support.

We can call 911, contact our local domestic violence organization, reach out to the crisis resources listed at the back of this book, or seek help and support from members of our support team.

When we feel unsafe, we remain in survival mode, our systems on high alert and attuned to the outer world. Once we feel safe, our healing can begin. We can access our internal environment and connect with our inner wisdom, allowing us to identify what we need to best support ourselves in our efforts to heal.

Today, I will acknowledge the seriousness of narcissistic abuse. If I find myself drawn back to the narcissist, I will assess my safety needs and risks and reach out for support in staying safe.

February 27

Secrets

Many of us did things while with the narcissist that were not aligned with our values. We were groomed to meet their needs and become who they wanted us to be. We changed ourselves to avoid being abandoned or risking losing their "love." Often, our need for love and approval outweighed our values, which is understandable considering our past trauma, unmet needs, and inner wounds.

The narcissist may hold secrets of things we've done or said, and even possess texts, photos, or emails as evidence. This can trigger intense fear that they'll use the information against us. We may tiptoe around them or maintain contact, trying to keep them from hurting us, which only drains us, gives energy to our fear, and feeds them narcissistic supply.

We have no control over what the narcissist does with information we don't want revealed, but we do have control over what we do with our fear. We can fully own our power by caring for ourselves, maintaining No Contact with the narcissist, and making the choice to continue healing and moving forward.

If the worst happens and our secrets are revealed, we can refuse to abandon ourselves and trust ourselves to deal with whatever comes up, one step at a time.

For today, I recognize that I don't have control over what the narcissist does. I will live my best life and deal with situations as they unfold rather than thinking ahead, getting lost in "what ifs," and trying to protect myself.

February 28

Saying No

Many of us learned long ago to accommodate people's wants and needs in order to keep the peace, finding that it was safer and easier to do so. "Yes" became our default.

When we begin practicing our "no," it can be uncomfortable and awkward. Explaining our "no" is unnecessary. People on the receiving end of a "no" may react, trying to engage with us in an old way of being so *they're* comfortable.

As we begin to love ourselves, saying no to the games, intimidation, control, and exploitation of others becomes easier. When we refuse to continue putting ourselves aside and handing over our precious energy to people who misuse it, they will either join us in a healthier way of being or move on to someone else with whom they can continue that dysfunctional behavior.

Our "no" is the gift that helps us know what our "yes" is. If we are used to going along with other peoples' wants and needs, we may be unaware of our own wants and needs. When we feel safe enough to begin saying no, we create the space to learn who we are and what we desire. Then, we will come to know what our "yes" is.

Today, I will practice my "no" when I feel the need to set a boundary or take care of myself, and I will observe how others react. I will also watch for, and celebrate, my "yes!"

February 29

Awareness

Awareness is required for change to happen. We cannot fix a problem if we don't know it's there.

During the narcissistic abuse relationship, we had compelling reasons for wanting to hold on to the narcissist, driven by past survival patterns. As a result, we didn't acknowledge the red flags as we soaked in all the "love" and good feelings that the narcissist gave us initially.

Many of us lacked the reference point of a healthy relationship as children, so we weren't even aware that the narcissist's behavior was abusive. To us, it seemed normal and even comfortable in a familiar sort of way.

Many of us have also experienced the pain of abandonment in our past. To avoid experiencing that ache again, we held on tightly to our abuser and excused the words and actions that hurt us. We tried to help the narcissist heal and once again become the person they appeared to be in the beginning of our relationship. Eventually, we found out we had undertaken an impossible task.

We become aware of things when we're ready, the timing of which can only be revealed from within us. We can identify the survival behaviors that protected us from hard things and kept us unaware, letting go of them when we're ready.

Today, I trust myself and my inner wisdom to make me aware of the things I'm ready to see, in the timing that fits me and my healing journey.

March 1

12-Step Programs

The first 12-Step Program, Alcoholics Anonymous, was created in 1953 to assist alcoholics in their recovery from alcohol addiction. Since then, many 12-Step groups have been created for things other than alcoholism.

One of those groups is Al-Anon, which serves families of alcoholics. It may be helpful for those of us recovering from narcissistic abuse who have also been affected by alcoholism in our families and adult relationships. Another supportive group is Co-Dependents Anonymous (Co-DA), which may be helpful for those of us with co-dependent traits that lead to difficulties in creating and maintaining healthy relationships.

In these programs, the twelve steps outline a path to spiritual progress through specific actions designed to shift our perspectives, and in turn, our reality. The steps guide us to call upon a Higher Power of our understanding and begin with our acceptance and acknowledgement of powerlessness over others' alcohol use (Al-Anon)—or over other people (Co-DA)—as we work to surrender our desire to control. The program has provided many people with the support they needed—and with the wisdom, strength, and hope of those who have traveled the road of recovery before them.

One survivor shared, "I was broken and barely functioning. It was in a 12-Step program that I found sanity and a sense of support that gave me courage and hope in those early days of recovering from narcissistic abuse."

Today, I will explore 12-Step programs further if they seem like a supportive step for me at this time.

March 2

Surrendering

Surrendering is letting go of our efforts to control, allowing life to flow naturally. Wanting to control people and situations isn't bad. In fact, it may have been one way we protected ourselves in the past.

As children, maintaining the illusion that we had some control over the out-of-control situation around us may have been the only thing that helped us feel like we could keep ourselves safe. Some of us hoped that if we kept our abuser happy, they wouldn't hurt us or others.

Sometimes our life has to become completely unbearable before we'll surrender our control over it. One survivor shared their story of trying to control everything they could to make their relationship with the narcissist work:

"I lost weight, loosened up, and tried not to feel or show emotion. I obsessed constantly, trying to understand why my relationship was crumbling and how to save it. Finally, exhausted and weakened at every level, I surrendered to the truth. My relationship with the narcissist was killing me. As I acknowledged that painful truth, a huge wave of relief washed over me. I no longer had to try to control the uncontrollable."

This person learned to put the focus on themselves, surrendered their control to their Source, and found their way to a better life.

Today, I will explore the idea of surrendering. I will examine where in my life I might need to release control—and what it would mean for me to trust this process.

March 3

Narcissistic Traits

We often hear people flippantly using the word "narcissist" in a way that wholly misrepresents the true meaning and impact of pathological narcissism and the destruction it brings. Someone who looks in the mirror often or is self-centered is not necessarily a narcissist.

Some people believe we're all a little narcissistic. While we may exhibit behaviors from time to time that appear to be like those of a narcissist, such as needing external validation or lacking empathy, the narcissist's pathological traits lead to behavior that is enduring, a pattern they exhibit across their lives, no matter the situation.

We may have been called a narcissist for putting ourselves first, setting boundaries, and practicing self-care. Some people refer to those behaviors as healthy narcissism while others believe they have nothing to do with narcissism. Either way, they are healthy behaviors that we practice for the good of ourselves and everyone around us—the opposite of what a narcissist does.

Narcissistic traits run along a spectrum. On one end, people may exhibit only a few pathological narcissistic traits, while on the other they have diagnosable narcissistic personality disorder. Unfortunately, as some of us well know, a narcissist can destroy another person with only one pathological trait, making it clear that there is no "safe" level of pathological narcissism.

Today, I will continue to practice and improve my self-care, knowing that the beautiful things I'm doing for myself are healthy, loving behaviors.

March 4

Narcissistic Tactics

Narcissists have an arsenal of abuse tactics they use to obtain narcissistic supply from us and increase their self-esteem, giving them a sense of power and superiority over us. The following are what some of them sound like:

Stonewalling. "I'm not discussing this *AGAIN*." • "Quit being ridiculous." • (Sometimes the dialog stops altogether, even for days.)

Triangulation. "My co-worker looks so sexy after losing weight." • "That friend of yours has such a nice way about them." • "My ex-spouse thought what you said was ridiculous, too."

Gaslighting. "I never said that." • "You're dreaming this all up." • "I didn't flirt. You're making way more of this than you need to."

Love Bombing. "You're the love of my life." • "We're soulmates." • "You know me better than anyone else."

Devaluation. "My friends don't understand what I see in you, but I love you and that's all that matters." • "Menopause or not, your weight gain isn't what I signed up for." • "You're not wearing that, are you?"

Projection. "Do you have your period? You're so emotional!" • "I'm not the problem. Look in the mirror!" • "Are you cheating on me?"

For today, I will remember that I was up against a master manipulator. I will forgive myself for getting caught up in the narcissist's abuse and allowing myself to be treated the way I was. I know I did the best I could with the wounds that I had.

March 5

Lack of Empathy

One characteristic that defines a narcissist is their lack of empathy. They are unwilling to consider the thoughts, feelings, and needs of others.

One survivor shared a moment early in their relationship when the narcissist's facade slipped for a moment, their lack of empathy evident.

"The narcissist stated that if anything ever happened to incapacitate me, a serious injury or illness, they would have to leave me and continue to live their life. I was caught in an agonizing bind between wanting to run far away from this person whom I suddenly didn't recognize—and desperately wanting to hold on to their 'love.' As I conveyed my shock, sadness, and disbelief, the narcissist soon backtracked, saying they didn't really mean what they'd said."

Many survivors of narcissistic abuse have experienced this painful truth when faced with a disabling health concern such as cancer, depression, or chronic pain. Many narcissists suddenly evaporate, unwilling to support their partner and making it clear that what their partner is going through is their own problem.

Many of us have wondered how we ever allowed ourselves to be with a person who demonstrated such a complete lack of empathy. It's helpful to remember that we were controlled and manipulated by someone who was masterful at drawing us in.

Today, or whenever I'm ready, I will revisit the painful moments when the narcissist lacked empathy. I will provide myself with all the love and support I needed at those times.

March 6

Seduction

It starts subtly. *We talked on the phone for hours. I feel heard for the first time ever. They see something in me that no one else ever has!*

Then it heats up. *I can't stop thinking about them. They surprised me with flowers and cooked me dinner. They opened my door and pulled out my chair for me. They're a great kisser. They're unlike anyone I've ever dated before!*

Then it hits us full force. *We danced the night away. Their touch makes me come alive. We walked along the beach under the moonlight. The sex is beyond amazing. Life with them is so exciting!*

Narcissists are masters of seduction. Using attention and affection, they extract information from us: our wants, needs, dreams, and past wounds. They use this information to manipulate us and give us experiences in the relationship that we've only dreamed of.

The problem is they can't maintain it, nor do they want to. Once the seduction has served its purpose of getting us hooked on them, they withdraw their energy, giving us less and less as time goes on.

Today, I will explore the ways that the narcissist seduced me, noticing which of my inner children were susceptible to the manipulation. I will connect with them to see what they need, and I will lovingly provide it in ways that are sustainable, safe, and real.

March 7

Release

Many feelings accumulate within us as we try to negotiate the insanity of narcissistic abuse. Often, we have no outlet because we are isolated from our support system, or we may be unable to fully grasp what's happening. Shame can also silence us if we believe that everything is our fault.

It's important to release the stuck energy of the painful emotions and move it out of our body. There are many ways to do this.

We can imagine the narcissist in the chair across from us or 100 miles away (whatever distance feels safe), and we can say everything we need to.

We can write them a letter that we know will never be sent, saying absolutely everything we want and need to say. Afterwards, we can rip it up or burn it.

We can find safe, physical ways to release, such as through dancing, singing, completing a vigorous workout, or hitting our mattress with a pillow.

We can throw rocks in the water, speaking our truth as each one leaves our hand. As our feelings are released into Mother Nature's waters, we can picture the energy we've released being purified and transformed back into love.

Many things come up and out when we're ready to release. It's important to reach out for help and support, even professional support, if we find ourselves overwhelmed by the process.

Today, I will try one of the above strategies to release the energy of the past.

March 8

Wholeness

When we are living through narcissistic abuse, especially the later stages of it, we can feel crazy, broken, lost, and empty. At some point, we may even lack the desire to keep going, feeling disconnected from ourselves, Source, and everyone around us.

Deep inside of us, though, there is a different reality taking place—something that is critical to understand at our lowest times. There is a flame, an energy that burns within us that cannot be extinguished. Our soul, the truest and highest expression of ourselves, remains connected to Source and is always waiting to be expressed.

When we are experiencing narcissistic abuse, we are in survival mode with the bulk of our energy being fed to our abuser. This allows little room for our soul's energy to fill our bodies and our lives, causing our flame to become an almost imperceptible flicker at times. However, even during our darkest night, there is a version of us that is whole and complete inside. No matter how far away we seem from that wholeness, it's always there.

Today, I will remember that there is a whole, healthy version of me inside no matter how impossible life may seem. I will take time to sense the energy of my soul, lit by Source's love, allowing it to radiate throughout me and bring me strength. I know that I can heal and create a life in which my entire being is infused with Source every moment.

March 9

Inner Knowing

Our inner knowing is our connection between ourselves, our soul, and Source. It's where our answers to healing and living an authentic life exist.

The narcissist used abuse tactics to make us doubt our inner knowing, causing us to defer to them as our authority on what to do and who to be. These tactics caused many of us to feel as if we'd completely lost the connection to ourselves and our Higher Power.

Our inner knowing is our greatest resource on our healing journey. It filters through all of the information we take in from outside of us, helping us determine what's true for us. Until we regain strength in our connection to ourselves, we may need information and support from trusted, qualified sources outside of us to help us make good decisions for ourselves.

Every human being is an intricate work of art. There is not another replica of us that exists anywhere. As such, there is no "correct" way to act, think, dress, or be, other than our way. Our owner's manual is written inside of us, powered by our connection to the Divine Energy that created us.

Today, I will practice connecting with my inner knowing in a safe, soothing, and quiet space, seeking shelter from the distractions of the world and my life. I will connect first with my bodily sensations and then go deeper to listen for the whispers of my inner knowing.

March 10

Stonewalling

Stonewalling, shutting down or refusing to communicate, is something that can happen during an argument or heated conversation, when we feel overwhelmed or emotionally flooded. We may also use stonewalling when the past trauma within us gets triggered by the intensity of the moment. We may stop talking, avoid eye contact, or even leave the room. This behavior can be a survival response or perhaps our best attempt at self-care in the moment.

Narcissists have a darker purpose for employing stonewalling. They use it intentionally as a manipulative technique to trigger us by refusing to acknowledge our needs and the truths that we may be attempting to bring to light.

When we look for accountability from them, they may unleash their narcissistic rage or threaten to leave us, triggering our overwhelm, pain, and fear, making certain we will back down. When we confront their poor behavior, they often roll their eyes at us and play the victim, minimize or ignore our concerns, and blame us for ruining their day. They may even refuse to talk to us afterwards—for what seems like an eternity.

Today, I will look at the ways that the narcissist used stonewalling to manipulate me, discovering what caused the pain and fear that made me susceptible to it. I will also determine if I use stonewalling, and I'll look at healthier ways to set boundaries and care for myself in overwhelming situations.

March 11

Feelings and Emotions

Feelings and emotions are our guides, calling out for our presence. They can cue us to people and situations that aren't safe for us, let us know when we're off course, or show us the beauty of life. They can also indicate the presence of old, pent-up energy needing release. Every feeling we have is valid because it's ours.

Feelings and emotions weren't welcome in our relationship with the narcissist. They avoided them—ours and their own—at all costs. If we felt anything, we were often looked at as crazy, weak, needy, or broken. Our emotions were a problem for the narcissist because we were making the moment about us instead of them and their needs.

Now, we can be the loving witness of our feelings and emotions. We can allow them to arise and release as needed, emptying the vast ocean of emotion within us. We can be present with the feelings and emotions of past traumas, as well as the present, allowing them to move through our bodies without holding on to them.

Today, I will take a breath and let the feelings that are right there arise. If I need support, I will reach out to a trusted source, knowing I have the right to ask for what I need. I will remember that I don't need to be fixed as I am not broken. I now know that it's okay to have feelings and emotions—and that I'm perfect as I am.

March 12

Blindsided

Narcissistic abuse tactics often leave us in utter disbelief, unable to comprehend how someone we love could be so cruel or thoughtless. Being attacked from our blind side, where we are the most vulnerable and can be easily caught off guard, leaves deep wounds.

One survivor shared that mere hours after they were intimate with the narcissist for the first time, a sacred moment for the survivor, the narcissist openly flirted with someone else and completely ignored the survivor, who felt worthless and heartbroken as they watched, in shock at the betrayal.

Another survivor shared that while on vacation, the narcissist's rage surfaced. They packed up the survivor's belongings and left them standing alone on a sidewalk in an unfamiliar city, devastated and outraged.

We may feel frustrated, wondering how we continually allowed ourselves to be blindsided by the abuser. We must remember that our vulnerability and openness are superpowers and gifts that were misused in the hands of an unsafe person.

Today, I will think about the times I was blindsided and the thoughts and feelings that emerged with that betrayal. I will be gentle with myself and curious about everything that arises within me. I will connect with my unhealed inner children who were devastated each time I was blindsided, invite them to tell their stories, and listen to them with compassion and understanding.

March 13

Dreams and Nightmares

We often process the unresolved trauma within us through our dreams. The following are several types of dreams associated with narcissistic abuse:

Empowerment Dreams. As the narcissist plays their abusive games, we speak up, ask them to leave, or walk away ourselves. These dreams are a gift, giving us hope or reminding us how far we've come.

"Good" Nightmares. The narcissist is kind, loving, and affectionate. Things between us are warm and wonderful. This truly is a nightmare as we wake up yearning for them, our heart shattered once again.

"Bad" Nightmares. The narcissist is after us, intending to hurt us. Or perhaps we're forced by circumstances to be around the narcissist and their new source of supply, our heart breaking as we watch them together. Maybe we dream that the narcissist is abusing us in the same ways they did while we were still with them. We awaken in excruciating pain, exhausted from intense emotions, with our focus back on the narcissist.

During these nightmares, it's as if the narcissist's vortex is reaching out to us via the energetic connection between us, trying to suck us back in as we sleep. We may awaken feeling attacked and frustrated, the trauma bond raging within us all over again after we've worked so hard to heal.

Today, I will practice extra self-care if I have one of these dreams, and I'll look for the information within them that shows me what I still need to heal.

March 14

Smear Campaigns

One survivor shared a tool that helped them get through a smear campaign. "I have a plaque adorned with the phrase: '*Every storm runs out of rain.*' These words gave me hope during the narcissist's smear campaign which nearly shattered me."

During and after our relationship, narcissists often spread lies and half-truths about us, attempting to destroy our reputation and our lives. They make us look abusive and crazy, so they look like the victim. It's heartbreaking when our family and friends believe them.

It's unimaginable that someone we loved so completely could turn on us and betray us in this way. The narcissist's allegations may bring up intense shame, pain, and fear, triggering our abandonment and persecution wounds from the past.

It's important to seek professional support, if needed, to heal the wounds that are brought to life from the intense triggering taking place, and it helps to have someone remind us that this hell won't last forever.

When we come to understand our own power and worth, healing our core survival wounds and awakening to the magnificent truth of who we are, we will disengage from the narcissist completely, having no need to defend or refute their allegations—and focusing on ourselves and our life instead.

Today, I will remember that I cannot control what the narcissist says or does, but I can control my response to it. I will also remember that what others think of me has absolutely nothing to do with me.

March 15

Identifying Our Inner Children

We may understand the concept of inner children but be unsure of how to go about connecting with our own. The following ideas and suggestions can assist us in becoming aware of and making the connection with our precious inner children.

When we're having a strong reaction to something, feeling intense emotions, we can ask ourselves, "*Who* is feeling this?" in an attempt to discern the age of this version of our inner child or get a picture of them in our mind's eye.

We can look back at our childhood photos and memories, reconnecting us to our younger selves to see if any moments stand out that relate to our current feelings or circumstances.

We can spend time with or observe a child so we can remember ourselves as children.

We can watch for signs of our inner children in our behavior. If we find ourselves eating large amounts of food, we can explore whether one of our inner children is seeking comfort through food or trying to numb themselves to avoid feeling. If we find ourselves on edge, feeling like we're ready to explode, we can calm our body down and attempt to connect with the inner child that is experiencing such big emotions, reassuring them that we're here and they're safe.

Today, with an open heart and mind, I will use my outer circumstances to bring me inside of myself, where I can identify and connect with my inner children.

March 16

Inner Work

While our intellect is an important healing tool, allowing us to learn and research information that can expand our awareness, perhaps the most powerful tool available to us is our inner work, the process of going within ourselves for healing.

When we dedicate time to focus on our inner world, being present with all that we discover there, deep healing can happen. Our answers lie within us, in the place where we connect with our soul's wisdom and with Source. It's there that we also hold unresolved past trauma wounds, our body often revealing them to us when we're ready to heal them. By witnessing and embracing all the dark corners inside of us, we leave our shame behind and are able to carry more light within us.

There's no wrong way to do our inner work. It's an intuitive process that unfolds step by step, each one emerging when we're ready for it. Perhaps we're reading a book and we discover a new healing modality that feels right for us, or a friend mentions a counselor they know, who turns out to be the right counselor for us.

Today, I will notice where I am on my journey with my inner work. If I'm at the beginning, I will look at the resources in this book and elsewhere to find my first step. If I've already traveled some miles on my healing journey, I will take a moment to acknowledge my courage and strength in continuing to heal and grow.

March 17

The Pause

How often have we reacted to someone and immediately wished we could take it back? We run into our ex after we've begun to heal and blurt out a "yes" when they suggest going for coffee. Someone sends us an angry message, and we furiously type up a response and press send. *Cue dramatic music.*

Sometimes people and situations trigger us. It feels like a life-or-death issue that must be taken care of *now*. This is a common trauma response, and it's an especially good time to pause.

If the issue isn't life-threatening, we don't have to respond immediately. We can take a moment to calm ourselves and assess the situation from the perspective of our inner wisdom. Then, from a place of awareness and empowerment, we can decide how to respond rather than react.

Many of us who gained more peace in our lives after establishing No Contact boundaries with a narcissist suddenly felt compelled to contact them again. This is an important time to take a hard stop instead of a pause to explore which of our inner children want to contact them and why. We can then meet our inner children's needs in a more loving way.

Today, I will practice pausing and coming back to a triggering situation after I gain perspective and information from within. In the stillness of the pause, as I sit with my thoughts, I will pay attention to the emotions I am feeling and their location in my body.

March 18

Obsessive Research About Narcissism

After we ended the relationship with the narcissist, we were left reeling, trying to survive the only way we knew.

We may have felt stripped of our confidence, power, and self-worth, but when we began researching narcissistic abuse, we felt things shift with our new understanding of what we'd just been through. There were words, stories, and research that captured the particular hell we'd experienced with the narcissist. Suddenly, we felt empowered and a little freer.

Researching is a valuable process—initially. Awareness is the first step to freedom and healing.

But some people don't stop there. They obsessively learn all there is to know about narcissistic abuse to arm themselves, attempting to feel powerful over the narcissist. This feeds the valid anger we hold inside and heightens feelings of self-righteous indignation.

Over time, though, our energy is drained, and we keep ourselves tied emotionally, mentally, and energetically to the narcissist. This process ultimately keeps us from the quiet space inside where our pain and our possibility for true healing and transformation resides.

Today, I will consider where I am in this process. If I am still researching information about narcissists, I will notice that without judgment. I will know that I'm doing the best I can with all that is arising on my healing journey. I will put the search aside, if even for five minutes, and see what is happening inside of me.

March 19

The Narcissist's "Truth"

What the narcissist says can be quite different than what they mean. Understanding that fact and recognizing the mechanics of narcissistic abuse can empower us, reducing our susceptibility to it in the future.

The following are examples of what the narcissist says *and what they mean*:

You'll never know how much I love you. *If I can make you believe that, you won't leave and make me start the exhausting process of love bombing a new partner.*

They're just an old friend. *We were involved, but I'll lie to you about it so you doubt your intuition. I'll also drop subtle hints at the truth to increase your insecurity.*

I wish you were more adventurous in bed like my exes. *Most of my exes wouldn't do what I'm asking either, but you have weaker boundaries, so I thought I'd at least try to guilt you into making my fantasies a reality.*

Can we remain friends? *I need you as a backup source of supply and to make my new partner jealous and insecure, allowing me to control them. I'll make them dislike you so the two of you won't talk and compare notes about me.*

Today, I will embrace any emotions that surface when I think about the narcissist's hidden agendas with me. I will breathe into the feelings, picturing the energy of them rising out of my body and being transformed back into pure love with the help of my Unseen Support.

March 20

Spring

New life and possibilities unfold as we step into the vivacious energy of spring. This is the time of year when Source reminds us that life is a series of cycles with the rebirth of spring always following even the darkest, coldest winters.

As we soak in spring's lively energy—hearing the birds sing again, seeing the vibrant colors emerging from the grays and whites of winter, and feeling the warmth of the sun on our skin—we are inspired to move forward.

We burst out of our chrysalis after months of transformation and preparation. A sense of awe ensues—and possibly even some hesitation.

Who are we now, as we try out our new wings, dropping further into our soul's truth?

We will learn as we go, discovering the unfolding miracles, a result of all the work we've done during our internal winter.

This sacred process is also at work in our cycles of healing and growth. It can feel like winter when we're facing our inner wounds or shadows within, but spring always comes. Then, we are blessed with new insights, understandings, and opportunities to come alive at an even deeper level than before. It's during the spring of our healing cycles that we reap the miracles and rewards of our hard work.

Today, I will embrace all of Source's nourishing, enlivening gifts of spring. If I feel like I'm experiencing winter within me, I will remember that spring will always follow.

March 21

Crazy

We are not crazy. Narcissistic abuse is crazy. It subtly provoked jealousy, insecurity, and self-loathing. The repeated psychological abuse and threats of abandonment left us begging for acceptance and approval from our abuser. We became highly emotional at times, reactions that were completely understandable under the circumstances. As we exploded, pushed to our limits, the narcissist sat back and calmly accused us of being crazy.

Sometimes, our friends and even our families turned against us as the narcissist spread lies designed to smear us and our reputation—an indescribably painful betrayal. For some, their own children turned against them.

The only way out is through.

We can ask for support as we deal with the agonizing feelings of powerlessness and betrayal that the abuse has created within us. The process of healing from narcissistic abuse can be too much to work through alone.

We can also take comfort in knowing that there are many who have also walked through this nightmare and reached the other side.

Today, I refuse the label of "crazy," or other similar labels, and I will remember that only I know the true insanity and severity of the abuse I've been through. I will do my best to be detached from other people's reactions, knowing that the people who are "my people" will be there when the dust settles. If no one is left, I will create a new support system that honors me and my inherent value.

March 22

Stockholm Syndrome

Encyclopedia Britannica (10 Sept. 2020, https://www.britannica.com/science/Stockholm-syndrome) defines Stockholm Syndrome, a term coined after a 1973 bank robbery attempt in Sweden, as "a psychological response wherein a captive begins to identify closely with his or her captors, as well as with their agenda and demands."

During narcissistic abuse, we bonded deeply with our abuser, willing to go along with their agendas and demands to hold on to the "love" they showed us. We were held captive by our hopes and dreams as well as the fear that our abuse triggered within us. Over time, we became dependent upon the narcissist. Their love and affection alone defined us, which left us craving both. We felt empathy for them, even as they abused us. If anyone attempted to intervene, we'd defend the narcissist and blame ourselves for the problems between us, convinced that others just didn't understand the situation.

Some of us encountered a similar trauma bond in childhood when our ability to bond with our caregivers was a matter of survival. We depended upon them to meet our needs and keep us safe, yet sometimes they were also our abusers. This created an incredibly complex mental and emotional bond with them as we tried to rationalize and cope with their abuse, unable to escape it.

Today, I will have compassion for myself, remembering that bonding with my abuser was a mechanism I used to survive the abuse.

March 23

Being a Victim

Many of us have heard the following:

- Why won't you stop thinking about them and move on with your life?
- It couldn't have been that bad.
- At a spiritual level, you chose it.
- You're overdramatizing.
- I really liked your ex.
- You can choose happiness.
- It's God's will for us to forgive.

We were victimized. Devastated by a narcissist, we earned the right to call ourselves a victim and to feel broken and alone, unsure if we would make it through the pain of loss. Well-meaning people in our lives gave us the message that we should be stronger and less emotional. We should forgive, think of the good, and let it go. They were uncomfortable with our strong feelings and couldn't understand what we'd been through.

Being a victim isn't weak or wrong. There is no need to fight, avoid, or change where we are. We can stay there as long as we need to without buying into society's shame about it. Self-acceptance is absolutely necessary in the process of healing and loving ourselves. We can accept our feelings even if we're the only one who does.

Today, though being a victim isn't where I want to stay forever, I will honor myself and respect the timing of my process. I will choose to surround myself with supportive people who do the same.

March 24

Joy

When we've lived in survival mode for most of our lives, we tend to be a very serious bunch. We're hypervigilant and ready to avert real and imagined danger at any given moment. Many of us never got to be joyful, curious, carefree children. Instead, we had to focus outside of ourselves and figure out how to meet others' needs, in hopes of getting our own met and surviving.

In contrast, joy is a boundless energy felt in the heart that comes from the connection to Source within us where our inner magic and sparkle lives. Experiencing joy may seem like a foreign concept at first, and may even be uncomfortable, as it is a feeling that leaves us extremely vulnerable. What if we open ourselves to the magnificent feeling of joy and it gets ripped away, like so many things in our lives have? It takes courage to allow joy a place in our lives.

Today, I will make a list of everything that sparks joy in my heart, embracing the feelings that arise. If I have no idea what brings me joy, I will tell Source that I'm ready to find out. Then, I will let it go, trusting that the Universe is conspiring to teach me about joy.

March 25

Exhaustion

The deep feeling of exhaustion we experienced while we were with the narcissist was our body's way of telling us that our inner resources were depleted and that change was necessary.

Empty from the continuing cycle of abuse, our superhero routine wasn't working anymore, which further reinforced all the narcissist's thoughts about us. Broken. Lazy. Inept. Crazy. Weak.

In hindsight, many of us wished we'd have listened to and honored our exhaustion, knowing there was a valid reason for it. The narcissist was triggering us and feeding off of our reactions, draining us of our vital energy.

The exhaustion we felt with the narcissist was one that couldn't be cured with sleep. This type of weariness required us to withdraw from the narcissist and consciously stop feeding them our energy. This applied even when we weren't physically present with them but still engaging at an energetic level.

When we preserve our precious energy for ourselves, we begin to come alive again.

Today, I will care for myself and address my exhaustion in whatever way is necessary at this time. If I need to rest or revitalize, I won't hesitate to make it a priority. Whether it's a walk in nature, even a short one, or a twenty-minute nap, I will do whatever is required to restore my vital energy and bring myself back to life.

March 26

Shame

Shame is the agonizing belief that we are somehow defective and undeserving of love. It disempowers and paralyzes us, shutting down the magnificence of who we truly are. Shame sits in our DNA, passed down to us through our genetic ancestry, and it lives in our bodies while we go to great lengths to avoid it.

As children growing up with dysfunctional caretakers, we were given appallingly inaccurate information about our value. It was too painful to acknowledge how abandoned and unloved we felt by those who were supposed to care for us, so we decided we must have caused our mistreatment. Something was wrong with us, and if we fixed it, *then* they'd love us. This illusion we held gave us a fleeting sense of power and hope as the shame within us grew.

In the narcissistic relationship, as in our childhood, feeling unloved and abandoned brought up unbearable pain. Again, we desperately tried to fix ourselves and meet the narcissist's needs so we wouldn't be faced with the crippling sense of shame buried within us. Like our caregivers, the narcissist could not give us what we needed to feel worthy, and it had nothing to do with us.

Today, I will talk about my shame with a safe, supportive person or with Source. I will explore which of my inner children are holding shame, and I'll show them great compassion and accurate reflections of their value.

March 27

Pressure

During the seduction phase of our relationship, the narcissist created an image in their mind of who they wanted us to be, slowly molding us to fit. They made suggestions for how we could change while showering us with "love" and affection.

Once we were hooked, the pressure was on. They pushed us to become that idealized image, disregarding who we were. Our ability to fit that image made them feel better about themselves—and, in their eyes, made us worthy of their love. When we fell short of their standards, they threatened abandonment, insisting they were doing it for our own good—to help us reach "our potential."

Many of us experienced pressure around sex. Some of us were expected to perform sexual acts that were outside of our comfort zone to please them. If we refused, we were called prudes or told we were cruel, unwilling to meet their needs after all they did for us.

After constant pressure, coercion, and threats of abandonment, some of us even started to believe we wanted the same things as the narcissist.

The prolonged pressure of narcissistic abuse eventually took its toll on us. Many of us ended up with chronic conditions like asthma and fibromyalgia, or mental health issues including complex post-traumatic stress disorder (C-PTSD), depression, and anxiety.

Today, I will explore the level of pressure in my narcissistic relationship and how it affected me physically, mentally, and emotionally.

March 28

New Life

As horrible as the narcissistic abuse was, it opened up the potential for us to create a new life for ourselves, the likes of which we'd only dreamed of.

However, before we reached the miracle of a new life, we faced the challenge of a lifetime—breaking our addiction to the narcissist, healing and loving ourselves, and releasing our old way of being. The damage that the narcissist inflicted on us triggered and exposed our past trauma wounds. It stripped away our facades and the defenses we used to keep the pain buried.

First, we entered into our raw and battered internal terrain. In this sacred space, we were able to heal what stood between us and our true, wild and free selves. In our vulnerability, we discovered our soul's truth. What a sacred gift that was.

When we were ready, we let go of our past victimization, all the way from birth to the present, and began to live the life that our soul intended for us, loved and held by Source. Limitless possibilities presented themselves. Our lives were pure potential.

Today, I will remember why I take the sometimes painful, intensive steps of healing from narcissistic abuse, always keeping the end goal in sight—a beautiful, nourishing life that reflects my goodness and light.

March 29

Confusion

Being in an intimate relationship with a narcissist can make us feel like we are constantly lost in confusion. The relationship goes from being the best thing we've ever had to an unimaginable, mind-bending nightmare.

We experience a constant stream of anxiety, questions, and thoughts running in the background of our minds. *What happened to the person I fell in love with? Should I stay or end the relationship? Would they cheat on me? What if I leave and it's the wrong thing to do?* We assess and try to make some sense of it all, unsure of which way to turn. We feel weary and uncomfortable in our own skin.

In truth, we are being controlled and manipulated by the narcissist to see things from their perception of reality. We aren't confused. We are being toyed with so the narcissist can feel powerful.

As we heal the wounds that made us susceptible to the narcissist's tactics, our mind stills, and we come back to our inner connection—the place of our steadfast knowing.

Today, I will pay attention to my state of mind. Is it reeling and spinning like it did when I was with the narcissist? Or is it calm and peaceful? If I ever feel confused again, I will remember to ground myself with the things I am certain about, to remind myself that I am not confused. Instead, I will notice what is confusing about the situation I am in.

March 30

Self-Righteousness

Narcissists often display self-righteousness, believing that they are superior to others and expecting to be treated accordingly. Then, they judge others against their perceived standard of self-perfection.

Victims of narcissistic abuse can also display tendencies of self-righteousness. After falling into the narcissist's skewed version of reality, we may have joined the narcissist in judging others, something that is not necessarily in our normal character. This judgment may even have been extended to members of our family, isolating us and giving the narcissist more control over us. Through our pain, many of us also judged the people that the narcissist used against us to make us jealous or insecure.

After we were drained of our resources and discarded, many of us felt extremely self-righteous, justified in our anger after the horrendous behavior of the narcissist that left us doubting our sanity and fighting to survive.

We can honor those feelings. They deserve our attention and care. At the same time, it's important to consider that while in self-righteousness, we are still focused on the narcissist, handing over our energy and power to them. Healing happens when we disengage from them completely and bring our focus and resources back to us—a difficult but transformative step.

Today, with curious, non-judgmental eyes, I will explore my relationship with self-righteousness and look at the root of that behavior within me.

March 31

Boundaries

Boundaries are our personal rules of engagement that we establish in relationships with others to create space in our lives for us to fully exist. They are loving self-care tools that provide us with a sense of safety and predictability, which is important for the healing and integration of our vulnerable inner children.

As children, many of us were not taught or allowed to have boundaries. Instead, we were left reacting to the circumstances around us. As adults, we can set boundaries and determine how we will respond if they are crossed, taking on a more active role in creating the life we desire.

To identify our boundaries, we must first determine our values. Suppose our former partner was unfaithful. We learned that respect, honesty, and trust were values we were no longer willing to compromise, and we set those boundaries immediately in new relationships.

Learning to set boundaries can be awkward and difficult initially, often triggering our fear of abandonment. There comes a point in our healing journey, though, when the price of putting ourselves aside to meet others' needs becomes too great. We set our boundaries, breathe deep, and let things unfold, unwilling to abandon ourselves any longer.

Today, I will explore where boundaries are present or lacking in my life. I will look at the things I value and decide which boundaries best fit me. I will practice saying "no" if it's something I'm not accustomed to doing.

April 1

Unacceptable Behavior

When we were raised with dysfunctional or toxic caretakers, we had unacceptable behavior modeled to us regularly. Emotional and mental abuse as well as physical or sexual violence may have been a part of our daily existence. That behavior may have seemed normal and even comfortable in some way. It was what we knew, and we associated it with "love," "home," and ironically, even "safety."

As we matured, we may have repeated the offensive behavior we observed, behaved in the exact opposite manner, determined not to repeat it, or found ourselves surrounded by it once again.

During our relationship with the narcissist, we were exposed to their continuous unacceptable behavior. Being that they were an expert manipulator and their injurious behavior may have seemed normal to us, we allowed it to continue, desensitized to it.

Now, we can establish our boundaries, what we will and will not accept. If someone doesn't respect us or the boundaries we've set, we can distance ourselves, refusing to engage with them.

Today, I will no longer put up with behavior that injures me. I will connect to my own values, wants, and needs, and acknowledge my inherent worthiness to be treated with love and respect.

April 2

Strength

Narcissistic abuse can wear us down until we feel completely sapped of strength. We may appear distraught—or even crazy—while the narcissist seems strong and composed. Regardless of how things look on the outside, the truth of what's happening on the inside is vastly different.

The truth is: We are much stronger than the narcissist.

Many narcissists are overwhelmed with shame and self-loathing from their past traumatic wounds, having disowned their true self, where their power and connection to Source is held. They are masterful manipulators, finding people who will support the false self they've created and feed them a steady source of narcissistic supply. Without it they quickly decline since they've locked away their inner resources. This actually makes them quite fragile, vulnerable, and dependent—not at all what they portray on the surface.

Surviving narcissistic abuse showed us how incredibly strong we are—as we fought to keep moving forward while our lives were falling apart around us. Now, after disengaging completely from the narcissist, we have the opportunity to discover an even greater strength—the Brave Love we have for ourselves as we embrace and heal the wounds that made us susceptible to being abused. We can use this powerful love to create a gentle, nourishing, vibrant life.

Today, I will explore my strength before, during, and after narcissistic abuse. Now that I can use my strength to thrive, not just survive, I will find new uses for it that support my healing, well-being, and expansion.

April 3

Journaling

During our experience with narcissistic abuse, journaling may have been a helpful way to explore our confusion, frustration, and pain. After the relationship ended, those entries became reminders of the reasons we were maintaining No Contact with the narcissist. Many of us created an I WILL NOT CALL list with the information from our journals. We kept both handy in case we were tempted to make contact.

Journaling may have also been a way to get out of our rational mind and into our heart. Our soul, connected to Source's infinite wisdom and love, could speak to us through our writing, bringing clarity while guiding and supporting us.

After the abusive relationship ended, one survivor read through their old journals, amazed at what they found. The truth of their inner wisdom was written in those pages, but they couldn't hear it at the time they wrote it. They put it aside in their pursuit of the "love" the narcissist showed them initially, their inner wisdom taking a backseat to their painful, unmet needs.

Journaling has also been a useful tool to help us access our wounded inner children who are waiting to be heard. Once we take the time to listen, they will share their wants, needs, feelings, and their pain, allowing us to honor and release it.

Today, I will lovingly focus inside, with pen to paper, allowing whatever is ready to be expressed and revealed to flow through me onto the page.

April 4

Survival

We're magnificent beings with physiological measures in place to help us survive trauma. When we perceive we're in danger, all available resources in our bodies are channeled to help us survive. The part of our brain that processes information goes offline, allowing our reactive brain to kick in and deal with the crisis at hand. There are four instinctive survival responses that can be triggered when we are faced with a threat or memories of it:

Fight. We stand ready to aggressively face the threat.

Flight. We flee to escape the threat.

Freeze. We freeze because the threat is too overwhelming.

Fawn. We put our needs aside and please others to avoid the threat.

In the narcissistic relationship, many of us learned not to fight or flee as we would risk further abuse or abandonment and lose the hope of ever experiencing the narcissist's "love" again.

Many of us coped by freezing—spacing out and feeling far away. We may also have felt overwhelmed and unable to move, make a choice, or form a thought.

When fawning, a common reaction to narcissistic abuse, we put aside our wants, needs, and values to keep things smooth and avoid the repercussions of the narcissist's rage and reactions. As a result, we felt unsure of who we were and looked to the narcissist to define us.

Today, I will do something special to honor my miraculous body for helping me survive narcissistic abuse.

April 5

Getting Sucked In

One survivor lamented, "I used to be confident in myself and my decisions. I was healthy, well respected in my career, and had a wonderful circle of friends. Now my life is a wreck. How did this happen?"

Many of us can relate to the above sentiments. We were baited and love bombed by a pro. Like a tracker, they watched our every move, determining whether we were worth the energy of the hunt. When they found our Achilles' heel—perhaps our fear of abandonment or betrayal—they discovered how to attach themselves to us by becoming exactly who we needed. They used manipulative tactics that were beyond anything we could've imagined.

Narcissists often lure in smart, powerful people who have wounds around intimacy. The stronger and more successful we were when the abuse started, the more powerful the narcissist felt as they stripped it all away from us.

First, we must be gentle and compassionate with ourselves. We are one of MANY intelligent, confident people who have experienced narcissistic abuse. We can now lovingly take ourselves, step by step, toward recovery, healing, and freedom.

Today, I will take a non-judgmental look at how I was drawn into a relationship with a narcissist. I will connect with my unhealed inner children who needed what the narcissist offered, finding a healthy way to meet those needs for myself.

April 6

The Burden of Another's Needs

In our relationship with the narcissist, we unknowingly took on the burden of meeting their insatiable needs. It didn't matter how much we gave. It was never enough. This took its toll on our well-being, depleting our vital energy and inner resources. The burden was as insidious as the abuse itself. The narcissist gradually placed responsibility for their happiness and satisfaction on our shoulders, unwilling to be responsible for themselves.

Many of us have known the burden of others' needs in the past. We may have had caregivers who were actually care*takers*. Their needs took priority over everything, including our well-being. We quickly learned to meet their needs and be who they wanted us to be, in hopes of getting at least some of our needs met. It was exhausting. Life wasn't supposed to be that hard, and we shouldn't have had to work to get our needs met. We deserved unconditional love, care, and devotion.

Now, as adults, we can create an abundant life in which we make our needs a priority. It is no longer an obligation to meet someone else's needs for them—it is a choice. We can surround ourselves with people who take responsibility for their own needs and who choose to be with us while we do the same.

Today, I will put down the burden of others' needs, and I will meet my own needs as an act of self-love.

April 7

Abandonment

Our greatest threat as children was abandonment by our caregivers. We learned quickly, even as toddlers, to carefully read them and act appropriately to ensure that our needs would be met. We became whoever we needed to be in order to stay safe and alive.

Those survival patterns were strengthened by the narcissist's constant threats of abandonment. So we silenced ourselves. We stayed close to home, watching over them, ensuring they didn't stray. We put aside our wants, needs, and passions, so we could remain attractive to them. We lost or gained weight, whitened our teeth, enlarged our breasts, participated in crazy sexual acts, or became funny and larger than life—even if we didn't feel that way.

When the pain of denying our own existence became greater than our fear of abandonment, we began making different choices.

As we come to understand how strong and capable we are, especially when we are connected to our soul, our fear of abandonment lessens. We can create boundaries to manage abandonment, surrounding ourselves with healthier people instead of being a victim to it. We can work to heal our core abandonment wounds and refuse to abandon ourselves any longer.

Today, I will look at the things I did to avoid abandonment, both as a child and in my relationship with the narcissist. I will remember that I am responsible for my own needs now, and any extra support I receive is a bonus.

April 8

Respecting Ourselves

As children, by observing the actions and words of our dysfunctional caretakers, many of us came to believe that we were not valuable or worthy of respect.

In actuality, their disrespectful actions and words had nothing to do with us and everything to do with their own mental health issues, patterning, wounds, and past traumas still held within them. Unfortunately, we internalized the painful messages they gave us, believing that we didn't measure up or deserve to be loved and respected.

The narcissist reinforced this grossly inaccurate belief many times after the love bombing phase was over. Our time, energy, thoughts, feelings, needs, wants, finances, and our bodies may all have been disrespected by the narcissist.

As we become aware of the erroneous messages that have defined us, we get to choose new definitions of who we are. We can now respect ourselves, setting boundaries and making sure our needs are met. It may feel uncomfortable at first, as we learn these new skills. We can even put distance between us and the people in our life that don't respect us.

We are magnificent beings.

There isn't another person like us on Earth.

We are worthy of respect because we exist.

No other qualifiers are required.

Today, I will love myself enough to see the truth about me and my value. I will cast off the messages that I received from the unhealthy people in my life, respect myself, and embrace my truth.

April 9

Fear

Fear on its own can be a useful emotion. It lets us know when there's a threat we need to be aware of, and it can keep us safe. Fear coupled with PTSD and unresolved trauma can cripple us, making us feel like we're never safe. It can be incredibly frustrating when the fear within us was created by abuse or neglect we didn't ask for or deserve.

Many of us are uncomfortable with our fear, causing us to suffer with it in shame and silence. When we express it, we're often told there's nothing to fear, giving us the message that having it is unacceptable.

What others don't understand is that healing our fear is a process, which we're doing our best to get through. Only we can ever know how hard we're working or what our path with fear is. The more we accept the fear within us, the easier it is to work with it.

Whatever our relationship with fear, we're perfect right where we are. When we're ready, we'll take another step forward in healing it. Sometimes, it's a long path, but we only need to take one step at a time, moving as we're guided to from within and reaching out for support when necessary.

Today, I will accept wherever I am with my fear, knowing there is a valid reason it's there. I will move at my own pace, trusting my process and loving myself through it all.

April 10

We Are Not Alone

When we entered the relationship with the narcissist, many of us had a strong support system in place. Isolation was a tactic the narcissist used to separate us from family and friends. They quickly became our sole source of support, making it easier to control us and pull us into their self-created narrative of reality without interference from outside.

They began by revealing judgments and criticisms of our support people, perhaps shaming us for "needing all of those people" as they attempted to isolate us.

This process left us feeling lost and alone within a world of chaos, confusion, and hurt. We felt no one could possibly understand what was happening because we couldn't comprehend it ourselves.

One survivor contemplated getting professional help while still in the relationship, but attempting to put their confusing, mind-bending experiences in a cohesive narrative to share with someone else seemed much too big and overwhelming. As a result, they stayed silent and alone.

In truth, we are never alone. There are survivors on the other side of narcissistic abuse who absolutely understand what we've been through, and our Source is always with us.

Today, I will reach out for support if I need to, even if I think my story won't make sense. I will embrace all my sources of support from this world and from the Unseen World. I will speak my truth even if it takes a while to put into words.

April 11

Responsibility

The narcissist conditioned us to believe that we were responsible for every undesirable thing that happened in the relationship. We were too difficult, selfish, needy, or weak.

We also took responsibility for the narcissist's needs. We wanted to ensure their continued happiness to avoid their narcissistic rage and abandonment. Feeling resentment was a cue that we'd taken on more than our share of responsibility.

Not my responsibility:

- Providing sex at the narcissist's every request.
- Putting my needs aside and stopping my life to ensure the narcissist was happy and faithful.
- Working myself to exhaustion to gain the narcissist's recognition and approval.
- Excusing the narcissist's inappropriate behavior.

My responsibility:

- Knowing and clearly communicating my wants and needs.
- Creating and ensuring my own happiness and peace.
- Respecting my body, mind, spirit, time, and energy by setting necessary boundaries.
- Speaking up when things or people hurt me.
- Keeping myself safe and sane.
- Filling myself up first and then giving to others.

Learning how to be responsible to ourselves when we weren't taught how to do so is a process that takes time and practice.

Today, I will explore what is actually my responsibility and what I've taken on that I need to give back to others.

April 12

Letting Go

Letting go of the narcissist, and our relationship with them, can be agonizing and may even seem impossible at times. Trying to hold on, we often create illusions that represent the reality we wish were true.

One illusion we hang on to is the idea that the narcissist is "family" and we will always be with them in some capacity, even if our intimate relationship is over.

Another illusion we create is that we have a sacred, everlasting soul connection with the narcissist that can never be broken.

An illusion that many of us have used to try and hang on is that in order to let go of the narcissist and find closure with them, we need to talk to them. Any attempts we made only strengthened the trauma bond and drained us as we provided them with more narcissistic supply and information to use against us in the future.

We will never get closure with the narcissist. It must come from within us.

Once we let go of the narcissist and make the connection with ourselves and our Source a priority, we come to realize that those are the most fulfilling, nourishing connections of all.

For today, I will have great love and compassion for myself as I steadfastly walk forward making this painful transition. I will remember why I am doing this, and I'll look forward to the miracles that follow such a difficult task.

April 13

Winning the Inner Battle

"We can choose short-term comfort for long-term pain, or short-term discomfort for long-term gain." — Dr. Courtney Paré

A battle raged within us during narcissistic abuse. On one side was our adult self, led by our soul's wisdom, who would never have stayed with an abuser. On the other side were our wounded inner children, starving for love and devotion. They would've rather died than be abandoned by the narcissist or be forced to give up the crumbs, which seemed like entire cakes, that the narcissist fed us during the love bombing phase.

After the relationship ended, our adult self had more room to exist, but our inner children fought harder to return to the narcissist, still attempting to get their needs met. When they won, we lost, as the pain of the trauma bond once again shattered us.

The path to healing is loving and accepting those inner children and meeting their needs ourselves. We can then walk forward as our adult selves to the best of our ability every day, knowing that maintaining No Contact and refusing to engage with the narcissist will catapult us forward so we can free ourselves from the vicious cycle of narcissistic abuse.

Today, if I am tempted to break No Contact, I will identify what I need and provide that to myself. I will remember that the discomfort of not engaging with the narcissist won't last forever, and it is leading to my freedom and a beautiful life.

April 14

Belonging to Ourselves

Many of us wander through life looking outside of ourselves for a sense of belonging, but the place we really yearn to belong is in our own skin.

Belonging to ourselves is loving and knowing ourselves so completely that nothing outside of us—others' beliefs, judgments, or expectations—could possibly make us waver from who we are.

Belonging to ourselves means total acceptance of who we are—our strengths *and* weaknesses. We know when to hold ourselves accountable whether with a gentle nudge or a supportive push forward when it's time to grow. We also know when it's time to be still and rest or go inward and connect with our soul self.

Belonging to ourselves offers a guarantee that we'll never be abandoned again. We don't need others' love, validation, or acceptance because we have our own. If someone freely offers us those things, we feel gratitude.

When we belong to ourselves, we recognize the divinity within us and treat ourselves with utmost respect, nourishing ourselves and flourishing as a result.

Belonging to ourselves means we follow our own rhythms, which may not make sense to anyone else, but that's okay. We know what we're doing.

This solid sense of belonging gives us the strength and courage to stand on our own and to bring our passion and purpose to the world.

Today, I will contemplate the concept of belonging to myself, and I will tune into the power, peace, and freedom that comes with that.

April 15

Embracing Our Inner Children

I was once told by a "spiritual guru" that the concept of the inner child was only the ego trying to sabotage us and there was no value in focusing on it. As I began to heal and discover my own truth, I took on a different perspective about the value of embracing my inner children.

I realized that my inner four-year-old who sees, feels, and senses everything had correctly assessed every toxic intimate partner I became involved with. I'd get a flash of knowing, and then a tension in my chest or a knot in my stomach, before the teenage part of me who was starved for love and acceptance dismissed the warning and jumped in.

I became aware of my inner five-year-old's intuitive survival skills after re-experiencing the memory of her running up to my alcoholic father and trying to make him laugh as he became belligerent. That moment marked the start of an exhausting pattern of trying to keep myself safe.

I also discovered that some of my very young inner children did not yet have language to convey what they experienced, but my body remembered what they couldn't express.

Beautiful things can happen when we embrace our inner children and see their value, including never again accepting another's belittling, shame, or disregard of them, and never again apologizing for their needs to make someone else comfortable.

Today, I will contemplate my thoughts and feelings about embracing my inner children.

April 16

Self-Sabotage

"Our deepest fear is not that we are inadequate. Our deepest fear is that we are powerful beyond measure. It is our light, not our darkness that most frightens us." — Marianne Williamson, *A Return to Love: Reflections on the Principles of "A Course in Miracles"*

We were strong in our recovery from narcissistic abuse, our life feeling exquisitely peaceful, until one day, seemingly out of nowhere, we broke No Contact with the narcissist. Once again, we were faced with the enormous task of getting out of the trauma bond and back onto our feet.

Why did we do that?

Maybe we're trying to keep ourselves hidden and our lives small. Our bodies still hold past experiences of persecution, a time when our inner light and power was seen as threatening to fearful people and was extinguished.

Perhaps we're wavering because letting go of our old way of being is painful. After knowing trauma our entire lives, we go through a process of grieving our old reality as we step into a peaceful, nourishing life.

Growth can be triggering. Overwhelmed by the dysfunction that surrounded us as children, we learned to keep our lives small, manageable, and safe. Living from our adult self and expanding our lives can trigger fear or overwhelm within us.

Today, I will explore with curiosity and self-compassion my ways of self-sabotaging. I will remember that I can get back on my feet and continue moving forward at any moment without shame or self-judgment.

April 17

Holes

When narcissists seduce us, they ask us many questions about ourselves. We feel seen and heard, maybe for the first time. In truth, they're identifying the holes within us, the past wounds that leave us vulnerable to their manipulation and control. They have no intention of supporting us with this information. Instead, they use it to more effectively extract our energy to meet their insatiable need for narcissistic supply.

Then, they assure us that they'll fill our holes.

"Your last partner left you?" they ask, perceiving our fear of abandonment. "I would never do that to someone. I'll always be here for you."

Yet they do exactly that. They abandon us by cheating or flirting with others as we stand by and watch—until they finally discard us completely.

When we look to a narcissist or anyone outside of us to fill our holes, we are trying to use a square peg to fill a round hole. Only we know how to fill our holes. Our inner children crave the patience, compassion, love, and acknowledgement they needed in the past and never received. We can become a reliable source of support for them now, bringing true healing and integration to ourselves. Anything extra we receive from others is a bonus.

Today, I will let go of trying to use others to fill my holes. I will dedicate my time and energy to creating a firm foundation of love and respect within myself. Then I will attract people who have done the same.

April 18

Reaction vs. Curiosity

Becoming curious about our strong emotional reactions to triggers can be an opportunity for healing and growth.

One survivor shared an upsetting pattern which happened often in their toxic relationship. At social events, their narcissistic partner would continually ignore them, instead flirting with and being attentive to other interested party guests. This behavior triggered intense feelings of hurt, anger, and humiliation in the survivor.

Again and again, the survivor reacted, like a car stuck in the mud, with engine revving and tires spinning. When a friend suggested they explore this pattern with curiosity, the survivor was taken aback by the new perspective they gained, which gave them the necessary traction to free themselves and move forward.

Bringing their focus inside, they saw how the narcissist's actions triggered their past feelings of worthlessness, feeding their outdated belief that they aren't enough.

Looking at the narcissist's behavior with curiosity, the survivor recognized the narcissist's high need for external validation—which required more than any one person could ever provide to them.

The survivor felt relief, recognizing that the narcissist's behaviors weren't about them at all. Instead, they were about the narcissist's insatiable need for narcissistic supply, which they needed to survive a life cut off from Source.

Today, I will think of a past reaction I had to the narcissist. I will bring my awareness inside of myself, exploring my response with curiosity.

April 19

Crumbs

We became spellbound by the narcissist's manipulation during the love bombing stage. We were seduced by their overflowing displays of "love," affection, and acceptance. It felt like we were receiving more than anyone had ever given us before, and we were elated to have found them.

As the relationship progressed into cycles of devaluation and devastation, we worked harder to try and recreate what we experienced in the beginning, giving more and more of ourselves. The narcissist took it all and doled out just enough crumbs to keep us engaged.

Their actions convinced us that the responsibility for their change of heart fell squarely on our shoulders. We worked to alter ourselves and better accommodate their wants and needs, hoping we'd be "loved" again. In truth, their radical changes had nothing to do with us and everything to do with the narcissistic abuse cycle.

During or after the relationship, as our illusions began to crumble, we became painfully aware that what we were actually receiving from the narcissist was crumbs. Unfortunately, they were the best crumbs we'd ever gotten from anyone, leaving us unaware that they were crumbs at all.

Today, I will no longer accept crumbs. I will remember that I deserve so much more. I am worthy of and am going for the entire cake! I will welcome mature love that flows freely into my life, not love that I must toil for. I now understand that isn't love at all.

April 20

Boundaries: Meeting Others' Needs

In intimate relationships, it's not our job to take on our partner's needs as our obligation, a concept that may be hard to grasp at first. It may even feel cold and heartless, the very idea triggering our fear of abandonment.

The following are other perspectives about meeting the narcissist's needs:

- The narcissist believed that if they made their needs known to us, we should and would meet them. *No.* Our needs mattered, too, and we had the right to say *no*—or *not right now.*
- It's okay if the narcissist didn't always get their needs met. No one does. We are all disappointed at times.
- We could have acknowledged their needs, but it wasn't our job to do anything with them. As adults, they had the ability to figure out other ways of getting their needs met.
- When someone states a need, we can ask ourselves, "Do I have any interest in meeting that need?" If we don't, it's always okay to say no.

As we explore life outside of taking responsibility for others' needs, we can practice saying no a lot at first until we have solid boundaries and know what we want for ourselves.

Today, I know that my life is about much more than just meeting the needs of others. I am here to live, love, and express the wonder of who I am.

April 21

Energy

We each exist at a specific energetic frequency, and our reality consists of things that match that frequency. When we are living out the truth of who we are, we vibrate at a high frequency, in tune with our Source. When we met the narcissist, we willingly compressed ourselves down to meet the narcissist's frequency and create equilibrium. We did this because of our past trauma, inner wounds, and unmet needs.

One survivor shared that the moment they made the decision to give their relationship with the narcissist another try, they felt themselves instantly "densify" (a term they created to describe the heaviness that overtook them). They felt the forward motion of their life come to a screeching, numbing halt. They understood that moving forward with the narcissist would necessitate existing in a diminished capacity—a heartbreaking realization for them.

As we heal our wounds and become devoted to ourselves, we raise our energetic frequency. We are strong, able to set boundaries, and no longer a vibrational match for the narcissist.

Today, I will explore how the work I'm doing is changing my vibration. Even if I temporarily go backwards, I will keep doing my healing work and look forward to finding out what and who I resonate with as I change my frequency.

April 22

Criticism

Criticism is judging the virtues and failings of some*thing*. It can be useful for evaluating works of art or job performance, behaviors, or attitude.

Criticism has no place being used on a human being. It's misguided to judge *who we are*, as we all have enormous inherent value. Each of us was created perfect, bringing a combination of unique gifts to this world.

We can gently acknowledge the things within ourselves we'd like to change and that don't fit anymore, but self-criticism has no value. When we fully accept ourselves as we are, we can receive and work with these awarenesses, allowing us to become the truest version of ourselves without adding judgment to the process. This results in deep healing.

But can't we criticize the narcissist after all they've done? That is a necessary and understandable stage we go through in our healing process. But as we put our focus back on ourselves and our lives, we acknowledge their destructive actions and accept who they are while maintaining No Contact and firm, clear boundaries to ensure our health, safety, and peace.

Today, I will remember that I never have to diminish myself again, no matter what. If there are things I need to change, I will be aware of them and gently move toward my goals without diminishing the magnificence of who I am.

April 23

Red Flags

In car racing, when the flagman throws a red flag, drivers know the track is unsafe, and the race stops immediately. In dating, our soul raises red flags for us, but due to the depth of our wounds and unmet needs inside, we don't always stop immediately. With the narcissist, we were unable to perceive our soul's red flags, focused instead on all the "love" they were showering us with.

Substance abuse and domestic violence are two of the more obvious red-flag relationship behaviors. When those things are "normal" to us, however, we don't see red flags. To survive and avoid the pain inside, we try not to see anything at all.

There are other, more subtle red-flag behaviors to watch for in potential partners, including lying, being obsessed with social media, acting controlling or jealous, refusing to apologize, and claiming that all their former partners were crazy. In addition, having significant differences in values with our potential partner in areas like sex, money, and work can be red flags.

We can also look inside ourselves for red flags, for things such as suddenly feeling stupid, insecure, or not good enough. We might also feel confused and doubt our perceptions of things happening in the relationship.

Today, I will hold a space of love and understanding for myself as I look back at the red flags I missed in the narcissistic relationship, learning more to help me recognize them sooner in the future.

April 24

Yellow Flags

While watching for red flags in a new partner's actions and attitudes, it's also important to look for yellow flags. These are annoyances in our partner's behavior we choose to monitor as they could turn into red flags.

Deciding whether a behavior is a yellow flag, red flag, or nothing at all is a determination each of us must make for ourselves after assessing all the information that we have.

Consider the following behaviors.

Interrupting others. Is this done innocently, or is it rude and done to control the conversation?

Swearing. Does it happen only with their best friends, or in public in front of anyone? Does it have a violent or threatening tone?

Being rude to us or others. Are they shaming, demanding, disrespectful, embarrassing, or inappropriate? Are they going through an incredibly stressful time in their life? Does this happen often?

Not wanting to make the relationship public. Are they trying to be responsible, perhaps not wanting their children to know about the relationship yet? Or are they evasive about the reason, which leaves us wondering?

We can share our concerns with our partner, their response providing further information. Are they defensive? Are they willing to work on the concern, expressing a desire to learn and grow?

Today, I will check in with my gut feelings as I assess possible yellow flags, maintaining the willingness to walk away if necessary, refusing to abandon myself or my needs again.

April 25

Passion

Passion can be described as a compelling sexual or romantic desire for someone, a strong feeling about a person or thing, a powerful inner drive and feeling of excitement about doing something, and an intense emotional feeling that causes us to act.

Often, we think of passion exclusively in a sexual or romantic context. But we are looking at someone's manifested passion every time we appreciate art, watch a movie, or read a book. Passion gives us the strength and commitment to persevere and reach our goals, which can be seen in the hard-earned success of an elite athlete or the work of a timeless musician.

Passion is an energetic force that originates within us. Finding our passion is finding our soul's truth. We each came to this world with unique gifts, and when we free ourselves from the past, letting go of all that we're not, we make room for those gifts and our true, wild, and free selves to emerge.

Some people create their entire lives around the expression of their passion, which becomes their purpose, supporting their physical, emotional, mental, and spiritual health, and keeping their inner sparkle bright.

Today, I will contemplate what passion means to me. As I grow and heal, I will pay attention to what activities bring out my passion and make me come alive.

April 26

Sex

Amid the mingling of bodies and energies during sex, the narcissist receives big hits of narcissistic supply. As a result, getting their sexual needs met may have been their top priority during our relationship, leaving some of us feeling drained, objectified, and alone.

The narcissist may have:

- Used sex as a reward or withheld it as a punishment.
- Shamed us by comparing our body or sexual performance to others.
- Incorporated props, sex toys, or other people to avoid intimacy with us during sex.
- Used abusive tactics to convince us that we wanted to engage in edgy, painful, and even dangerous sexual activities.

Our bodies are sacred, wondrous creations. We're all perfect exactly as we are. There is no ideal sized body, breasts, hips, or legs. There is no right or wrong way to have sex.

Now, out of the relationship, we can redefine sex for ourselves according to *our* wants and needs. Do we want love notes? Romance? Soft and slow touches? Lots of eye contact? Do we enjoy role playing? Outdoor sex? Sex once a week? Multiple times a night? Multiple partners?

What we want matters.

Today, I will explore what good sex looks and feels like for me. I will honor all that arises within me, and I will reach out for support if I need it. I will remember that I never have to engage in sex out of obligation again—only by choice—when and how it feels good to me.

April 27

Worthiness

Do you have any idea how worthy you are of being loved? The very fact that you exist makes it so. You are the only one like you on this entire planet. No one else brings the gifts you bring or sparkles quite the way you do.

In the past, we may not have received the love, devotion, and respect that was rightfully ours. As a result, we weren't able to see our own value and didn't respect ourselves. We gravitated toward familiar situations that did not support us.

Now, we can discover our worthiness and provide ourselves with the love and devotion we missed, by going inside to witness the truth of who we are. We can discover our wants and needs, set boundaries that support us, and address the wounds that have kept us accepting less than we deserve. Then, we can engage with people and situations that support our true worthiness.

Today, I will spend time honoring the beauty of who I am, inside and out. I will explore the people and situations in my life to see if they support the truth of who I am now or if they reinforce what I believed about myself in the past.

April 28

Obsessive Thoughts

Where there is narcissistic abuse, there are obsessive thoughts. Without deep inner healing, these agonizing intrusions can persist.

Working with our inner children, healing and releasing our trauma wounds, and refusing to abandon ourselves are all important steps in facilitating the healing process. The following tools can help us cope with obsessive thoughts as we work on our recovery from narcissistic abuse:

- **Maintaining No Contact** to diminish triggers that increase our obsessive thoughts.
- **Moving our body** to release pent-up energy.
- **Practicing guided meditation** to refocus our minds and relax our bodies.
- **Accepting** our thoughts—because when we fight them, they get stronger.
- **Connecting with our inner children** who obsess so we can reassure them and meet their needs.
- **Getting lost** in our favorite music or an engaging activity to refocus our attention.
- **Becoming the curious observer** of our thoughts to gain a different perspective.
- **Cutting energetic cords** with the narcissist.
- **Spending time in nature**, soaking in Her grounded, nourishing goodness.
- **Reaching out for support.**

Today, I will try one of the tools listed above if I am ruminating about the narcissist, remembering that as I do my inner work, I am taking the steps to resolve any obsessive thoughts and free myself from the effects of narcissistic abuse.

April 29

Miracles

Healing from narcissistic abuse is a process that requires hard work and a commitment to ourselves. The healing miracles that can happen make every moment worth it in the end.

As we disengage from the narcissist, we may encounter things that seem more painful than being with the narcissist, such as braving the cravings caused by the trauma bond within us or enduring a smear campaign initiated by the narcissist.

During those painful times, it's important to remember that we are creating space within us for something fresh to emerge—a life full of new experiences and relationships we may never have dreamed possible. Our new life will be sustainable because we are creating it for ourselves in partnership with Source.

All our hard work will pay off. One survivor shared their story: "I can still remember the day when the maddening reel of endless thoughts about the narcissist that ran in the background of my consciousness just stopped. I suddenly realized my mind was quiet and I was thinking of things other than the narcissist. I consider that a miracle."

Today, I will remember that miracles will come if I stay focused, to the best of my ability, on doing the things that will bring me into a new reality. I will meet and deepen the relationships with myself and Source, and together we will create a life that inspires me and reflects the amazing beauty of who I truly am inside.

April 30

Pampering Ourselves

Life can be overwhelming, demanding much of us. When we're always on the go, it's easy to forget about the soul magic within us that awaits expression. When we free ourselves from the monotony of everyday life, even for a moment, it has space to emerge. Pampering ourselves, something that looks different for each of us, is one way to bring about that freedom.

We can pamper our adult selves with a massage or a hot bath with salts, essential oils, and relaxing music. We can get lost in the book we've been wanting to read or take time for a stress-releasing run or game of golf. Pampering could also be sitting outside under the full moon, letting the wind play in our hair as we connect to the wildness deep within us.

We can also pamper our inner children, whether in our minds or in real life, giving them the fun and care they may have missed. This could include a day of fun by ourselves or with others—making sandcastles, running up and down the beach with wild abandon, having a dance party in the living room, or making a blanket fort and reading a book by flashlight. It's healing and okay to do those things, even as adults!

Today, I will put aside all my obligations for a moment and discover what my heart yearns to do. Then, I will make it happen, freeing my soul magic in the process.

♥

May 1

Vulnerability

Seduced by the narcissist, we were instantly drawn in. Thinking we'd found "the one," we became vulnerable, revealing everything about ourselves including our deepest wounds and fears. After the love bombing stage, the narcissist used our vulnerability against us, wounding us where it hurt the most and playing on our greatest fears. We learned to hide our precious selves away deep inside, building walls of protection around our heart—a survival skill many of us perfected long ago.

Embarking on our healing journey, we began to peel off our layers of protection as we healed their corresponding wounds. After building up enough courage, confidence, and trust in ourselves, we reclaimed our radiant vulnerability and the power and freedom that comes with it. Once again, we felt comfortable in our own skin. Vulnerability made intimacy possible as our focus began to shift from protection to connection.

We lived without fear of being exposed because we knew, loved, and accepted every part of ourselves. We set and maintained boundaries to create a life that supported our vulnerability. We took new relationships slowly, knowing others must earn our trust and the right to be close to our radiant, vulnerable selves that we worked so hard to unearth.

Today, I will explore my vulnerability. Whether it's hidden away, I've reclaimed it, or I'm still peeling and healing, I will lovingly accept whatever I find, seeing it as my strength instead of my weakness.

May 2

One Step at a Time

Taking life one step at a time helps us stay in the present moment and allows us to deal with anything that arises in manageable chunks while we prioritize our self-care. This leads to more peace within us.

After our toxic relationship, our lives were upended. Many of us were exhausted and in survival mode, lacking the inner capacity to manage our lives normally. Faced with overwhelming feelings and physical symptoms, we were often forced to take things one hour, one minute, or even one second at a time, unable to get through more than that, dealing only with what was right in front of us.

We can maintain the focus on taking things one step at a time with most things in our life, such as getting through only one problem, one appointment, or one day of No Contact at a time. This is a loving, compassionate way to care for ourselves and make our life more manageable.

When we have a big problem to work through, it can feel overwhelming and intimidating at first glance. However, when we tackle just one part of it at a time, the problem becomes more manageable, and completing a part of it gives us a feeling of accomplishment and proof that we are making progress.

Today, I will focus on taking life one step at a time when I am feeling overwhelmed, remembering that changing my perspective will change my experience.

May 3

Worry

Worrying, a fearful and often paralyzing thought process, is a coping mechanism many of us have used. When we've survived trauma and abuse, the world feels unsafe, and we see potential threats everywhere, giving us much to worry about.

When we worry, we're usually focusing on worst-case scenarios. Remaining in those scenarios is often a protective measure we learned early in life. Then, we don't have as far to fall when the next painful thing happens. We're already there.

When we worry, we are projecting our precious energy and attention outside of ourselves to the future. It is stressful and affects us physically, mentally, emotionally, and spiritually. Instead, we can now find different coping mechanisms that allow us to use our time and inner resources in a healthier way, supporting our continued healing.

Managing the anxiety behind our worry is an empowering way to refocus our energy inward. We can accomplish this by practicing focused breathing exercises, getting enough sleep, working with our inner children holding the anxiety, moving our bodies through exercise or soulful dancing, practicing meditation or yoga, or reaching out for support.

Today, I will explore and honor my past relationship with worry. I will identify one new coping mechanism to use the next time I find myself worrying.

May 4

Money

Some of us lost large amounts of money to the narcissist as they disregarded what was fair and right, focusing only on their own needs. It is inconceivable to us that someone we loved and gave ourselves to so completely could treat us that way. A shocking, yet predictable betrayal.

Some of us had to let our money go. We walked away to save our lives, learning that we are the most precious resource we have. Others fought for what was ours, and in the process, we found our voice and learned how to support ourselves.

Now, focused on our growth and healing, we can consider the money we lost as tuition. When it's time, we will see all the wisdom we gained in our relationship with the narcissist, and we'll know a new strength and self-confidence.

Moving into a new life, we can now explore and deepen our relationship with money, ensuring we will make different choices with it in the future.

What is our history with money? What messages were we given about it growing up? What fears do we have about money? What are some positive, exciting things we would do with more of it?

Today, I will honor the feelings I have about the money I lost to the narcissist, but I won't get stuck there. I will remember that I can now create a conscious, joyful, and innovative relationship with money.

May 5

Caretaking

Caretaking, prioritizing others' needs while putting our own aside, is a survival skill that many of us learned early in life. Growing up in a dysfunctional family, we attempted to meet our parents' needs in hopes that they would meet ours—a matter of safety and survival. We cared more about others and their lives than they did, often gaining positive attention and a sense of value as a result.

Carrying this behavior into our adult lives, we were easy targets for narcissists. We looked to their needs to decide our next moves, and we read their feelings to determine our value. This gave them a sense of great power as they shaped us into who they wanted us to be.

While caretaking the narcissist, we were often forced to face our pattern of self-abandonment—a partner to caretaking. Our inner children became angry, even rageful, after they and their needs had been put aside too many times, causing some of us to blow up or shut down completely. The narcissist declared us crazy to whomever would listen.

For today, I know that my life is about so much more than taking care of others. I will honor all the feelings that emerge as I look with great love and understanding at my self-abandonment and caretaking behaviors. I will take the time to discover who I am and what my needs are as I create a life in which I have space to fully exist.

May 6

Unavailability

As children, when our caretakers were wrapped up in their own dysfunction, illness, or distractions, we learned that they were unavailable—mentally, emotionally, and sometimes even physically. We adjusted accordingly to survive.

As adults, many of us found ourselves in unhealthy relationships in which we felt incredibly alone, even after we'd given all of ourselves. *Why?* Often, we were repeating the pattern we'd learned well in childhood: being drawn to people who were unavailable.

Sometimes, we were attracted to people who were married or already had a partner. We may also have been drawn to those who had an addiction or traveled a lot for work, preventing them from being available. The narcissist was the pinnacle of unavailability after banishing their true, available self from their reality.

As we begin to create a life that supports our truth, we learn to be available for ourselves, breaking generational patterns of abandonment. When we're ready, we can explore availability and intimacy with others *at a pace that works for us*. Being with someone who is available can be frightening at first. It can leave us feeling incredibly vulnerable. But we can set boundaries, creating a safe space in which to explore.

Today, I will look at my history of intimate relationships to determine whether I've been attracted to unavailability. After exploring past patterns and identifying what I'd like to create in the future, I will put in my "order" to the Universe, trusting that it will unfold in divine timing.

May 7

Leaving a Toxic Relationship

Once we're out of the abusive relationship, we hope and pray that we're done with narcissistic abuse forever. However, some of us go back, the pull of the trauma bond and past patterning still too strong to override.

If we are faced with leaving a toxic relationship, we can do so consciously. Once we make the decision to leave our partner, it's wise to plan our exit safely and strategically. When we inform them of our intentions, it may trigger abandonment and rejection wounds within them, and we may see a dark side of them we didn't know existed.

If we have any concerns about our physical safety, it's critical to take precautions to avoid putting ourselves in danger. We can immediately call 911 if our safety is ever in question. We can also contact our local domestic violence support organization.

We can move our important documents and other valued possessions prior to telling our partner that we're leaving. We can ask safe, trusted people for help with our move even if we could do it alone because it's important to give ourselves support in getting through this. Not only are we leaving a relationship, but we're also breaking generational patterns of abuse, fear, and powerlessness that have resided within our cells and DNA.

Today, if I'm not in physical danger, I will take time to think things through, seek support, and plan according to my needs, leaving once everything is in place.

Taking Action

We can hold a daily intention of taking action to move ourselves forward on our healing journey from narcissistic abuse. We can take whatever sized step we're capable of in the moment, which at times might be just beyond where we thought our limit was.

After our toxic relationship ended, many of us felt completely exhausted and unable to take any action. Resting and being gentle with ourselves *was* taking action after the constant drama and trauma we had been through.

As we faced our inner wounds, we sometimes felt frozen or stuck. At those times, even taking a tiny step—setting up a needed appointment or making ourselves something to eat—was success.

As we began to get back on our feet, we learned to take steady steps forward. We experienced how continued healthy actions formed good habits, moving us toward the lives we desired.

When we were ready, we took big steps forward. Initiating legal action to recoup the money we'd lost to the narcissist, going back to school to get a degree, or moving out of our familiar location to start a new life were all big steps forward.

Today, I will hold the intention of taking action each day, to move me in the direction of my dreams. I will not put aside my needs to do so. Instead, I will work with myself exactly where I am, even if that action is a tiny step forward.

May 9

Unseen Support

With the intensity and demands of our day-to-day lives, it's easy to forget that there is an Unseen Realm that exists beyond the three-dimensional world we live in. We can connect with that realm for rest, rejuvenation, healing, inspiration, and reflections of who we truly are. It's there that we have the support of spiritual guides who are accessible to assist us in navigating this earthly existence.

We can connect with Source in its many forms such as angels, archangels, ascended masters, goddesses, spirits, and guides. They can be people we've known in this lifetime, such as friends and relatives who've passed away—a beloved grandparent or a friend who left this world too soon. They can also be those we know of who are guiding and inspiring us now from afar—spiritual figures like Jesus, Mother Mary, or Buddha, and those whose words have touched our heart, inspiring, expanding, and strengthening us like Martin Luther King, Jr., or Albert Einstein.

Each of us has a "team" of Unseen Support that surrounds us and works with us as we learn and grow in this earthly classroom. Perhaps they are behind the beautiful synchronicities that surprise us, or the gentle, inner nudges and strong gut feelings we sometimes receive.

Today, I will contemplate the Unseen Support which surrounds me. I will connect with my "team" when I need a reminder of who I really am, a spirit in a "human suit" having an earthly experience.

May 10

Healthy Connection

In the narcissistic relationship, we had no room to exist. Like a blank whiteboard, our authentic stories were erased as the narcissist wrote all over us. They wrote stories of who they wanted us to be and pushed us to change, a process they constantly monitored and controlled. Looking "our best," we helped them secure greater amounts of narcissistic supply. We worked hard to fit their narrative, trying to protect ourselves from the pain of their abuse and abandonment.

In a healthy intimate relationship, there is space for both people to be themselves and to experience one another's authentic stories. We are seen as a human being with our own valid thoughts and feelings, not as an object to meet our partner's needs. We explore whether a committed relationship is something we both desire, being honest about our feelings even if that means going our own separate ways.

Committing to a healthy intimate relationship is a process of choosing ourselves and someone else at the same time. We get to have boundaries *and* be loved, something many of us believed impossible. When conflict arises, we remain connected as we explore the issue, having deep compassion for one another while maintaining our autonomy and honoring our own wants and needs.

Today, I will pay close attention to how the energy of the above situations resonates in my body—to help me recognize inner cues for healthy connection as I venture back out into the dating world.

May 11

Energy Showers

Everything is energy. We are all vibrating energy, our physical bodies denser than our invisible energy fields that surround us. Sometimes, an energetic cleansing or clearing can be helpful when we're holding heavy energy—ours, someone else's, or the world's. We can take on heavy energy in a number of ways, including:

- Being around someone else's negativity.
- Re-engaging with the narcissist and taking on their energy.
- Being in pain—physically, mentally, or emotionally.
- Feeling overwhelmed with other people's energy, as in a crowded public place.
- Experiencing or witnessing a natural disaster.

One tool to help us maintain our energy health is an "energy shower." Taking whatever time we need, we can quiet our body and mind, picturing a huge reservoir of sparkling energy above our heads that is connected to our Source. We can see it coming down, washing over and through us, infusing every cell with the vibrant living energy that created us. It cleanses us as rain cleanses pollen from the air, raising our vibration and transforming the dense energy we were holding back into love and light.

Inspired by our truth within, we can get creative. What color is the energy? Perhaps a sparkling pink and gold or a brilliant, swirling turquoise? Does it wash over us in waves or lightly sprinkle down on us? Is it warm or cool? Does it move fast or slow?

Today, I will shower myself with the energy of light, love, and joy!

May 12

Parenting With a Narcissist

Attempting to co-parent with a narcissist can be a nightmare when they refuse to cooperate with us for the good of our children and instead use them as pawns to trigger and disempower us. For example, if the narcissist is playing rough with our child and we express concern for the child's safety, the narcissist will increase the intensity of their play as we watch, feeling powerful as we stand by helpless and afraid.

When our children's custody or placement is determined legally, we must accept that we cannot control what happens to them while in the narcissist's care. We can work to grieve the anguish that comes with that understanding while continuing to document and report our concerns.

We can work through our past trauma and powerlessness that has been triggered by the narcissist, healing ourselves so we can be fully present with our children as a positive force in their lives.

We can set firm boundaries, allowing us to disengage from the narcissist and begin to heal. We then come to accept that our child will live in two separate worlds, and we stop feeding the narcissist our energy, making their efforts at control useless. Then, our children are no longer caught in the middle.

Today, I will focus on my healing, knowing it's the best way to support my children. I will use my voice and my power when necessary to advocate for their best interests and my own.

May 13

Finding Our Authentic Self

When we live from our authentic self, our soul's truth, we feel alive, and life feels like an adventure. Source flows freely, inspiring love and connection within us. We speak and act genuinely, living by our own values and beliefs. We put aside our false personas and stop trying to please others at our own expense, willing to face abandonment or any other consequence of being authentic.

In the process of moving into our authenticity, we often step back from or let go of people and things that have supported an old version of us. This can include toxic relationship partners, unhealthy friends and family members, as well as alcohol and other substances that we used to avoid ourselves. This letting go process creates space for our true self to emerge.

Then, we have the sacred honor of discovering and manifesting our authentic self. We can explore our values and authentic characteristics with tools such as personal inventories, meditation, and creative outlets. We can pay attention to what makes us come alive, examining our past to see when we felt the most free and authentic, and bringing more of that into our life.

When we express our authentic self, we're no longer willing to abandon ourselves, our safety, or our wants, needs, and desires. It's from this place that miracles emerge.

Today, I will contemplate where I am on the journey to finding my authentic self.

May 14

Possessiveness

In the beginning, we felt valued and wanted when the narcissist acted possessively toward us. We craved this kind of attention because of our inner wounds and past unmet needs. It gave us a sense of safety and belonging. Our inner children felt honored that someone finally "loved" us enough to "care" that much.

Some examples of the narcissist's possessiveness can be seen in the following behaviors:

- Calling multiple times when we're unavailable and then leaving a message saying they're going to come over to "make sure we're okay" if they don't hear from us soon.
- "Educating" us about how our family members, children, and friends are unhealthy, encouraging us to cut ties with them.
- Monitoring our phone calls while we're talking, or interrogating us afterwards.
- Getting upset when we make plans with our friends.
- Telling us how to dress or to change our appearance.
- Having few friends themselves and relying on us as their sole support.

Later, we discovered that being possessed was much different than the love and belonging we were seeking. The narcissist's power and control over us became a suffocating force.

As we become devoted to ourselves and filled with Source, we no longer look for someone else to provide us with a sense of value or belonging.

Today, I will examine the possessiveness in my past relationships, as well as my reaction to it, using that information to create healthy relationships in the future.

May 15

Inner Children and Their Superpowers

Inside each one of us dwell our magical inner children, their essence pure love and joy. They possess an innocence and exuberance that feeds our creativity and lights us up from the inside.

Each unique expression of our inner child, created at different ages by the effects of childhood trauma, possesses a "superpower." Some of these traits were with us when we entered this world. Others developed in response to the trauma and chaos surrounding us.

Survivors share stories of their inner children's superpowers:

"When I paint, I feel joyful and free as I channel the energy of my inner two-year-old. While they can throw quite an inner tantrum at times, they are the passion behind my art."

"I call my inner five-year-old 'the fantasizer.' All my life they've worked hard to help me survive by making things appear much better than they are. In my relationship with the narcissist, their gift made things complicated, but in my career as a playwright, their creativity is invaluable."

"My inner seven-year-old possesses considerable strength and tenacity, having worked tirelessly to keep me safe. It was healing to channel their Herculean efforts toward moving my life forward instead of surviving threats."

A key to our inner transformation is finding our inner children's superpowers and channeling them in a way that supports our healing and our brave new life.

Today, I will contemplate my inner children's superpowers.

May 16

Being in Our Bodies

Our body holds our highest potential as well as the pain of our past traumas, both of which can frighten us.

To survive the pain of the past, we learned to pull our energy and attention out of our body to avoid feeling the things that were overwhelming us. We welcomed the relief of a degree of numbness from the pain.

As we heal, we can gently bring our awareness back into our body and set the necessary boundaries to begin feeling safer in it. We can begin paying attention to our feelings and sensations, positive or negative, which we've avoided for so long. In addition to encountering painful feelings from abuse or neglect that we've suffered, we can also experience the warmth of sunshine on our face, the awe in our heart inspired by a sunset that paints the sky in brilliant colors all around us, or the peace and tranquility of a quiet moment. We can even dance and feel joy!

Today, I will breathe in for a count of four and breathe out for a count of six until I am relaxed. I will then pay attention to what I feel or sense within. I will allow my body to release what it needs to and move as it desires. Whenever I am ready, I will embrace my past pain as well as my greatest potential, both of which live within me.

May 17

Anger

In our society, expressing anger is viewed as normal and acceptable for men, while women are often viewed as being out-of-control or crazy for doing so. Feeling our anger can be messy but necessary to prevent it from building up inside.

The intensity of our anger is proportionate to our lack of self-care and the degree to which we've abandoned ourselves. The magnitude of anger within our inner children can be surprising, but understandable, after having to put ourselves and our needs aside for so long and receiving only crumbs back. We exhausted ourselves trying to earn the love and acceptance we deserve simply because we exist.

To help us heal our anger caused by narcissistic abuse, we can envision a still-painful situation with the narcissist and consider how we wish we had responded in that moment. We can pretend the narcissist is in front of us and write, say, or act out a reimagined scene. We can also use these tools with our inner children who are angry, letting their words, actions, and emotions flow, honoring and releasing how they felt being mistreated by the narcissist or other people who hurt them in the past.

Today, I will embrace and express my anger, doing my best to take responsibility for it so it is released safely. I will reach out for professional support if I need help dealing with my anger. No matter what, I will show myself compassion, understanding, and love.

May 18

Hoovering

Hoovering is a manipulation tactic that some narcissists use. Like a vacuum cleaner, they suck their victim back in, attempting to regain power and control over them.

For example, we receive a text, e-mail, phone call, or even a personal visit from the narcissist after not having had contact with them for over a year.

"Hi darling, I miss you." "I'll never love anyone else like I loved you." "We have a bond that just doesn't seem to go away."

Narcissists also hoover by proxy, talking with our family members, friends, or even our children, telling them how much they "love" and miss us.

Narcissists often hoover us back in just as we are moving forward with our lives. There are victims who continue to be hoovered by the narcissist even after the narcissist is with a new partner. Hoovering can confuse us into thinking that the narcissist misses us or still "loves" us. Instead, they're ensuring that we are still a viable source of narcissistic supply, there when they need us.

Hoovering keeps us in limbo with one foot in our old reality and one in the new. It destabilizes us and keeps us stuck in the cycle of abuse, making it impossible to fully move forward into the healing and life that awaits us.

Today, I will assess whether I have been hoovered by the narcissist. If so, I will look within to determine what made me susceptible to this manipulation tactic.

May 19

Savior to Victim

In the beginning of our relationship with the narcissist, during the love bombing phase of the narcissistic abuse cycle, our partner asked many questions about us and our life. In response to their show of interest, concern, and "love," we opened ourselves completely, trusting them with our deepest wounds and fears. They became our **savior**, compassionately supporting us like no one had ever before, acknowledging our strength, and perhaps even doing "loving" things to help us heal.

As the narcissist moved into the next stages of abuse, the devaluation and discard phases, they used what they'd learned to gain power over us. Suddenly they didn't see us as strong—but weak and broken. When we showed emotion or expressed our needs, the narcissist reacted with frustration and condescension.

They threatened abandonment, claiming they were tired of being a **victim** to our issues.

They attributed any difficulties in our relationship to us and our past, bypassing their own abusive behavior that was injuring us and retriggering our past wounds, their vortex of abuse creating a destructive tornado within us.

Today, I will remember that no one can save me from anything I went through in the past, nor is it anyone's job to do so. Fueled by my connection to Source, I am my own savior, and what will heal me is the love, devotion, and commitment I give to myself.

May 20

Guilt

As highly sensitive, empathic children, many of us could sense the incredible amount of pain that our narcissistic parents or caretakers kept hidden deep inside. Easily manipulated when they played the victim, we walked on eggshells and felt enormous guilt if we added any more to the burden they already carried. We met their needs, putting our own aside, while they neglected and even abused us, destroying our trust in ourselves, others, and life.

Many of us carried that pattern into our relationship with the narcissist. When we couldn't or wouldn't meet the narcissist's excessive needs, they played the victim, trying to convince us that having our own needs meant we were selfish. This triggered our guilt from the past and made it nearly impossible to set boundaries. We tried to please the narcissist to avoid the discomfort of the guilt, careful not to hurt them in any way.

As we heal, we may still be susceptible to taking that pattern of guilt into new relationships, putting the burden of others' needs on our shoulders even when that person doesn't have those expectations of us.

Today, I will contemplate my patterns of taking on others' guilt, paying attention to any relationships in which I am currently engaged in that behavior. I will explore my susceptibility, looking closely at how others' emotions and pain affect me inside. I will take responsibility for my own experience instead of making their feelings my burden.

May 21

Testing Boundaries

In the beginning of our relationship, the narcissist performed many tests to evaluate whether we were able to set boundaries, and if so, how strong they were.

Narcissists often try things like speaking to us disrespectfully, flirting with others in front of us, or doing sexually inappropriate things in public, all to gauge our reaction. They may attempt to push us past our boundaries during sex, telling us we're being immature or that we need to loosen up. They might also maintain close contact with former lovers—backup sources of supply—to see how far into our relationship we'll allow them.

When we voiced our upset at their inappropriate actions, we often saw their inner monster emerge, acting as if we were despicable human beings for not tolerating their abusive behavior. In response, they often used threats of abandonment to control us. They informed us that we did something reprehensible by expressing our feelings, that we negatively affected the relationship, and that we'd lose them if this behavior of ours continued.

Each time we didn't set a boundary when we needed to, we gave the narcissist permission to treat us poorly, ensuring that they would push their inappropriate behavior further the next time.

Today, I will practice setting the boundaries I need to set in order to feel safe and maintain my self-care. I will say and do what I need to, without shame or hesitation, knowing it is my right to set my personal boundaries.

May 22

Asking for Help

Asking for help can be difficult for many of us. There is vulnerability involved in doing so as we expose our weaknesses and needs and let go of our facade of "having it all together."

Other reasons why asking for help can feel challenging include:

- We feel ashamed and think we should be able to handle things on our own because other people do.
- We don't think we deserve help, as evidenced by a past history of being unsupported by those who didn't have enough inner resources themselves, much less enough to give to us.
- We believe no one understands us anyway, so asking for help seems futile.
- We are overwhelmed by anxiety, depression, or other mental health challenges that cause us to shut down, making it difficult and even painful to reach out for help.
- In truth, asking for help is a sign of strength.

Help and support will assist the progress of our healing so that we can live the beautiful new life that awaits us. We don't have to do it all by ourselves anymore. Source stands ready to send help and support when we can allow it in.

Today, I will ask for help with something, big or small, paying attention to my thoughts and feelings in doing so. I will remind myself that I am worthy of help and support.

May 23

Crisis as Opportunity

For many survivors, narcissistic abuse is one of the most intense crises we will experience. We were pushed to our limits, unsure if we would survive the relationship or the aftershock that followed when it ended.

As we get further along the road of our recovery journey, after some of our pent-up emotions have had the space to flow freely and we've healed our wounds enough to lessen the unrelenting pain of the trauma bond, many of us have found deep healing in realizing the gifts and opportunities that our experience with narcissistic abuse provided.

One survivor shared, "Narcissistic abuse completely broke me open and brought my deepest wounds of the past to the surface. Surviving it required me to connect with my formerly abandoned inner children that held the pain, and to love them as never before. In the end, I uncovered the miracle of who I really am, someone I hadn't had the pleasure of meeting before now."

It's not a requirement to find gifts in our experience with the narcissist. Some of us may never share that perspective, and that's okay.

Today, I will try on the possibility that there were opportunities in the abuse that I encountered. If that fits for me, I will explore the gifts I've received in the process. If it doesn't, I will put it aside for now, or forever, honoring my feelings exactly as they are.

May 24

Expectations

Expectations are strong thoughts or beliefs we hold about the correct way that something should be done or someone should behave. Our expectations are fueled by our own needs and desires. The more expectations we have, the greater our chance of being disappointed.

The narcissist had many confusing, unrealistic expectations of us, wanting us to look, act, speak, and think in the manner they judged appropriate. We took on their expectations as our own, believing they were ours to meet, which often left us resentful as we neglected our own needs and truth. We also had unrealistic expectations of the narcissist, based upon their misleading behavior during the love bombing stage. We wanted them to remain loving and meet our needs, something they were incapable of.

When we experience the weight of others' expectations, we can now respond in a way that is self-supporting, saying no if we need to, without guilt. We can let people be exactly who they are and see if they're a fit for us.

Today, if I find myself feeling resentful, I will look at what my expectations were, explore the reality of the situation, and adjust accordingly. I will remember to stay in the moment, allowing life to unfold without weighty expectations. I know that the Universe often has people and things in store for me that are far more wonderful than my expectations.

May 25

Going Back(wards)

After our relationship with the narcissist ends, we're extremely susceptible to being pulled back into their vortex. They skillfully remind us of the good times, tenderly pointing out that "special connection" between us. They tell us they'll never love anyone like they love us, or anything else we yearn to hear. This may lead to a phone call, a sexual encounter, or even a reunion with them.

We go back as many times as it takes—until we don't need to go back anymore. Until we've healed enough of the wounds that caused us to be manipulated by the narcissist and we can maintain No Contact.

If we go back, there is no value in shaming ourselves. We can keep our eyes wide open, watching how we participate and which inner children are in action as we fall back into the illusions. We can observe things about the narcissist that we were blind to in the past.

It's important to consider that each time we go back, the abuse becomes more severe, even dangerous in some cases. Everything we say will likely be used against us at some point. Going back will diminish us, touching everyone and everything close to us in some way.

Today, I will look at the realities of making the choice to re-enter the relationship with the narcissist. Regardless of the choice I make, I will continue to do something healing and loving for myself every day.

May 26

Attachment

In her book *The Complex PTSD Workbook: A Mind-Body Approach to Regaining Emotional Control & Becoming Whole*, Arielle Schwartz, PhD, defines attachment as "an emotional bond between two people, initially a caregiver and an infant, which provides a foundation for healthy relationships later in life. Secure attachment forms when we can depend on a safe, predictable, attuned, and loving caregiver during infancy and early childhood."

Dr. Schwartz goes on to say that "healthy attachment is associated with the ability to learn emotional regulation and stress tolerance, and the development of healthy boundaries."

Based on this definition, we can see how having inconsistent, over-involved, neglectful, or abusive caregivers can impact our health and ability to connect with others.

As adults lacking the experience of secure attachment in childhood, we may have gravitated toward those who were unavailable to support us because we believed we didn't deserve support, clung anxiously to others, protected ourselves by maintaining a safe distance from people, or become abusive like the caregivers that hurt us.

One survivor shared that after the narcissist left them and then returned for more narcissistic supply, the survivor believed the narcissist's reappearance was evidence of their love. Without a foundation of healthy attachment, the survivor lacked the understanding that someone who loves us doesn't abandon us.

Today, as I consider my attachment to my caregivers, I will reach out for support if needed, remembering that this can be a deep, tender topic that can bring up much within me.

May 27

Will

Many of us have gotten through difficult moments in our lives by the sheer force of our will. Unfortunately, our will alone doesn't have the power to move us beyond the effects of narcissistic abuse. We can't will away the trauma bond in our brain—or the excruciating pain that follows separation from the narcissist.

It can take time to heal from narcissistic abuse, but as we do, we are also healing our past and creating a solid foundation for a new life. We turn inward and face the pain of our past wounds which made us susceptible to the narcissist's manipulations. Once held deep within us, the narcissist reopened these wounds, bringing them to the surface of our consciousness to be healed.

We reclaim our inner children and hold them close, providing them the acknowledgement, love, safety, and support we didn't receive as children. Connecting with Source and handing our lives, our will, and our healing over to this sacred energy creates new depth and healing possibilities within us.

Our will can be helpful in our healing. When we want to break No Contact with the narcissist or skip necessary self-care activities, our will can often steer us in the right direction if we've healed enough of the wounds behind these self-sabotaging actions.

Today, I will connect with my will. I will breathe into the place in my body where my will resides, feeling its strength and remembering times it has served me well.

May 28

Narcissistic Injury

Though narcissists move with an air of confidence, they are quite fragile inside. Having disowned and exiled their true self, which they see as unacceptable and unable to meet their needs, they built armor around themselves in the form of the false self that they present to the world.

When the narcissist feels any real or imagined slight, criticism, correction, or something that doesn't adequately represent their false self or maintain their superiority, they often react strongly, out of proportion to the situation at hand. This happens when there is a crack in their armor, allowing emotions and feelings of low self-esteem to come through from the true self that are too much for the narcissist to bear.

An example of narcissistic injury: a narcissist receives correction or criticism at work. Because that feedback goes against the image of power and perfection maintained by the narcissist's false self, they are unable and unwilling to consider the information and discover how to improve their performance. Instead, they obsess and complain about it to others, insisting that management is out to get them or doesn't see their value.

Today, I will think about whether I encountered this behavior with the narcissist. I will remember that the abusive behavior occurred because of the narcissist's insecurities, not because they were stronger, more competent, or superior to me.

May 29

Resentment

Resentment is the feeling of being treated unfairly, something we know well as victims of narcissistic abuse. It is created when we lack boundaries and give more of ourselves than we're comfortable with, especially to someone who only takes while giving little or nothing back to us. When our needs and expectations aren't met, our resentment builds.

Holding on to resentment is not wrong. It is justified after the abuse we endured, but it is a heavy burden to carry, sapping us of our life force just like the narcissist did. When we're ready, we can work through our feelings and cut the cords of resentment toward the narcissist, setting ourselves free and opening up to love, joy, and our connection with Source.

If we aren't sure how, we can ask for support or hand our feelings of resentment over to Source, asking for resolution. Our willingness begins the process of healing resentments.

We can't change what happened with the narcissist, but we can now make choices to support ourselves, including not tolerating behavior from others that disrespects us and our boundaries.

Today, I will sit with any resentments I still have toward the narcissist. I will write them down or acknowledge them to myself. Then, I will explore my expectations to see when and how my resentment grew. I will also look at my boundaries or lack of them in each situation and decide how I will set more effective ones next time.

May 30

Circular Arguments

Circular arguments were the heated moments we experienced with the narcissist, which often occurred as we attempted to confront their inappropriate behavior or address the effects that their unreasonable expectations were having on us. We entered the argument clear and strong, hoping for an adult conversation. We left it feeling beat up, exhausted, and confused, asking ourselves what the hell just happened.

In response to our valid concerns, the narcissist projected everything back onto us, threatened us, accused us of being crazy, brought up something that they felt *we* did to *them*, or talked incessantly, seemingly just to hear their own voice.

In circular arguments, the narcissist didn't speak to communicate. They spoke to confuse and diminish us, playing on our fears and vulnerabilities to gain power over us. As we reacted, our emotions escalated, and we were unintentionally providing them with copious amounts of narcissistic supply, fulfilling the narcissist's true agenda.

If we ever find ourselves in another circular argument, becoming overwhelmed and reactive, we can take a step back, recognizing that we're likely being manipulated. We can excuse ourselves by saying, "This conversation isn't working for me," and committing to our own self-care.

Today, I will remember that the best course of action in a circular argument is refusing to engage. I will remove my energy from abusive situations and communication that drains me, and I will reinvest that energy into healthy interactions that support me.

May 31

Needing a Fallback Person

Contrary to outward appearances of strength and independence, the narcissist requires many solid, reliable sources of narcissistic supply to help them feel less vulnerable to abandonment by others and to keep the barrier strong between their false self and the true self they've abandoned. It's essential to their very survival. As a result, they keep at least one fallback person at the ready, a potential intimate partner to ensure their needs will be met.

During our relationship, if the narcissist was bored or we weren't providing them with enough narcissistic supply, as we might have been meeting our own needs or busy with our life, they reached out to other sources of supply.

No matter how long we were together, after our relationship ended, the narcissist quickly had a new source of supply. In some cases, the narcissist already had our replacement and was seeing them before our relationship ended.

Seeing how fast the narcissist moved on was inconceivable after how deeply we loved them. However, what we must remember is that for them, it was a matter of survival—sheer mechanics of maintaining their false persona to avoid the pain of their self-abandonment.

Today, I will vow never to be someone's fallback person again. I will also remember that it wasn't about me being replaceable and insignificant. It was about the narcissist trying to survive.

June 1

Flying Monkeys

During and after narcissistic relationships, narcissists often recruit people to do their dirty work. These people are known as the narcissist's "flying monkeys," a name inspired by the movie *The Wizard of Oz*.

The narcissist portrayed themselves as the victim in our relationship, detailing the horrible things we'd done to them—which ironically were often the things they'd done to us.

It was devastating when the narcissist enlisted people we loved and trusted—family, friends, and even colleagues, who turned against us after having been drawn into the narcissist's lies and games.

One survivor's reputation and trust were shattered as several family members became the narcissist's flying monkeys. Persuaded by the narcissist's manufactured tales of woe, they stood up against the survivor in court during their divorce from the narcissist, creating lasting impacts for the survivor and their children.

While we can't control what the narcissist does or how their lies and misrepresentations are received, we can focus on ourselves and our healing, disengaging from the situation as much as possible. In addition to maintaining No Contact with the narcissist, we can also do so with their flying monkeys to minimize painful triggers and to help us stay focused on ourselves and our new reality.

Today, I will explore and honor my deep feelings emerging at this time. I will remember that while it feels impossible at times, many others have survived narcissistic abuse and flying monkeys, and have gone on to heal themselves and live beautiful lives.

June 2

Trauma Symptoms

The trauma of narcissistic abuse can wreak havoc on our mental, emotional, and physical health, greatly exacerbating already existing conditions.

Some typical symptoms include:

- **Mental Health Symptoms.** Dissociation, hypervigilance, intrusive thoughts, anxiety, depression, feeling suicidal, self-harming behaviors, social anxiety, agoraphobia, and panic attacks.
- **Emotional Health Symptoms.** Overwhelming fear, sorrow, anger, and shame, helplessness and hopelessness, a decrease in our self-esteem and sense of worth, and frustration with the continued effects of the trauma bond.
- **Physical Health Symptoms.** Fibromyalgia and chronic fatigue syndrome, adrenal fatigue, asthma, stomach aches, headaches, and exhaustion.

It's important for us to get the support we need, especially from professionals who are educated in and familiar with working with trauma and narcissistic abuse, as we continue on our inner healing journey.

If we feel suicidal, it's critical to get immediate support whether by contacting our local crisis line, dialing 911, or going to a hospital emergency room. There are also resources available at the back of this book.

Today, I will take steps to ensure I have the support I need in the process of healing from narcissistic abuse, knowing that I don't have to do it alone or try to muscle my way through it. I will remember that many have gone through this process before me and the collective energy of their healing surrounds and supports me.

June 3

People Are People

When the narcissistic relationship ended, we may have felt isolated and alone, like no one could possibly understand what we'd just been through. While this is a very normal feeling, a broader view of the situation can sometimes offer us a more hopeful perspective.

Narcissistic abuse is universal. It knows no bounds.

Gender makes no difference. Both women and men experience it.

Intelligence doesn't protect us. Even a genius can fall prey to narcissistic abuse.

Financial status doesn't insulate us from it. It affects people living in poverty as well as those with great wealth.

It happens to Black, Indigenous, and People of Color.

Sexual identity doesn't prevent it. It happens to heterosexual people as well as those who identify as LGBTQIA2S+.

It happens to people of all religions, regardless of ideologies.

It happens to those in all types of relationships, including heteronormative, queer, polyamorous, married, dating, or any other configuration of people in relationship.

When looked at broadly, this information ties us together, showing us that underneath all that divides us, people are people. People everywhere have wounds that create narcissistic personalities, just as people everywhere have wounds that make them susceptible to narcissists.

Today, I will take comfort in knowing that I'm not alone in what I'm going through, and I will choose to see the connectedness between all people rather than focusing on the things that divide us.

June 4

Hate

After the level of pain, betrayal, and psychic destruction we experienced at the hands of the narcissist, it's not abnormal to have feelings of hatred toward them, even if it's not in our character. Many of us have felt this way.

Does it make us bad people? No! It makes us human, having a normal reaction to a highly abusive situation. The feeling of hate is just energy to be released from within us.

From a self-care perspective, it isn't wrong to feel hatred. It does take a lot of energy, though, to maintain that feeling and state of mind, and our energy is still engaged with the narcissist. We are focused on them and not on our healing.

To help ourselves move through feelings of hate, we can lean into the feelings and accept that they're there. The kindest thing we can do for ourselves is to allow and honor the feelings as long as necessary, but not a moment longer.

In a quiet, safe space, we can connect with our inner children that feel this strong emotion and ask them what they need. If we feel stuck in hatred, we can reach out for support to help us move through it.

Today, I will show myself compassion and understanding. I will not judge any feeling, including hate, that arises within me. I know that there is a good reason it's there. I will trust myself to know what I need according to my inner wisdom.

June 5

Strengths

Initially, the narcissist was attracted to our strengths. As they praised us for each strength, we felt seen and loved.

Tired of working hard to reel us in and certain we wouldn't leave, they began to devalue us, trying to convince us that our strengths were, in fact, weaknesses.

In the beginning, they loved our intelligence.

Later, they were threatened by it and worked hard to diminish us so they were the intelligent one.

In the beginning, they loved our independence.

Later, they called it selfishness, expecting us to be available to meet their needs.

In the beginning, they loved our innate creativity.

Later, they tried to control us and our creativity, shutting down our inner creative flow.

In the beginning, they loved how real we were.

Later, they transformed us into the person they thought was the "best version" of us.

In the beginning, they loved what a good parent we were.

Later, the narcissist insisted we were coddling our children, creating distance between us and them. This ensured that the narcissist continued to receive maximum narcissistic supply from us.

The very strengths that the narcissist called weaknesses are what will carry us through our healing journey to freedom.

Today, I will identify and appreciate my strengths, never again allowing anyone to diminish them.

June 6

Repelling Narcissists

As loving, tolerant empaths, we are highly attractive to narcissists. Developing skills to repel them can support a peaceful journey into our new and true life.

Ideas for repelling narcissists:

- **Needing nothing from them.** When someone shows up as our savior, we don't participate in their game because we don't need to be saved. We know we're capable of getting our own needs met.
- **Speaking our truth.** If someone does something that makes us uncomfortable, such as making an inappropriate comment, we can tell them how we feel.
- **Doing what we need to do**—*every single day*. We can decide what to do with our precious life each day. If it includes someone else, great. If not, then we go solo without an ounce of guilt.
- **Taking intimacy slow.** Narcissists try pulling us in quickly because it takes a lot of energy for them to seduce us. We can go slowly with someone new. The slower we go, the less interested they will be if they're a narcissist.
- **Knowing our personal values and setting boundaries accordingly.** Narcissists want to call the shots. They don't want to live within someone else's boundaries.
- **Limiting the personal, intimate information we share about ourselves.** We can choose not to become vulnerable right away. This leaves a narcissist with nowhere to attach themselves to us.

Today, I will try on these strategies for empowering myself, remembering that developing new habits takes practice, and I don't have to do it perfectly.

June 7

Grooming

In the beginning, the narcissist lovingly gazed into our eyes, fascinated with us. They expressed heartfelt sentiments that made us glow. Like a predator, they were actually observing us, listening to our every word and monitoring the shifts in our body language. They identified our vulnerabilities, the strength of our boundaries, and the presence of a support system that could interfere with their control and engulfment of us and our lives.

They asked many questions, hunting for information, and we felt seen, heard, and known. They shared details about themselves, perhaps even divulging "a secret" that no one else knew. They listened carefully to how we'd been hurt in the past and lovingly reassured us that those things would never happen with them, giving us a false sense of safety. They gained our trust and bonded with us deeply before we even knew what was happening.

Next, they tested our boundaries to see what they could get away with. They trained us to be someone we weren't, attempting to control our appearance, our sexual performance, and anything else that would mold us to fit into their self-centered, self-created version of reality. They shamed us if we tried to set limits—and subtly transformed us until we didn't recognize ourselves anymore.

Today, I will acknowledge and be grateful for my awareness of the things that I was unable to see in the past. I will remember that awareness leads to empowerment.

June 8

Divine Timing

Healing from narcissistic abuse and toxic relationships is a journey that just takes time. Regardless of the efforts we put in to heal quickly, we can heal and release only what we're ready to, as each milestone in our deep inner healing forms another piece of our strengthening foundation. We can take comfort in the blossoming connection with ourselves as well as the miracles and growth that happen along the way, making each step worthwhile.

Some of us are great at manifesting our ideas and meeting our goals. These skills work well for many things, but when it comes to our healing, the magic is in aligning our awareness with Source. Slowing down and quieting ourselves allows us to hear the intuitive whisper that reveals our next step while we embrace the divine timing that is woven into our journey.

When we flow freely with divine energy and trust its timing, our soul's highest outcomes emerge. Life has a way of working out in the most unexpected fashion. Things happen that we couldn't have imagined possible from our human perspective.

Today, I will let go of my grip on my recovery from narcissistic abuse and toxic relationships. Instead of assuming I know best, I will let the magic of each next step unfold, trusting in the wisdom of divine timing. When things get tough, I will remember to reach out to Source and the Unseen Support that surrounds me every moment.

June 9

Physical Abuse

This post may be triggering for those who have experienced physical abuse.

Some people are physically abused in ways that are straightforward. Others experience it in more convoluted ways. One survivor of narcissistic abuse described a painful experience and the healing that followed.

"I loved the narcissist beyond words, and I was terrified they'd leave me. I tried hard to be the person they wanted me to be. At some point, unhealthy things started to seem normal as I got sucked deeper into their abnormal reality.

"The narcissist told me I needed to be more adventurous and loosen up during sex, or they'd leave. Trying to be adventurous, I suggested they whip me, hoping it would placate them. At that moment, I truly believed I wanted it to happen. When it did, I felt very differently. Wanting to be hit wasn't something that came from inside of me, and I knew I would never allow it to happen again. I felt degraded but remained silent, unwilling to lose the narcissist.

"After the relationship ended, I discovered a therapy called Brainspotting. During one session, my upper body repeatedly jerked forward as if I was being hit. I was thunderstruck when I realized that my body was releasing the physical abuse from that incident. Truly amazing!"

As we can see from this survivor's account, our bodies always remember.

Today, I will get the professional support I need to assist me in unpacking my experience with physical abuse.

June 10

Being Alone

For many of us, the thought of being alone is painful.

We may feel that we're better off being with someone even if they are abusive because being alone in the world feels too frightening. If we've been victimized by having our sense of safety in the world and in our bodies compromised in some way, we may want the security of having a partner there to protect us.

Not having established a connection with ourselves and our value yet, many of us need people around us who provide us with confirmation that we're acceptable and that we belong. Being alone would be painful without that external validation.

We can honor all of the thoughts and feelings we have inside about being alone. They're there for a good reason, and they are valid because they're ours.

Being alone requires strength and courage, and we become willing and able to stand on our own when we're ready. As we heal, we learn to trust that we can handle whatever comes our way. We begin to recognize ourselves as capable adults.

Today, I will take time to explore my thoughts and feelings about being alone. I will think of times that I enjoyed while alone—even if they were just brief moments. I will seek out new adventures, activities, and ways to enjoy myself when I am alone.

June 11

Addiction to the Narcissist

During the love bombing stage, the narcissist freely doled out their "love." Swooning, we easily shared our heart and soul, revealing our deepest wounds and greatest fears. Once we were addicted, they withheld their "love" and played on our weaknesses to gain power over us. To keep us engaged, they provided an occasional hit of "love," knowing we craved what they controlled.

During intense moments with the narcissist, such as betrayal or threatened abandonment, our brain released a flood of chemicals, causing a rush of feelings in our body. Though painful, we became addicted to the intensity. These chemicals are why we break No Contact with the narcissist, and why it can seem like they're still alive within us even when we maintain No Contact, as our brain and body yearn for that pleasing chemical rush.

At its root, our addiction is related to our unresolved traumas and wounds and our efforts to medicate or avoid them.

Our healing can include exploring our inner terrain and uncovering the wounds that made us susceptible to this addictive process, identifying which inner children are holding them and what they need to heal. Then, we can release the trauma from our body. This process often requires the insightful, steadfast support of a professional therapist, psychologist, or qualified coach.

Today, with self-love and compassion, I will explore whether I'm still addicted to the narcissist. If I am, and I'm ready, I will contemplate options to support my healing.

June 12

Reclaiming Our Own Life

Prior to the narcissistic relationship, many of us never had room to exist as the magnificent beings we truly were. Our childhood may have been consumed by caring for those around us, including the people that were supposed to be caring for us.

In our relationship with the narcissist, we played a similar role. Perhaps we were exhausted and just wanted to relax and read a book before bed. The narcissist wanted sex, so we put our book and our needs aside and provided what they wanted. Maybe we were looking forward to a quiet night together with our partner, but the narcissist wanted to go out and party, yearning for more external validation than we alone could give them. We got ourselves ready and went out with them.

Narcissistic abuse relationships magnify the painful pattern of putting our needs aside and meeting those of another, bringing it back to life within us. This gives us the opportunity to see it and choose another way. An awareness that shifted one survivor's perspective while they were still in the relationship was to consider what they would do just for one day if they were single and there was no one else to please.

Today, I will cherish the freedom I have outside of the abusive relationship. I will take the opportunity to start a new life, a life that is about me. Not only do I have permission to be selfish; it's required.

June 13

Seducing Ourselves

While the narcissist was incredibly gifted in the art of seduction, if we take a deeper look within, we may find that we're quite skilled in it ourselves. Our self-seduction is often a survival mechanism that we adopted long ago to make difficult circumstances bearable.

Our thoughts of self-seduction with the narcissist can take many forms.

They're behaving this way because of their traumatic childhood, and they're doing the best they can. With enough time, my love will heal them.

I don't need to protect myself (physically, financially, legally, etc...). I trust them completely and know we'll be together forever.

If I show them enough love and respect, they'll do the same for me.

I will get help for my "issues." If I fix myself, then I won't lose the narcissist.

No one will ever love me like the narcissist. They always come back.

They will mature and change their ways eventually.

Although I'm maintaining No Contact, I NEED to contact them because...

Today, I will remember that I did the best I could in my relationship with the narcissist, considering the unhealed wounds and unmet needs within me. I will look at the ways I seduced myself, compassionately bringing my inner patterns to my awareness to prevent me from repeating them in the future.

June 14

Dating After Narcissistic Abuse

Are we ready to date again after narcissistic abuse? There isn't a right answer, but these are some personal milestones to consider meeting before we do:

- We love ourselves and our life.
- We know how to nourish ourselves and meet our own needs.
- We aren't yearning for a partner.
- We are clear on our goals and the life we desire.
- We greet life straight on without numbing out often.

These are concerns to watch for in a potential partner:

- They try to change who we are.
- They frequently talk about their exes.
- They bring up long-term commitment early on.
- They tell us how we should parent our children.
- There is an imbalance in their giving and receiving.
- They discuss sex before being emotionally intimate with us.

Here are some ideas about how to return to the dating world:

- Go slow.
- Don't try to do it perfectly. We learn as we go.
- Become the observer, watching ourselves and them.
- Stay alert and watch for red and yellow flags.
- Be crystal clear about our boundaries.

Today, I will remember that I can date again whenever I feel ready. If it doesn't feel right, I can change my mind at any time.

June 15

Inner Children in Our Life

We can sometimes feel our inner children's state of being in our daily life. Though we may not realize it initially, when we take time to connect within, we may find that our inner children need support or reassurance.

Below are several instances that could indicate our inner children's presence in our life.

With little food in the refrigerator, we feel lost, lacking motivation and any idea of what to cook. Felt by the inner child, these are valid feelings, as young children don't know how to plan or cook meals. This could also be felt by someone who experienced poverty or neglect in childhood, a bare refrigerator triggering memories of similar conditions from the past.

Strong fear reactions that seem to come out of nowhere. This could indicate that unbeknownst to us, something triggered intense feelings that our inner child has held and that we've worked hard to avoid.

An emotional moment when we are firmly positioned on a negotiable matter, unwilling to explore compromise. When our inner children interact with others instead of our adult selves, communication can become chaotic.

There are also times when our inner children show up in a more supportive way, allowing us to be playful, let go, and thoroughly enjoy the moment, something that can be challenging for many trauma survivors.

Today, I will look for evidence of my inner children's presence in my life, paying attention to their needs when they make themselves apparent.

June 16

Levels of Narcissistic Supply

Narcissists employ a system of gaining narcissistic supply, guaranteeing that their insatiable need is always met, ensuring their very survival.

Numerous ideas exist about classifying and defining that process. The following is the system that fits my experiences as well as those of the people I've worked with.

Level 1 is the narcissist's closest source of supply. This is typically their spouse, partner, or child whom the narcissist has vigorously tested for their ability to withstand abuse and continue providing narcissistic supply. As the relationship proceeds, the narcissist devalues and exploits their primary source often, confident that the source will continue to meet their needs.

Level 2 sources are people the narcissist turns to if their primary source isn't meeting their voracious need for supply. They consist mostly of former or potential Level 1 sources. The narcissist keeps Level 2 sources readily available by doling out crumbs of affection and attention, should the need to replace their current primary source arise.

Level 3 are the people who aren't up to the narcissist's standards for Level 1 or 2 supply but from whom they can still receive narcissistic supply. These can include restaurant servers, store clerks, clients, former "flings," or even random strangers.

Today, I will review my relationship with the narcissist to see if this information fits my experience. I will use it to help me heal, better understanding the dynamics that were powering the abuse I endured.

June 17

Enabling

To enable is to make an unhealthy situation possible. Many of us have taken responsibility for people who weren't taking responsibility for themselves, enabling unhealthy behaviors in them. Some cues that we may be enabling include:

- Being more concerned about someone else's life, health, or success than they are.
- Doing things for others that they could do for themselves.
- Making excuses for someone's inappropriate behavior.
- Feeling resentment for enabling others at our own expense.

Unbeknownst to us, we enabled the narcissist to continue their abusive behaviors, thinking we were being loving partners. Some of our enabling behaviors included:

- Blaming ourselves for their abusive behavior and trying to change who we were.
- Letting the narcissist control us, as it seemed respectful or just easier to do so.
- Agreeing with the narcissist's version of reality, knowing it was unhealthy for us.
- Not taking care of ourselves by setting boundaries or walking away when we were being abused.
- Defending our partner and their behavior to others.

Our habit of enabling, a survival mechanism formed long ago, can be broken. It's important to keep our focus on what's best for us. Then, we can make choices and set boundaries that support us and maintain our health and well-being.

Today, I will remember that it's not self-ish to focus on me. It's self-love and self-care.

June 18

Forgiving the Narcissist

There is no right way to heal. Sometimes, the most loving gift we can give ourselves is the permission not to forgive—if that's what we need. Ironically, some have found that doing so paved their way toward forgiveness. More important than forgiveness is honoring ourselves right where we're at.

Forgiving the narcissist is tricky business. Some of us moved directly into forgiveness after the abuse, thinking we were doing the "right thing." Instead, we were abandoning ourselves, bypassing our pain—and our need for deep healing.

In the healing process, our heart can open a bit, giving us a glimpse of forgiveness. When we're still susceptible to the narcissist's grip, our inner addict can take that and run with it, causing some of us to break No Contact. After offering our love and forgiveness to the narcissist, supplying them with our hard-earned energy, we are ravaged by the trauma bond once again with more mountains to move to get ourselves out.

If we move into forgiveness, gifts definitely come to us in that new place, but we don't have to forgive if we're not ready.

Today, I will keep the focus on myself and my recovery needs. If I am feeling forgiveness toward the narcissist, I will embrace and honor that feeling. I will hold the beautiful energy of it within me, knowing that my forgiveness is a gift I give to myself.

June 19

Gaslighting: What It Sounds Like

Gaslighting is an insidious form of psychological abuse designed to make us doubt our perception of reality and question our mental health. The narcissist presented what we knew to be true as false—and withheld information that misled us. We felt confused and overwhelmed, questioning not only our sanity, but our very identity as our dependency on them grew.

Narcissists often say one thing *and mean* something far more harmful when gaslighting.

You're imagining things. *I'm denying what's true so you'll doubt yourself and I'll have more power over you.*

You're too sensitive. *I'll criticize you for having a healthy reaction to my abusive behavior.*

Here we go again! *You're calling out my inappropriate behavior and I won't be accountable for it.*

I never said/did that. *If I make you question yourself, you won't look at what I'm doing to you.*

You're crazy and you need help. *I'll make you believe you're crazy for having emotions so you don't focus on my issues.*

I can't handle your jealousy. *I'll flirt when and with whom I want to. If that's a problem, I'll put you in your place by leaving.*

I told you that this morning. You forgot already? *I'm threatened by your strength and intelligence, so I'll lie and convince you you're losing your mind.*

Today, I will embrace all the feelings that arise when I remember the narcissist's gaslighting, knowing that feeling and expressing my needs does not make me crazy.

June 20

Gaslighting: How It Feels

To control and disempower us, the narcissist used gaslighting to feed us a false version of reality, making us question our thoughts, feelings, recollections, judgments, and even our sanity.

We were in a position of constantly having to defend ourselves. As our insecurity grew, we ensured that we had facts to back up everything we said to the narcissist. In moments of potential confrontation with them, when we lacked the facts we needed to justify our position, we shut down, becoming voiceless and unable to own and express our inner truth.

The narcissist's continual gaslighting left us feeling tormented. Even though we knew there was something wrong, we couldn't put words to what was happening to us, causing agonizing confusion within us. Because gaslighting doesn't "look like" abuse, we convinced ourselves it was our imagination. We were unsuccessful in our efforts to find relief, eventually becoming numb to our thoughts and feelings as this mind-bending abuse drained us of our vital energy.

We believed no one could possibly understand what we were going through, leaving us hesitant to reach out for the help and support we so desperately needed.

Today, I will honor my intellect, perceptions, and inner knowing. I will speak my truth without wavering, trusting all that comes from within me.

June 21

The Gifts of Summer

Summer brings with it warmth, inspiration, and hope. New experiences call to us, beckoning us to blossom into the updated version of ourselves that we have labored to embody.

We move, dance, connect, and celebrate. Our body is softer and our mind more at ease. There is much to delight our senses as we welcome the familiar smell of fresh cut grass and the taste of a juicy chunk of watermelon. Frogs and crickets chirp as we fall asleep under the light of the moon. Gentle waves lap against the shore, and gulls screech overhead. The sun warms our skin and we relax, feeling fully alive.

In addition to experiencing summer, we can internalize it as a state of being that we create within us. This can be a beautiful tool in our healing journey as we work hard to move through the winter of our trauma. After an exhausting day or a challenging moment, we can invite in the radiant warmth of our inner summer, immersing ourselves in its light. Once we're full, we can shine that light outward, warming the world around us.

Today, I will explore my favorite parts of summer, including the rich sensory details that make me come alive. When I need warmth, inspiration, and hope within, I will quiet my mind and take a few deep breaths as I call forth my inner summer.

June 22

Cravings

We wake up one day missing the narcissist fiercely, engulfed by cravings for them. We remember their gentle side—and the loving things they said and did. The feeling is visceral as if we're fully connected and they're alive within us again. We wonder if (and even hope that) they're thinking about us and feeling us as strongly.

After a day, a month, or a year spent obsessing about them, resentment builds, threatening to implode us—especially if we've been in contact with them and have given them our energy and love, once again receiving paltry crumbs or nothing at all back. We realize they're still with someone else, we're still alone and hurting, and we've just abandoned ourselves and our lives once again.

Sometimes, the cravings are triggered by thoughts, dreams, a sighting of them in person or on social media, an anniversary date that we may or may not remember, or nothing at all.

When these cravings hit, we can breathe into the feelings that have taken over our body, becoming curious and embracing them without judgment. We can explore whether there is a need behind the craving. Are we looking for some excitement? Physical touch? Socialization? A protector? Once we identify the need, we can meet it in healthy ways that support us.

Today, I will explore present or past cravings to learn more about how my body reacts and what it is/was looking for—so I can keep myself safe and sane.

June 23

Communicating Boundaries

Learning to set boundaries is similar to speaking a new language. Finding the right words and the confidence with which to use them can be challenging. It can be especially tricky when we enter the dating world again. It is empowering to walk into new situations already knowing what our boundaries are and some possible ways to articulate them.

The following phrases are some examples of ways we can communicate our boundaries:

Thanks, but I'll pass.
That doesn't work for me.
That's unacceptable to me. I'm not comfortable with that.
I don't allow myself to be treated that way.
I hear and respect what you're saying, and...
I will do..., and the rest of it doesn't work for me.
I respect your point of view, and mine is different.
I'll need time to consider that before I answer you.
No. (It's a complete sentence. No explanation required.)
I'm looking for different things than you are, but I wish you the best.
That's more personal information than I'm comfortable hearing right now.
I didn't feel the connection I'm looking for, but I appreciate the fun we had.
I'm not interested in an ongoing relationship with you, but thank you for this experience.

Being patient and compassionate with ourselves is important as we learn this valuable new skill.

Today, I will practice communicating boundaries, either to myself or with someone else, to see which words and phrases fit who I am.

June 24

Embracing Serenity

Chaotic and overwhelming are words that many of us can use to describe a number of things in our lives—our childhood, our inner state, our physical surroundings, and most certainly our narcissistic abuse relationship.

As we do our inner healing work, many things change within us. These changes then manifest in our lives, reflecting our new internal state back to us. Serenity is one of these changes, a gift of our recovery efforts.

Embracing our newfound serenity can be challenging as life becomes quieter inside and out. When chaos and overwhelm have been our normal states, we may not feel alive without them. They may serve as a distraction from the painful things inside that we don't want to face. We may even be addicted to them, our brain and nervous system conditioned to be on high alert. Letting go of that stimulation can be uncomfortable at first as we adjust to a new way of being.

Embracing serenity allows our body and brain to rest and heal. It also invites us to enter our inner world, where we can connect with our soul's wisdom and the powerful love of Source, claiming our authentic self and a life that reflects it.

Today, I will explore the serenity within me. If I have resistance to it, I will just observe that and be curious about it. I will pay attention to my serenity as I enter new relationships, choosing only those that support it.

June 25

Narcissist and Empath Connection

Narcissist + Empath = Danger.

Empaths are sensitive people who are highly in tune with the emotions of others and often put other peoples' needs before their own. They possess an abundance of empathy and bring great love and compassion to their relationships. When someone is in need, they strongly desire to help. Setting boundaries can be a challenge for empaths, who dislike conflict.

All of these wonderful qualities are also what make empaths susceptible to narcissistic abuse. The narcissist sees an opportunity to be with someone who will easily fulfill their needs.

Sometimes, the narcissist will construct a story of woe to draw the empath in. Other times, empaths can see beyond the narcissist's false persona, sensing the wounds that lie within them. The empath then attempts to use love (their superpower) to help the narcissist heal—a futile effort which allows the narcissist to drain the empath of their vital energy, which they use for narcissistic supply.

As the abuse progresses, the narcissist can diminish the empath to the point that their entire sense of self is tied to the "love" and approval they receive from the narcissist. Only when the narcissist doles out crumbs of "love," they feel worthy. And unfortunately, after a past history of trauma, the empath often has a high tolerance for pain.

Today, I will explore more about myself as an empath if that fits. I will honor the special qualities I possess and respect the challenges I face.

June 26

Grace

Grace is an unprompted, often mystical gift from Source that blesses us and our lives. We can be delightfully surprised and even awed when we loosen our grip of control and allow our Source's energy to support us and play in our lives.

We can follow Source's lead and give ourselves grace. When we make a mistake or behave in a way that doesn't reflect who we are, we can bless ourselves with compassion, understanding, and love, remembering that we're human and are not designed to be perfect. This practice quickly brings us back to our true selves.

Filled with our own grace, we can then extend it to others. Through the eyes of grace, we recognize that others are doing their best, allowing us to offer them the same love and patience that we give ourselves.

We gave the narcissist grace time and time again, believing we saw glimpses of their banished true self. We hoped that with enough love, they'd find their way to us. As we healed, we came to realize that giving grace to abuse results in self-abandonment.

Saving the narcissist wasn't our job. We found that removing ourselves from their abuse, instead of giving them grace, was an essential part of our survival and self-care.

For today, I will contemplate grace and be aware of Source's radiant energy surrounding me. I will extend grace to myself often as I learn and grow on my healing journey.

June 27

Shutting Down

As the narcissist's abuse intensified, life became overwhelming. Sometimes we felt exhausted, and other times we felt nothing at all.

One survivor described their alarm after watching a glorious sunset and feeling absolutely nothing. At that moment, they realized they were in dangerous territory, but still they held on. They continued to abandon themselves to avoid being abandoned by the narcissist, who they hoped would return to the person they were in the beginning of the relationship—an impossibility, since that person never actually existed.

Shutting down is a survival mechanism many of us learned at a young age while living through abuse or neglect. During narcissistic abuse, as the pressure, expectations, judgements, and mind games began to take a toll, we resurrected that survival mechanism, shutting down to cushion the blows we were dealt when it no longer felt safe to be vulnerable.

Today, I will explore how I used the survival mechanism of shutting down to endure narcissistic abuse. I will look at why I shut myself down and what triggered me to feel unsafe. I will tune into the inner children that shut me down, showing them gratitude for their efforts in helping me cope with abuse, and exploring other ways to handle unsafe situations with them.

June 28

Caring for Ourselves

Narcissistic abuse kept us in a state of inner chaos, our overly sensitive nervous systems on high alert for continuing threats.

Our bodies are designed to effectively respond to occasional threats by using our survival responses of fight, flight, freeze, and fawn. After the threat has passed, it is natural for the human body to heal, recharge, and return to normal functioning.

In our toxic relationship, the threats were continuous. Because our body didn't have time to heal and recharge, we became more exhausted as time went on. By the end of the relationship, many of us were depleted and even physically ill.

As we proceed on our healing journey, we learn that we're not weak or lazy if we rest or practice self-care. In fact, our bodies need us to do just that so we can heal from the destructive abuse we've been through.

Other self-care steps we can take include:

- Reaching out to a professional who is familiar with narcissistic abuse.
- Taking on a reasonable workload and saying no to the rest.
- Giving ourselves down-time to be still and process what's coming up inside of us.
- Pampering ourselves by creating a soulful, nourishing experience.
- Taking a walk in nature's healing energy to connect with ourselves and our Source.

Today, if necessary, I will reduce my expectations of myself to only those things I must do. I will give myself grace as I practice self-care whenever I can—without apology.

June 29

Boundaries: Time and Energy

We have a limited amount of time and energy available to us every day. If we use these resources wisely, we can invest them into learning more about our authentic selves, living our true purpose, and sharing our unique gifts with the world.

Seeing how important and limited our time and energy are, we have the right—and even the responsibility—to set boundaries around them. After years of using our resources to support others in our misguided efforts to survive and get our needs met, it'll take practice to learn to use them to support ourselves again.

The following questions can help us increase our awareness: Where does our energy go each day? What is it meant to be used for? What boundaries do we choose to put around our energy? As we refocus our energy on ourselves, it increases, regenerates our health, and fuels us to live our best life.

We are given the gift of twenty-four hours of pure potential every day—and the choice of how to use that time. What will we decide to do with such an offering? How different would our lives be if we channeled that time toward things that support us and make our soul sing?

Today, I will pay close attention to how I invest my time and energy. I will consider how I can better use my resources to support me, and I will set my boundaries accordingly.

June 30

Intensity After Narcissistic Abuse

After the narcissistic abuse relationship ended, we struggled to survive and make sense of what we'd just been through, faced with a new life we hadn't asked for. **We were intense.**

We didn't mean to be intense, but we'd lived through unspeakable abuse. The experience was intense, as was the withdrawal from it.

We talked about the abuse...*a lot*. We tried to make sense of it intellectually, which was an impossible task to accomplish. Finally, we dove into ourselves, and our journey toward true healing began.

Our emotions were intense. We cried often—and for good reason, stunned that someone we loved so much could have treated us the way they did.

We oozed the feelings that were coming up for us. Some well-meaning people were uncomfortable with that, especially when we were experiencing anger. Never having been through narcissistic abuse, they couldn't have imagined what we were going through.

We weren't simply grieving a failed relationship. We were left depleted, sometimes chronically ill, tasked with putting back together not only the shattered pieces of our reality, but also those of our very identity.

Today, I will have great compassion for my intensity after narcissistic abuse, remembering that it was completely normal after what I'd been through. I will know with all my heart that I did my very best in every moment, and I'll let go of self-judgment in favor of self-love.

♥

July 1

Empaths and Highly Sensitive People

Many of us are *empaths* and *highly sensitive people (HSP)*. Some of our common characteristics include:

- Feeling emotions deeply.
- Often feeling misunderstood and like we don't fit in.
- Being perceived as too sensitive.
- Being caring and compassionate.
- Needing time alone to process and recharge.
- Being highly attuned to other people's feelings.
- Having difficulty with change—and with criticism.
- Being sensitive to light, sounds, and smells.
- Desiring different things from life than other people do.
- Preferring quiet, more peaceful activities.
- Being unable to tolerate witnessing violence and abuse.
- Being easily overwhelmed by time pressure and busyness.
- Processing information more deeply than other people do.
- Constantly overthinking things and searching for meaning.

One difference—HSPs are typically introverts while empaths may be introverts or extroverts.

Also, as empaths, we not only attune to others' feelings, but internalize their energy, feeling what they're experiencing within us. Being highly empathic is also common in those of us who are intuitive and deeply connected to the spiritual realm.

Today, I will consider whether I fit the criteria listed above, learning more about myself to further appreciate who I am.

July 2

Empaths and Highly Sensitive People: Gifts and Challenges

Being an empath or highly sensitive person (HSP) comes with both gifts and challenges. Some of the gifts include:

- **Sensing deeply,** we can experience miracles where others see ordinary beauty or everyday occurrences. Watching a fiery sunrise or being captivated by the full moon's light can inspire and enliven us, connecting us directly to Source.

- **Experiencing others' feelings deeply** allows us to bring love, understanding, and compassion to situations and people, making us great helpers in roles such as counselors, nurses, and teachers.

- **Having rich, imaginative inner worlds** fuels our creative pursuits and ensures that we are never bored.

Below are some of the challenges:

- **Being easily overwhelmed** by conflict, time pressure, and change, or by things that others enjoy, such as scary or violent movies or a crowded sporting event.

- **Being judged and misunderstood by others** for being sensitive, being mislabeled as having anxiety or mental health issues instead of being recognized for our strengths.

- **Having difficulty with things seen as normal or exciting by others** such as moving, traveling, or starting a new job.

Learning more about ourselves allows us to create a life in which we can embrace our beautiful sensitivities and navigate more gently through the challenges.

Today, I will look at my own personal gifts and challenges of being an empath, HSP, or simply being me.

July 3

Empaths and Highly Sensitive People: Self-Care

As the ancient adage goes, *with great power comes great responsibility.* Being empathic and highly sensitive allows us to perceive things that others cannot. Embracing this gift requires us to commit to our self-care practice.

Loving things we can do to support ourselves include:

- Ensuring we have ample time alone to calm ourselves, process our thoughts and feelings, and recharge.
- Avoiding violence, tragedy, or horror in books, films, and other media, which can emotionally drain us and retrigger past trauma within us.
- Setting healthy boundaries in busy environments, only staying and interacting as long as we feel comfortable.
- Setting boundaries to maintain the integrity of our energy field. We can picture a protective "bubble" of Source's high-vibrating energy around us. Only love and light can enter it, while everything else bounces off its surface.
- Creating a soothing place for ourselves, in the world or in our mind, where we can go when we need to feel calm and safe.
- Saying no to the things that compromise us, whether that's a tightly packed schedule, someone who drains our energy, or the belief that we must be perfect.
- Incorporating inspiring, positive things into our life each day, such as reading affirmation cards or books, walking in nature, or dancing to a song we enjoy while moving stagnant energy out of our body.

Today, I will incorporate at least one new thing into my life that will support my sensitivity.

July 4

Empaths and Highly Sensitive People: Wounded Sensitivity

When the amazing gifts of empaths and highly sensitive people were met with abuse and neglect by our caretakers, we developed incredibly effective, intuitive survival mechanisms.

We used our gift of heightened sensitivity to monitor the inner state of everyone around us, remaining hypervigilant as we worked to discover what was required to stay safe. One survivor shared that upon returning home from school each day, they knew if their parents were drinking alcohol the moment they cracked open the door, instantly feeling the altered energy.

We also used our gifts of empathy and compassion to care for our wounded caretakers so they would be present for us and keep us safe. Earning their approval and being valued for doing so cemented this caretaking pattern into our survival repertoire—and made us an easy target for narcissists.

Gifted with the ability to internalize our caretakers' feelings, we sensed with agonizing accuracy their inner battles and struggles. To survive, we found ways to numb ourselves. We may have used shopping, overeating, or consuming TV or social media to avoid feeling our pain. As we grew older, some of us turned to alcohol, drugs, and sex.

Today, I will be especially gentle and compassionate with myself as I contemplate my childhood experiences and survival mechanisms. I will prioritize my self-care and reach out for support as I access the feelings I've held within me for so long.

July 5

Empaths and Highly Sensitive People: the Narcissist

When we met the narcissist, our sensitive traits and their self-serving nature collided with a *bang*. With our vulnerability, propensity to please, and weakened boundaries, the narcissist calculated that we'd easily provide them with narcissistic supply, with little effort needed on their part. They pretended to be *the one* who would meet all of our needs. We were putty in their hands, believing our search had finally ended.

During the love bombing phase, our sensitivity deadened as the narcissist shaped us into someone else. One survivor described the distress they experienced while taking a walk in nature, the sun on their skin and beauty all around. Normally making their heart explode with love and inspiration, they felt absolutely nothing. At that moment, they realized they couldn't maintain their sensitivity *and* have the narcissist's "love."

During the devaluation and discard phases, we assumed the narcissist's abuse was caused by their inner wounds. We believed that if we loved them enough, they would heal and meet our needs again as they had in the beginning. We freely gave them our vibrant energy until we were depleted. Then, the narcissist moved on.

Today, I will contemplate where I am on my journey to reclaiming my sensitivity and embodying my authentic self. I will take comfort in knowing that the work I'm doing will allow me to manifest the truest version of myself, perhaps one that I haven't even met yet.

July 6

Empaths and Highly Sensitive People: Reclamation

After a lifetime of shutting down our gifts of sensitivity or using them solely to survive our circumstances, we can now fully reclaim them and embrace their intended purpose.

As we own our gifts, we come to realize our extraordinary value. We no longer live with our attention focused outward, looking for external appraisals of our worth or making attempts to fit in. Instead, we go where we're valued and appreciated, our outer world matching our inner world.

Instead of jumping to fix things when someone is upset with us, fearing abandonment, we sit with the discomfort that arises. We now know that being abandoned isn't possible—because we're working hard to never abandon ourselves again.

We learn that we're not responsible for others' reactions, only our own. We can use our reactions as an invitation to explore our inner world, to gain a better understanding of what our discomfort is showing us and what we still need to heal.

The way we interact with people changes as we learn to set boundaries, making our sensitivity, vulnerability, and open heart strengths instead of weaknesses. We become a living example demonstrating that strength and sensitivity can coexist. In fact, we are showing humanity a new way to love. As our world makes a grand shift, our gifts are invaluable.

Today, I will continue working to realize my value and appreciate my gifts of sensitivity, grateful to be on this amazing healing journey.

July 7

Trauma Triggers

When we carry unhealed wounds from the past within us, certain things can trigger the trauma they hold, causing our body and mind to react as if it's happening in the present moment. It's important to learn about and recognize our trauma triggers. This way, we'll know how to care for ourselves when we're in a triggered state even if it makes someone else uncomfortable.

The narcissist often triggered our past trauma—sometimes on purpose. Then, they shamed us for the way our mind and body reacted, our inner children reeling. Some of us were triggered by the smell of alcohol on their breath or their reckless behavior, reminding us of unsafe people from our past. We became instantly upset for no apparent reason, or we began dissociating, too overwhelmed to deal with the trauma triggers.

We needed compassion, understanding, and support. Instead, the narcissist judged us, telling us we were broken and should be beyond this. They threatened to leave us, showing no empathy for what we'd been through, concerned only with how our trauma was affecting them.

Healing the wounds of our past takes time. As we move through this process, we can compassionately support ourselves and take responsibility for our needs. Then, we can teach the people in our life how to support us in working with our trauma and prioritizing our self-care.

Today, I will compassionately care for myself, managing my trauma symptoms in whatever way I need to. I will surround myself with people who respect and support me in that process.

July 8

Managing Our Trauma Triggers

When our unhealed trauma from the past is triggered within us, we may experience symptoms such as panic, shakiness, intense emotions or body sensations, dissociation (spacing out), or overwhelm.

There are several strategies we can use to manage our trauma symptoms after we've been triggered:

Breathing Exercises. Conscious breathing helps to relax our body and refocus our attention. We can inhale for four seconds, hold our breath for four, exhale for four, and hold for four before our next inhalation.

Visualization. We can visualize divine healing energy pouring through the top of our head, filling every cell with Source's love and light. As it does so, it pushes out the discordant energy of the trauma, which goes to our Source to be blessed and transformed back into love.

Grounding Techniques. We can use the 5-4-3-2-1 technique, which asks us to focus on and say out loud the following: five things we see around us, four things we hear, three things we sense with our body, two things we smell, and one thing we taste. This can help bring us fully back into the present moment.

If we experience frequent trauma triggers, it may be important to seek professional support to assist us in processing and releasing the trauma within us.

Today, I will explore the most effective techniques for managing my trauma symptoms so I can use them the next time I am overwhelmed by a trauma trigger.

July 9

New Beginnings

Each day brings with it an invitation for us to start fresh amidst the hope and promise of new beginnings.

Every moment affords us that same opportunity if we choose it. Regardless of what happened in the past, whether a year or a moment ago, we have the power to create a new beginning at any time.

We can tune into our intuition and our heart's desires to set the course for our new beginning. Some important questions we can ask ourselves and even journal about include:

- What would we like to see shift within ourselves and our life?
- What new things would we try if we knew that we could not fail?
- What people or things have we outgrown and are ready to let go of?
- What have we put aside that has been patiently awaiting our attention?
- How will we support our authentic self this year?
- What can we do to bring more beauty, peace, and joy into our life?
- What messages does our inner wisdom have for us?

Today, I will celebrate the new experiences and opportunities awaiting me, remembering that I have the power and ability to make a different choice and create something new at any moment.

July 10

Daily Practices

Incorporating consistent daily practices into our lives can provide a supportive structure around us, helping us to remain focused on ourselves. They serve as a daily reminder of our commitment to our self-care and healing.

Some daily practices that may be helpful include:

- **Journaling**. We can journal in a structured manner, writing about specific topics each day, or as a tool for free expression, letting our thoughts emerge naturally. Looking back at our old journals can be valuable in our recovery from narcissistic abuse, giving us a true perspective of where we were if ever we attempt to minimize the impact of the abuse.
- **Gratitude**. The practice of expressing gratitude can improve our mood and open our heart, bringing our awareness back to love rather than fear or disconnection. We can wake up and journal about gratitude, or start the day by thinking of several things we're grateful for. We can also wait until bedtime to appreciate the moments that brought us gratitude during the day.
- **Intention**. We can set intentions to manifest specific things in our lives, or we can simply set the intention of being in Source's flow from moment to moment, in tune with our soul's wisdom. We can have long-range intentions, intentions for the day, and even intentions for the next ten minutes.

Today, I will explore which daily practices would be supportive for me at this time. If I'm ready, I will implement one of them today.

July 11

Conflicting Needs

During our time with the narcissist, we had to negotiate three sets of conflicting needs. The first was the narcissist's needs, which completely overwhelmed us and left us little time and energy for our own personal needs.

Next were the needs of our inner children. Extensive at times, their needs competed with those of the narcissist. Because of our intense fear of abandonment and rejection, the narcissist's needs almost always won out, taking priority over our own. Our inner children didn't feel safe with the narcissist and needed our care, compassion, acceptance, and love. We had little or nothing to give them, so we pushed their needs aside. Their cries for support got louder as their pain and overpowering emotions disrupted our adult life.

Finally, we had our adult needs. Meeting them allowed us to have a smoother life and accomplish our adult tasks, which often suffered greatly during our time with the narcissist.

All of these needs swirled around us like a tornado.

Now, we're creating a life in which our needs matter. We set boundaries with others, allowing us to prioritize the needs of our adult self and inner children, creating balance and harmony in our life.

Today, I will explore what my needs are—physical, sexual, mental, emotional, spiritual, and financial—without censoring anything for fear that they are too much. Exploring with no limits, I'll let my soul lead the way.

July 12

Fun

When we've been living in survival mode for most of our lives and someone suggests we need to have more fun, we may scratch our heads, unsure of where to even begin.

We might need to ask for help. Young children are great teachers of fun. Watching them or engaging with them can help us understand how to lighten up and enjoy life.

Our inner children can also be great resources in helping us understand how to have fun. We can ask them what they would enjoy doing. By doing so, we are validating them and acknowledging their needs, steps that lead to our overall healing.

Here are some fun ideas to get us started: rolling sideways down a grassy hill, playing a board game, finding shapes in the clouds, drawing or painting, building a fort, singing and dancing, baking, playing tag, going swimming, playing with a pet, telling jokes, going on a bike ride, getting ice cream, paddling a canoe, or watching a funny TV show.

Our attempts to have fun may seem awkward at first, but if we keep at it, we'll get the hang of it.

Today, I will ask my inner children for ideas as I brainstorm ways to have fun. I will choose one thing I enjoy and take some time to play, even if it's only 10 minutes.

July 13

Sobriety

When we are in a narcissistic abuse relationship, our brains become addicted to the huge chemical rushes that are released, both when we are overwhelmed with emotion in the bad moments and when the sweet relief comes as the narcissist returns and gives us crumbs of affection.

Recovering addicts have stated that quitting highly addictive substances was easier than breaking free from a narcissist—a powerful reference point.

While the narcissist's "love" and affection were magnetic to our inner children who yearned to get their needs met, the freedom to be our adult selves and live our soul's truth is unsurpassed by any "fix" the narcissist ever provided.

We must respect the power that this addiction has and acknowledge that we will often default to a place of powerlessness and need when exposed to the narcissist—until we heal the wounds and trauma stored within us that made us susceptible to their manipulation in the first place. Implementing No Contact (or Modified Contact, if necessary) with our abuser is an absolute necessity in the process of maintaining our sobriety.

Today, if I'm tempted to break No Contact, I will take a hard stop and put my entire focus on myself. First, I will determine what I am truly yearning for. Then, I will move my body to allow the energy that is building up within me to move through me. Finally, I will reach out to my support team, attend a support group meeting, or seek professional assistance.

July 14

Adult vs. Child Communication

The quality of our communication with others can depend upon who is speaking—our adult self or our inner children.

When healthy adults communicate, they are able to have engaging, productive conversations. Mature adults can use the information they have to resolve issues and calmly make good decisions.

When we have inner children in adult bodies trying to work out a complex situation, at odds with the process and one another, little gets accomplished as they are often unable to explore options or compromise.

When communication goes awry, we can look within to determine if our inner children are involved. *Are we in fighting mode? Are we hurting and wanting to hurt back? Are we angry and putting up a wall to protect ourselves?* These questions give us valuable information about our inner state. If we are grounded in our adult self, then the communication issues may be stemming from another person in the conversation.

With the narcissist, it may have appeared as if their inner child was present at times. *However, did they really show us that vulnerable part of themselves that they've exiled so far from their lives? Or was it the false persona's attempt to reel us in with manufactured vulnerability?* We may never know for sure.

Today, I will watch myself in conversation to determine who is speaking. I will listen to and honor what my inner children have to say, meeting their needs so I can have uninterrupted adult conversations.

July 15

Befriending Our Inner Children

Beautiful, unexpected changes can happen within us when our inner children feel safe, held, known, and loved. Befriending them may seem a bit odd at first, but the healing that follows can be significant. Listed below are activities we can explore with our inner children.

- **Hold space for them.** We can visualize them with us while we are completely present, loving and accepting everything about them. We can also work with a professional who will hold space for us as we take this deep, soulful journey inward.

- **Play with them.** In our mind or in real life, we can enjoy a magically-spun ball of cotton candy with them, ride a horse, paint our fingernails, look for bugs, or have a tea party.

- **Create a safe place for them.** Whether a treehouse in the mountains, a tent on the beach, or a magical place halfway between heaven and earth, we can create a place in our mind where our inner children feel completely safe. We can include loved ones or pets who've passed, a spiritual presence, or any other support they identify with. Here, they can be children again in a place that's filled with overflowing love, fun, and support.

There are many wonderful things we can do with our inner children when we let our heart lead the way!

Today, I will choose one activity to do with one or more of my inner children.

July 16

Meditation

Meditation can be a great addition to our self-care routine. We can incorporate meditation seats, music, candles, singing bowls, or incense, but we truly only need ourselves and our breath.

Some people prefer a formal meditation practice that helps them deepen their attention and awareness while others meditate simply to connect within and relax. Some choose to sit in silence while others prefer to do guided or even walking meditations. Our own definition of meditation is all that matters. If it gets us out of our minds and into our hearts, it's meditation.

Through meditation we can create a state of peace and tranquility within us, giving our overburdened systems a chance to rest and rejuvenate after the stress of narcissistic abuse. Many have reported amazing changes in themselves and their lives after as little as 10 minutes of meditation per day on a consistent basis.

Today, I will examine what meditation means to me. If I've never meditated before, I will go outside of my comfort zone and give it a try, checking in with myself to see what type of meditation feels right for me at this moment.

July 17

Masks

All of us have masks that we wear as we navigate life. Many of us began using them in childhood as a strategy to protect ourselves when we felt vulnerable, overwhelmed, or somehow not enough.

In the beginning, during the love bombing stage, the narcissist wore their mask of undying love and devotion. Later, the mask of their false self emerged, which they use to keep their true, exiled self hidden.

We wore masks, too, trying to be what we thought the narcissist wanted us to be so we wouldn't lose the "love" they so freely gave us. After the love bombing stage, we worked tirelessly trying to hide behind a mask, but our wounded inner children became too loud for that, crying for acknowledgement and relief from the abuse being inflicted upon us. Our masks became useless. We were wide open and vulnerable.

The difference between our camouflage and the narcissist's is that we use our masks to cope, but take them off with safe, supportive people. The narcissist will never take that risk, choosing instead to live permanently as the false self to avoid the pain and disconnection they carry inside.

Today, I will notice when and with whom I share my authentic self. I will honor the masks I've used with gratitude, for helping me feel safe. I will explore which masks, if any, I'm ready to put aside, knowing that I can safely embrace myself and my true essence.

July 18

Nurturing

Nurturing is the process of caring for someone and supporting their healthy growth and development by being loving and attentive—and providing nourishment, protection, and safety.

Some of us grew up in families that provided little nurturing. Guided by our survival instincts, we often learned to nurture others in hopes that they'd meet our needs. As a result, many of us didn't learn to nurture ourselves and haven't yet created a consistent practice of doing so.

As we commit to our healing and come to understand the value of nurturing ourselves, we may discover that we aren't sure where to begin with this act of self-love, not only for our adult selves but also for our inner children.

For our inner children, nurturing experiences can include swinging on a swing or glider, taking a timeout to breathe and connect on a stressful day, and making ourselves a delicious, colorful meal. What other nurturing activities would our inner children enjoy?

Our adult selves may appreciate a massage or yoga class, supporting our bodies with nourishing herbs and vitamins, or listening to inspiring podcasts. We may also feel nurtured by simple things such as spending a moment with our beloved pet, feeling the warmth of the sun on our face, or appreciating our child's beautiful smile.

Today, I will take one step toward establishing a regular practice of nurturing myself at a pace that works for me and allows me to enjoy every moment of it.

July 19

Abuse Amnesia

One reason we stay in abusive relationships is abuse amnesia, which often began in childhood. Abused by a caretaker or family member, we created an effective way to cope with the pain and shame while still functioning alongside the person who hurt us. We completely forgot the abuse.

Then, we carried this pattern into our relationship with the narcissist, unable to face the truth of their abuse and unwilling to risk their abandonment. If they emotionally destroyed us in private one moment, we were often seen in public shortly after, looking happy and in love, already disconnected from the abusive incident.

If we've used abuse amnesia to survive, there are things we can do to support ourselves in remembering and breaking the pattern.

- Exploring our abusive relationship with a trusted professional can often help us feel safe enough to remember.
- When we begin recalling details of the abuse, we can write them down, demonstrating our commitment and readiness to remember.
- We can refuse to be silent any longer. The moment someone disrespects or hurts us, we can call it out on the spot, a practice that takes time to master.
- We can explore our pattern of forgetting without judgment, grateful for a coping mechanism that may have saved our life.

Our memories of abuse come when we're ready for them.

Today, I will ensure that I have a strong support system around me for my adult self and my inner children when I begin to remember.

July 20

Feeling Lost

Some days we feel lost. We may think it's wrong to feel that way, but allowing and embracing our feelings is a healthy way to support ourselves. Perhaps an experience has triggered our past trauma and is stirring up overwhelming emotions. Maybe things in our life are changing so fast we don't know which way to turn.

Sometimes we feel most adrift just before we find our way forward.

Feeling lost doesn't mean we *are* lost. Feelings aren't facts. Even though we may be feeling adrift, we're clear and present deep within. Our soul is our inner compass and knows exactly where we are. We can go within and sit with our feelings, creating space for our inner wisdom to guide us in working through them and getting to our truth.

After narcissistic abuse, we may have felt like we completely lost ourselves, having lived so far away from who we truly are. The narcissist slowly stripped us of our identity, transforming us into the person they wanted us to become. Looking in the mirror, we may not have recognized ourselves. Even then, we weren't lost. All that was necessary was for us to turn inward once again and make our way back home.

Today, if I am feeling lost, I will not judge myself or try to fix how I feel. Instead, I will become curious about the feeling, looking to my soul's wisdom for the best way to support myself.

July 21

Independence

Many of us craved independence while we were being controlled and manipulated by the narcissist, hardly able to breathe. We wanted to have room in our lives for our own thoughts and actions.

Some of us reclaimed our independence by walking away from the narcissist. For others, we yearned for our freedom, but the thought of losing the narcissist was unbearable. We regained our independence when the narcissist walked away from us.

Sitting with our newfound independence, many of us felt overwhelmed, unsure of what to do with it after having been defined and controlled by the narcissist so completely.

Here are some things to remember when our independence feels uncomfortable:

Take things slow and be deliberate. If something doesn't require immediate action, we can sit with it until we sense the right move to make. We no longer have to rush around trying to please anyone else.

Reach out for support. Our newfound independence can bring up a lot within us. Getting support for ourselves can be invaluable.

Reach in for support. Turning inward for support, we are fully connected with Source's comfort, love, and hope.

Our independence won't always feel this way. One day, we may decide that there's nothing so sweet as the freedom to exist exactly as we are.

Today, even if I don't know what to do with my independence, I will continue moving forward one step at a time, knowing that it will lead me to beautiful things.

July 22

Retraumatization

After our experience with narcissistic abuse, our well-meaning family, friends, and even our counselors may have retraumatized us due to their inability to comprehend what we endured. This is important to recognize so we don't take their lack of support personally. Instead, we can find supportive people who do understand what we've experienced.

Some of us chose or were mandated to see a therapist with our narcissistic (ex-)partner. Because of our reactivity to the narcissist and their ability to appear calm and composed, we were often labeled as conflicted or overly emotional. When we found the courage to speak our truth, our words were often dismissed and our message lost.

In individual therapy, we may have sounded overly dramatic to a counselor who didn't understand trauma or narcissistic abuse as we accurately discussed the narcissist's behavior. Many of us became hypervigilant during our sessions, able to sense precisely what the counselor thought or felt. If we perceived even the slightest look or vocal inflection signaling their disbelief, disapproval, or disregard, we experienced another betrayal, leading to further feelings of abandonment and distrust.

It's important to have people supporting us who explicitly understand narcissistic abuse so we can rely on their empathic support and accurate reflections even when they lovingly challenge us.

Today, I will voice my concerns if I feel that someone on my support team misinterpreted my words or dismissed my experiences. If necessary, I'll replace them with someone who better understands trauma and narcissistic abuse.

July 23

People-Pleasing

As a result of the dysfunction we were raised with and the inaccurate messages we received about ourselves, many of us thought our worth was determined only by what we could provide to others. We adopted people-pleasing behaviors to avoid abandonment and ensure we received love and acceptance, sacrificing ourselves and our needs in the process.

Certain people in our lives benefited greatly from our people-pleasing behaviors. When we realized and owned our inherent value, identified our needs, and set boundaries to get those needs met, their lives became uncomfortable. Those we'd always put before ourselves didn't appreciate our new way of being.

In the beginning of our toxic relationship, we quickly morphed into who the narcissist wanted us to be, unwilling to lose their "love." As time went on, we became exhausted and resentful. We began reconsidering those people-pleasing behaviors as our pain inside grew. We lacked the energy to ensure that everyone around us always had everything they needed. We stopped rearranging our lives to ensure their every desire was fulfilled, resentful at how much our desires were neglected.

Knowing that we are extraordinary, a divine expression of the Universe, we now make ourselves a priority in our own life.

Today, I will remember that my value comes from who I am, not what I do. I will honor and care for myself, accepting that those who don't like the empowered, real version of me will go their own way.

July 24

Playing With Fire

When we have been wounded in certain ways or we struggle with addictions and mental health issues, there are things that can be dangerous for us that are harmless for other people. Our self-care requirements can feel like a burden to shoulder, but when we look around, we realize that everyone is carrying something heavy.

For the alcoholic, one sip can lead to a life-long binge.

For the addict, one hit can lead to death and destruction.

For the anorexic, withholding food can lead to a dangerous relapse.

For someone with OCD, giving in to anxiety and performing compulsive rituals to find relief can begin an all-consuming cycle.

For survivors of narcissistic abuse, re-engaging with the narcissist can reactivate the trauma bond within us, leading to out-of-control emotions and behaviors as well as the abandonment of ourselves and others who need us. No longer being supported by a solid inner foundation, we quickly become overpowered again by the narcissist. Going back to them can be dangerous, as the abuse often escalates each time we do.

Today, I will choose my sobriety and self-care over the momentary relief of playing with fire. If I don't feel like I can make that choice for an entire day, I will choose it for an hour or even the next five minutes.

July 25

Capacity

Capacity, the amount we're capable of, is a concept we must consider in our self-care practice and our interactions with others.

Capacity was something the narcissist couldn't comprehend. They viewed us as objects, there to meet their needs, with no understanding that our capacity to do so was limited—by the hours in a day and the amount of energy within us.

Many of us are highly sensitive people, empaths, and/or survivors of chronic trauma. Our nervous systems often have a limited capacity for incoming sensory stimuli. Exceeding that capacity can make us feel overwhelmed and exhausted, needing time to recharge. The narcissist may have judged us for that, unable to understand our reluctance to go out and have fun after a long day at work.

We can never know someone else's true capacity because we're all unique and there are many factors that determine it. There were times when the narcissist thought we should be working harder on something. Though we may have had the physical capacity, their abuse was draining our mental and emotional capacities, affecting our performance in all areas of our life.

Because we can't truly understand someone else's capacity, it serves us and others when we assume they're doing their best and act accordingly. This is also a supportive, compassionate perspective to take with ourselves.

Today, I will thoughtfully consider what my capacity is for things that seem overwhelming in my life, no longer allowing others' ideas or expectations to influence me.

July 26

Autonomy

Autonomy is having the freedom to act according to our own values and interests. Since our autonomy comes from within, no one can take it from us. We give it away, many of us trained to do so from a young age, when our lives were dictated by others' wants, needs, rules, choices, and dysfunctions. Often, we unknowingly traded our autonomy for the love, acceptance, and security we needed to survive and hoped to receive.

Any autonomy we possessed when we entered the narcissistic relationship was soon overridden. The narcissist demanded our time and energy, leaving little to none for our own pursuits. Any attempts at maintaining our autonomy were quickly squashed. The narcissist may have called us selfish, shaming us for our wants and needs, or they worked to fill our lives with their own wants, needs, and agendas, keeping us disconnected from ourselves.

Determining our values and setting boundaries accordingly supports us in maintaining our autonomy and taking our place in our lives. We become internally focused, governed by what's within us, instead of looking outside of ourselves for our boundaries, value, and definition.

When we reclaim our autonomy, it's common for the people in our lives who don't support that change to exit, creating room for others who do.

Today, I will contemplate the relationship I have with my autonomy. I will embrace my values and interests, maintaining space for them no matter who or what else is in my life.

July 27

Communicating Our Needs

Beginning to communicate our needs can feel like speaking a foreign language. It can be intimidating at first if we've never experienced it before.

There is no need too great for us to voice. All our needs are valid, beautiful, and important because they're ours, and we have the right to ask for help to meet them. The person we ask may agree to help us meet part or all of our needs. They may also refuse if they're unable or unwilling to help. Then, we can meet the need ourselves, ask for someone else's help, or let it go.

One person cannot meet all our needs, something we found out after depleting ourselves trying to do so for the narcissist. Their needs were their own, not our burden to carry or our obligation to meet. The narcissist was able to manipulate us into meeting their needs though, knowing we were addicted to their "love" and unwilling to risk losing it.

When we communicate our needs, we honor our adult self and our inner children who didn't have a voice.

Today, I will look within to identify any current needs that I haven't yet communicated. I will decide whether I can meet them myself or if I need to ask for assistance with them. Then, I will communicate my needs to someone who may be able to help.

July 28

Sacrifice

Over and over, we convinced ourselves that there were good reasons to sacrifice our wants, needs, values, and dreams for the narcissist's own.

Some of these scenarios may seem familiar.

The narcissist has done so much for me. I can cancel dinner with my friends tonight.

These heels are killing my feet, but since my partner thinks I look sexy, I'll wear them.

I should probably try a threesome with my partner. Their sexual needs matter, too.

They're right. Taking that new class would take too much time away from us.

I know they didn't mean to slap me. I was being argumentative.

It hurts when they flirt with someone else right in front of me, but I am gaining weight.

They're probably right. I need to loosen up. I will try those drugs.

I never have time alone, but that's probably too much to expect.

They were rude to the server, but there are so many other great things about them.

The pattern of putting ourselves and our lives aside turns into us feeling obligated to do more for the narcissist as the abuse escalates, so we won't have to face the terror of abandonment that lies on the other side of our decision to support ourselves.

Today, I will explore how I convinced myself to put aside what was important to me. I will reclaim those things for myself now.

July 29

Costs of Narcissistic Abuse

When we were infiltrated by the narcissist's toxicity, overwhelmed by their needs, and fighting to prove our worth to them, it was impossible for us to be fully present in our lives. This lack of presence was costly for many of us.

Our relationships suffered. Some of us became distant from friends, family members, and even our children. Our relationship with ourselves, our very foundation, suffered most.

Some of us made impactful financial decisions. We lost money, houses, businesses, and vehicles to the narcissist. Our jobs and careers suffered as we often lacked the capacity to perform up to our normal standards, exhausted and overwhelmed much of the time.

Our physical health suffered from the significant stress we were under while navigating the narcissist's abuse and attempting to live up to their expectations. For some of us, this resulted in chronic illnesses. Narcissistic abuse exacerbated our existing mental health conditions and created new ones, further impacting our lives.

Though the costs of our experience with narcissistic abuse were steep, it's possible for us to heal and reclaim what we've lost—and even create a new life that's better than we could have ever imagined, based upon the solid foundation we're building.

Today, I will look at the costs of my narcissistic relationship with love and compassion for myself. I do so to learn and heal, not to judge myself for anything, remembering that I did the best I could in impossible circumstances.

July 30

Persecution

In our past lives or in the present, we may have been oppressed, harassed, injured, or killed for standing up, speaking, owning our power, knowing too much, or being viewed as a threat to those in authority. We carry within us the memories of our experiences and those of our ancestors, which are passed down the generational lines.

Present day triggers can reactivate those traumas and bring our fear of persecution back to life. Our bodies don't forget. This fear keeps us from living authentically and makes us magnetic to narcissists.

When we're afraid to speak up and we lack the ability to stand in our own authority, narcissists know we won't have boundaries in place to deter their agendas. Sensing our need to be accepted and our desire to please, they know we'll work hard to maintain the relationship, with little effort required from them.

When we recognize these persecution wounds within us, we can work to release these memories from our physical and energetic bodies. This helps our inner children feel safer to exist, and we come together as a more integrated person, moving deeper into the autonomy of our authentic self.

Today, now that I have a clearer understanding of why I couldn't speak up, defend myself, or leave the relationship with the narcissist, I will honor my feelings of persecution with respect and presence, trusting Source to provide me with my next step to move out of persecution and into empowerment.

July 31

Comparison

It's human nature to compare ourselves to other people—or at least to our perception of them—and then judge ourselves accordingly.

Narcissists often use the abuse tactic of triangulation, which further ingrains this pattern into us. They use other people's good qualities against us, pointing out where we don't quite measure up. This can provoke a strong reaction within us, providing them with large amounts of narcissistic supply.

Their abusive behavior often makes us feel less beautiful, worthy, healthy, and strong. This is beyond devastating coming from someone we love, and it affects our entire sense of self.

Our freedom comes from understanding that we all have challenges and pain within us. Remember that leggy, muscular, or attractive person the narcissist just pointed out or flirted with? Outside of the head games and illusions the narcissist created about them, they have fears and insecurities just like us. Their heart yearns for true acceptance and devotion, just like ours.

Physical bodies come in all shapes and sizes. One isn't better than another. They're merely vessels for the magnificent energy that we all carry within us. This is where our untouchable beauty, depth, wisdom, and peace lies—qualities the narcissist does not value or relate to.

Today, I will slip on my love glasses and turn my gaze inward. I will note the unique and wondrous things that make me special and different from everyone else. I will celebrate everything about myself, even the rough edges.

August 1

Caring for Our Open Heart

Considering the possibility of living with an open heart can be frightening for those of us who've been deeply wounded. Sometimes we'd rather protect ourselves by keeping it closed forever. Once we experience life with an open heart, however, we may never want to shut it again.

In living with an open heart, we learn to love with the spirit of a child and the wisdom of an adult. We maintain healthy boundaries, which are appropriate in every situation and relationship. Sometimes, they're enormous and completely impermeable, while other times they're smaller, more open, but always present.

We support our inner children, meeting their needs and earning their trust, preventing them from reaching out to the narcissist for "support" before we even realize what's happened. We no longer hand our heart, thoughts, or anything else to people who harm us.

We keep the energy field within and around our body clear and flowing. We can visualize our heart beating with Source's expansive energy in its very center, growing larger with every beat. Eventually, it fills our entire body and energy field, pushing out any dense, negative, or disruptive energies. With angelic assistance, those energies are transformed back into love and light.

Today, I will contemplate living my life with an open heart, remembering that I can choose to do so when I'm ready. I will explore ways that feel right for me to care for my open heart.

August 2

Unrealistic Sexual Expectations

Many narcissists' preoccupation with living out their sexual fantasies and urges can be obsessive, unrealistic, and inappropriate. They may use gaslighting to shame and manipulate us, insisting that their expectations are normal and reasonable. We try to convince ourselves to meet those expectations, often judging ourselves harshly for being uncomfortable with them.

Unlike the movies or magazines that feed many peoples' unrealistic expectations, we aren't celebrities, nor do most of us look like one. We have cellulite, wrinkles, and we aren't airbrushed or altered. We don't always look sexy while having sex either, which can be messy, sweaty, and awkward because we're human beings.

The pressure narcissists place on us to perform during sex and meet their needs can cause incredible amounts of stress within us, which can adversely affect our self-esteem, health, job, relationships, and especially, our sexual performance.

It's important to work through and heal the feelings about the abusive experiences we had with the narcissist. When we're ready, we can then explore our own sexual wants and needs—what intrigues us, gives our body pleasure, and makes our senses come alive. With that knowledge, we can walk into our next relationship when the time is right, clear about our sexual boundaries and expectations, able to enjoy intimacy and sexual connection without abandoning our integrity.

Today, or whenever I'm ready, I will find the gentle, loving support I need to help myself heal from my toxic sexual experiences with the narcissist.

August 3

Value-Based Decisions

Values are the qualities and behaviors we believe in, that are important to us, and that impact all areas of our life. Our core values can include things like prosperity, simplicity, dependability, autonomy, or happiness. When we act according to our internal, soul-based values, our life comes into alignment with our authentic self.

Our values can guide our decisions as we move beyond the influences of the past and create a solid foundation in the present. In determining our values, we can set aside everything we've been told is important—and all ideas of how things are supposed to be. Instead, we get to explore what's important to *us* and what will drive us forward into the new, expansive life we're creating.

Knowing our values allows us to establish our priorities and make value-based decisions that support them. Living without knowledge of our values is like building a house without a blueprint.

We can often discern what we value in relationships by looking at the things that hurt us in the past. Our values are often the opposite. If our ex-partner lied to us, we may discover that we value honesty, integrity, and respect. We can then use that knowledge as a map for our future, to make decisions that support us, nourish us, and improve our life.

Today, I will begin to explore my values. I will remember decisions I've made in the past that were in alignment with them and those that were not.

August 4

False Selves

In the beginning of our relationship with the narcissist, they presented themselves as a kind, loving, empathetic person with whom we fell deeply in love. In truth, they met us with a false self that concealed their manipulative, self-serving agendas.

Because of our past traumas, we also entered the relationship with a false self. We tucked our true self away, carefully protecting it and the pain it held, with walls, masks, defense mechanisms, needs, coping strategies, and even addictions.

The narcissist worked to change us, molding us into the person they believed would bring them the narcissistic supply—attention and admiration—they required to survive. They manipulated and controlled us, creating their own idealized version of us, taking us even further away from who we really are.

Once our narcissist-inspired false self was firmly in place, the narcissist's facade began to slip, revealing the person who'd always been beneath it. Then, we began to experience the abusive sting of devaluation. As the abuse intensified, we tucked our true self away even deeper within us.

As we heal from narcissistic abuse, we are healing the past wounds that caused us to need false selves, giving us the courage and strength to unearth our true self within us.

Today, I will embrace the process of shedding the false selves I've created to survive. I will find the gold of my one authentic self that lies within me, just beyond my past.

August 5

Facing Our Past

Facing our past can be a challenging endeavor as we venture into the places within us that we've worked hard to avoid. The good news is that once we heal our past, we can let it go and open to the endless gifts that exist in the present.

Facing our past is an intuitive process that unfolds over time. Each new layer presents itself to be healed as we're ready. Sometimes, we initiate the process. Other times, we aren't given a choice, as our body demands that we face what we can't hold in any longer. This can be intense at times, but we can seek the support we need and cultivate a loving self-care practice that nourishes us as we commit to our healing journey.

The incredible gifts of facing our past are revealed as we go. After the most difficult moments, there is often a miracle awaiting us, reminding us why we're doing this work and urging us forward. We may choose to forgive those who hurt us—though we don't forget—letting go and freeing up our energy to live. We find our voice and learn to set boundaries, creating a safe, nurturing life in which we can blossom. We come to know and love ourselves, revealing our radiance within.

Today, I will remember that facing my past is a brave and worthwhile effort. One step at a time, it can propel me into a new life after narcissistic abuse.

August 6

Finding Our Voice

As children, we were taught to be polite and were often silenced by our adults. If we voiced discomfort about someone who made us feel unsafe, we may have been scolded for being rude.

When raised in dysfunctional families, we were told—directly or indirectly—not to talk about what was really happening. Sometimes, our voice refused to be silenced, though, manifesting its message as a physical or psychological illness instead.

The narcissist worked hard to silence us. When we brought up their hurtful behavior, they gaslighted us, making us sound crazy. They minimized our concerns, making us sound overly dramatic. We measured our words carefully, trying to keep the peace while also being heard. Eventually, we said little.

The narcissist could even silence our voice after the relationship by leveling a smear campaign against us. When we spoke the truth about them, we sounded crazy according to the stories they told.

Now, we can reclaim our voice. It's helpful to first create safety for ourselves by setting boundaries and breaking contact with those who are unhealthy for us. We can practice speaking our truth with safe people such as a therapist or trusted friend. We can sing, scream, whisper, or chant, allowing whatever is inside of us to come out. Writing is another powerful way for us to set our voice free.

Today, I will remember that I am worthy of being heard. What I think, feel, and have to say is valid and meaningful.

August 7

Nature's Touch

Nature, the dynamic, energetic presence that surrounds us can be a powerful resource on our healing journey.

When we hurt, nature envelops us in her soothing embrace, her breathtaking views, comforting sounds, and calming aromas. She absorbs our pain, tears, and overwhelming emotions as we surrender to the healing of our hearts. Nature's nourishing energy can reach even our most guarded inner spaces, slowly and gently opening us to our Source's love.

Nature inspires us, powerfully connecting us with our Unseen Support. She reflects to us the truth of who we are, stirring up our hopes and dreams, moving us toward a beautiful new life.

Nature's winds awaken our creativity and cleanse our energy. The golden rays of her sun warm us, bringing light to every cell within us, enlivening and expanding us. Moving or still, her waters invite us to reflect. They soften and expand us, often inspiring us to ponder the great mysteries of life. The vivid colors and sweet fragrances of her flowers remind us that joy and hope are alive, no matter the circumstances.

As we pull ourselves from the grip of narcissistic abuse, we can connect with nature for healing and rejuvenation. Though we may resist making that connection, once we do, things often begin to make sense again.

Today, I will remember the miracles and gifts that nature holds for me, no matter the season. I will include her as part of my support team.

August 8

Armor

When we had to fight to survive abuse, neglect, or difficult circumstances, we developed survival skills to make it through. Armoring is one of those skills, our attempt at protecting ourselves against the threat at hand.

Some of us who've experienced sexual abuse armor ourselves with body weight. As our size increases, we feel less vulnerable to attack. In addition, food provides comfort and was often our only source of loving nourishment in childhood.

We can armor ourselves by body building, creating a protective physique around us. Sometimes, we armor not by building our muscles but by contracting them, keeping ourselves in a perpetual state of tension, always ready for incoming threats.

We can also armor ourselves with our intellect, filtering everything through our mind and avoiding our heart—where our painful feelings are stored.

We armor ourselves to become stronger, but what makes us strong is seeing the threat, noticing our desire to armor, and choosing to stay present. We remain in our power, connected with ourselves, Source, and the situation. There is nothing stronger.

Letting go of our chosen survival skills takes time. As we heal our wounds and consistently show up for ourselves, creating a life in which we don't need armor, it becomes easier to let them go.

Today, I will notice my ways of armoring myself and consider whether there are any that I'm ready to let go of, trusting myself and my Source to get me through anything that arises.

August 9

Integrity

Integrity is living by strong morals and ethics in all that we do, even when it's not easy or popular to do so.

The narcissist didn't value integrity. They valued whatever helped them meet their need for narcissistic supply. Instead of focusing on their own integrity, or lack thereof, they honed in on ours. When they were abusive and we reacted strongly, stepping out of our integrity, the narcissist shamed us for having acted that way. Our reaction became the focus rather than their abusive behavior, leaving us feeling ashamed for what we'd done or said.

We may have hurt ourselves or others by acting outside of our integrity as we were pulled deeper into the narcissist's reality. Perhaps we became involved in things like stealing, doing illegal drugs, driving while intoxicated, or participating in unsafe sexual activities—all to stay in the favor of the narcissist and avoid abandonment.

If we acted outside of our integrity while with the narcissist, it's important to remember that we were being controlled and manipulated by someone very skilled at doing so. Trying to avoid the shame we feel about things we did (or didn't do) disempowers us. Instead, we can embrace and honor those painful feelings, with support if necessary, compassionately forgiving ourselves and committing to a life lived in integrity with our morals and values.

Today, I will continue to heal and move beyond my past, remembering that I did the best I could in every moment.

August 10

Jealousy

During our relationship with the narcissist, many of us were led to believe that we had a problem with jealousy. Perhaps the narcissist even suggested that we needed help.

At the same time, they frequently talked about, talked to, and flirted with their exes, their "friends," and people we didn't know. In addition, they regularly shared the details of conversations they'd had with other available, interested people. They constantly prodded our insecurities and then called us jealous.

Did we have a jealousy problem? Or a narcissist problem?

We were reacting normally to abuse.

Our childhood experiences may have contributed to our feelings of "jealousy." Some of us witnessed a parent/caregiver who had affairs or flirted inappropriately with people other than their spouse or our other parent/caregiver, threatening our security. Others had a narcissistic parent/caregiver who played family members against one another, doling out their energy and attention to those they deemed worthy, while withholding it from everyone else. This left us fighting for what we needed, pitted against our other family members in the process. The people who were supposed to support us, who were part of our foundation, were now our adversaries—a complex, traumatizing situation for a child to navigate.

Today, I will explore the root of my jealous feelings, knowing they are there for a valid reason. Instead of judging myself for them, I will seek to understand and lovingly heal the insecurities that live within me.

August 11

Excitement

If we grew up in a chaotic family environment with lots of stimulation, our nervous system was often in high gear, causing us to crave excitement. Many of us needed it to know we were alive, often feeling lost without it.

Life with the narcissist contained plenty of excitement, which they thrived on. It provided them with narcissistic supply and distracted them from the things inside they wanted to avoid.

After giving so much of our energy to the narcissist, we began to dread the excitement they craved. What some of us really wanted was a quiet night at home spent reading a book or a cozy dinner with our partner—instead of another wild night out in town or a lively gathering with friends.

As we began to heal from narcissistic abuse, we discovered that our life was changing dramatically, and we craved a different kind of excitement, grounded in our truth. Our new definition of excitement may have included watching the fiery colors that fill the sky as the sun rises over the horizon, taking a long hike in the woods, paddling a kayak on a calm summer evening, meeting a friend for coffee, or starting a new creative passion project.

Today, I will look at how my relationship with excitement has changed as I heal from my past and step into a new, soul-driven life.

August 12

Seeking Relief

In our relationship with the narcissist, seeking relief was a behavior that became cemented within us after the repeated cycles of narcissistic abuse we endured.

In the devaluation phase, the narcissist was often manipulative and cruel. We walked on eggshells trying to make things better, convinced it was our fault.

After, they would return to the idealization phase, once again offering us kindness, affection, and attention. We had value again, and the relief was immense. We felt as though we could conquer anything with the narcissist at our side. Intuitively, though, we felt that something was amiss because we didn't feel that way on our own. As an addict needs a dealer, we needed them to feel *that* good.

As the abuse escalated, the periods of idealization became shorter. Resentful and depleted, we realized the good times didn't feel as good to us as they once had.

After the relationship ended, it was that relief we craved, even momentarily, to end the excruciating pain we felt while working to maintain No Contact. Intellectually, we wanted nothing to do with the narcissist after the damage they'd done, but the cravings of the trauma bond, something we couldn't quite put into words, made us stay with them or desire to go back.

Today, I will contemplate my experiences with seeking relief, looking at the ways that behavioral pattern has affected my life. If needed, I will reach out for support in working through any challenging patterns.

August 13

Lowering Our Expectations

"I can still remember the exact moment I realized the 'honeymoon period' was over," one survivor recalled. "The flowers stopped coming. The romantic gestures and utmost respect I was shown were replaced with subtle and not-so-subtle glances and comments of disapproval. I thought it was just a normal shift in the relationship. In actuality, I was being treated differently. I began lowering my expectations, excusing the narcissist's poor behavior because I felt that the remarkable person I met initially must still be in there somewhere."

As children, avoiding abandonment by our caregivers was a matter of our survival. We molded ourselves into who we thought they would accept to be fed—physically, mentally, and emotionally—even if we received only crumbs. We carried that survival pattern into adulthood, letting the narcissist's declining behavior slide rather than risk losing what once felt like the relationship of our dreams.

We lower our expectations until we are no longer able to carry the pain of doing so or have discovered that we are worthy of love and devotion and that we deserve to be respected and treated with kindness.

Today, I will reflect on my life and notice how I lowered my expectations when I was with the narcissist. I will explore how and when those patterns were established in me as a child or young adult. I know that I have the ability and the right to uphold my standards of how I desire to be treated.

August 14

God Box

Dealing with overwhelming thoughts, feelings, and situations that we can't control can be challenging. Perhaps the narcissist is smearing us to others, and we're obsessively thinking of ways to defend ourselves and to stop the damage they're causing. Sometimes, the best thing we can do is step back and hand our concerns over to Source, bringing the focus back onto ourselves and trusting that everything will work out in the end.

One helpful tool that gives us a tangible way to surrender difficult things is the God box. It can also be called a Goddess box, Buddha box, Source box, or any other label that inspires us and fits our needs. We can take any box, decorate it if we desire, and transform it into a sacred container.

When we find ourselves worrying about something, we can write our thoughts, feelings, and concerns down on a piece of paper and place it in the box. The act of closing the lid is a representation of us letting the situation go and trusting in Source's wisdom to guide us and give us the courage and strength to manage whatever comes our way. It can be interesting to go back and read the pieces of paper later to see how situations were resolved.

Today, if it feels like a tool that will work for me, I will create a God box and begin handing things over to Source instead of hanging on to or trying to control them.

August 15

Reparenting Our Inner Children

Many of us lacked a reliable caregiver in childhood. We couldn't depend on the adults around us to meet our needs for love, safety, and belonging, or to give us the information we needed to understand ourselves and our place in the world. However, we can now give our inner children what they missed along the way.

When we are faced with adult issues, our exhausted inner children who think they must fix everything by themselves can leave us feeling overwhelmed. Setting boundaries helps them feel safe. Once we reassure them that these issues aren't theirs to deal with and that we'll take care of everything, they often feel relieved and take their proper place as children, allowing our overwhelm to subside.

Our inner children also need to learn about the basics to bring more stability into our life. One survivor shared that as they began to heal patterns from a chaotic childhood, they held a steady focus on doing "normal things," maintaining regular cleaning, eating, and self-care routines, which were inconsistent in childhood. Doing so formed a foundation that brought order to the rest of their life.

As we reparent our inner children, they have room to exist as the children they are instead of the mini adult they had to become in order to survive. We give them what they need to finally integrate into our system of self, with our inner adult leading the way.

Today, I will look for opportunities to lovingly educate and reparent my inner child.

August 16

The Bullshit Standard

The Bullshit Standard is a set of unspoken, shame-inducing rules that dictate who or what is acceptable. People conveniently pull out the Bullshit Standard when they are uncomfortable with others' feelings, thoughts, needs, or behaviors as shown in the following examples:

- Still shattered and stuck in a trauma bond with the narcissist, someone tells us, "You should be over this already. Get on with your life."

    Exactly who determined the appropriate timing of my devastation? Perhaps it's easier to dismiss my pain than look at your own.

- Men are weak and women are crazy if they display emotions.

    Who declared that nonsense as truth? How much lower would our suicide rate be if that belief changed? We are human. We have emotions. Period.

- A child falls down and cries. Their parent declares, "You're not hurt. You're fine."

    Really? And you know that, how? What are you avoiding inside of yourself by denying your child's feelings?

- The narcissist tells their partner not to speak too loud, need too much, and for God's sake, they can't appear crazy, weak, or broken, no matter what they've been through.

    So, I should quit existing so you can feel better about yourself?

I call bullshit on the Bullshit Standard. The only standard that matters is our inner truth.

Today, I have the right to exist exactly as I am. I will live by my own inner authority, meeting my needs and honoring my truth, preserving my unique magnificence.

August 17

Perfectionism

Perfectionism, a standard we set for ourselves or others, requires perfection *as we define it* and rejects anything less.

Perfectionism is a survival mechanism we developed along our journey of life—a strategy we employed to stay safe and get our needs met. Perhaps believing we could do something perfectly, or *be* perfect, gave us a feeling of control or a sense of value we were otherwise lacking. Whatever the reason, we can appreciate that it served us in some way.

If we look closely at the concept of perfection, we'll find it's an illusion. To define perfection, we would need to employ a standard for comparison.

Whose standard would we use? The ever-elusive "Bullshit Standard"? In truth, no standards are needed, nor is the pressure that comes with them. We came into this world to have our own unique experiences and lessons. Only we know what those are and how to live them every day. That is perfection.

As we heal and move further into our ideal life, we can revisit and release our perfectionistic tendencies when we're ready. Then, we'll realize that it's impossible to be imperfect!

Today, I will explore my perfectionistic tendencies as I open my mind to a more expansive view of perfection. I will take a moment to breathe, with my hands on my heart, feeling and knowing my perfection within.

August 18

Overgiving

Giving more than we had to give—to someone who didn't give us much back—was once a way to survive. We gave without thinking of ourselves while trying to avoid abandonment, keep ourselves and others safe, and gain approval from those too caught up in their own dysfunction to value us.

When we lack boundaries and gain a sense of worth by giving to others, many of us give more than may be appropriate and much more than we give to ourselves. When coupling those traits with our past pattern of seeking people who are unavailable to meet our needs, overgiving feels normal. But as our inner and outer resources become depleted, we often become exhausted and resentful.

As we heal and attract healthier people into our lives, different rules apply. Learning to have boundaries and consider ourselves in relationships can feel unfamiliar and uncomfortable initially. When we overgive to healthier people, it feels awkward and can be a signal to the receiver that we lack self-esteem. Learning a new way of being may not be a graceful process, but we can be gentle with ourselves and remember that we're moving mountains inside of us.

Today, I will be conscious of what I give to others, and I will consider myself and my needs in those interactions. In situations that don't warrant my giving, when I receive little to nothing back, I will reevaluate. I will practice great self-compassion as I heal from overgiving.

August 19

Presence

Being present in each moment can be difficult when we are accustomed to finding ways to avoid doing so, whether by distracting ourselves or keeping our attention on the past or future. Sometimes, we have painful things knocking on the door of our consciousness that we don't want to see or feel, making the present moment the last place we want to be.

Our presence in each moment offers many gifts:

- Experiencing true connection to ourselves, Source, and others.
- Finding a sense of peace.
- Unlocking our creativity.
- Witnessing the beauty of life and feeling our Creator's love.
- Opening ourselves, which allows Source to speak to us and through us.
- Living up to our potential in all that we do.

To begin increasing our ability to be present in the moment, we can simply focus on what we're doing right now, even speaking it aloud. "I'm driving my car. I'm drinking my coffee." This keeps us in the here and now.

To help us relax into the present, it can be helpful to accept the moment just as it is, trusting that we're right where we're meant to be, doing exactly what we're meant to be doing, as directed by our inner wisdom, which guides us to the experiences we came here to have.

Today, I will focus on keeping my awareness in the present moment, observing the effects of doing so.

August 20

Hard Work

Recovering from narcissistic abuse may be the hardest work we'll ever do. We aren't just recovering from a break-up. We're attempting to put together the broken pieces of who we are, regain our dismantled sense of self, and deal with our past wounds that the narcissist newly reopened.

It takes incredible courage and strength to be present with ourselves through the excruciating pain of withdrawal from the trauma bond and to continue moving forward instead of going back to the narcissist.

Not everyone does the hard work of healing from narcissistic abuse. Some people find ways to numb the pain they feel. Others return to the destructive "relief" of another love bombing cycle. Like us, they're doing the best they can with the tools they have.

We can honor ourselves for making the choice to do the hard work.

It's important to remember that we don't have to do this work alone. We can reach out for assistance from professionals and members of our support team while calling on our Unseen Support that is always with us.

Our hard work will pay off as we are blessed with the gifts of knowing a new peace of mind and finding our way home to our true self.

Today, I will take a moment to acknowledge the hard work I've done so far on my healing journey. I will honor myself for my tenacity and my commitment to caring for myself and moving forward into my blossoming life.

August 21

Making Decisions

There are times when we must make decisions or take action even if we're unsure of the right move to make.

We may have various inner voices weighing in on the decision—perhaps those of a protector, saboteur, or our inner children, drowning out our soul's voice and causing confusion.

Intellectually, we can try to understand and organize the facts involved in making a decision by weighing the pros and cons. We can also educate ourselves about the issue at hand in order to make an informed decision. Or we can ask other people for their perspectives, listening for any of their thoughts that resonate with us.

Intuitively, we can reach clarity on a decision by bringing our attention to the stillness within us. We can also get in touch with our gut feelings and look for cues in our body telling us what our right move is.

If we still haven't reached a decision, we can focus on our heart and ask ourselves, "What would love do?" Love, the high-vibrational energy that flows through us from Source, supports the truth of who we are. Asking that question awakens wisdom within us.

No matter what decision we make, there is no need to judge it as right or wrong. All outcomes can be used as opportunities to learn and grow.

Today, when faced with a decision I need to make, I will experiment with different ways of deciding, finding those that work well for me.

August 22

Innocence

Inside, we hold an innocence that is untouchable. It's the part of us that's completely connected to Source and filled with pure love and joy. No matter what we've done or what's been done to us, we can go within and reclaim that innocence.

As children, many of us dealt with things far beyond our age, causing us to bury our innocence deep inside, away from the dysfunction that surrounded us. After the narcissistic relationship, it may have felt like we had lost our innocence completely, having done things that went against who we were.

However, we didn't lose our innocence, nor will we ever.

It's from our innocence that we truly see, love, and connect with all people. It's also from this place that we see beauty, magic, and miracles in the everyday moments. As we embody our innocence, we are a reflection for others, inviting them to remember their own.

As we continue to love and support ourselves, doing our inner healing work, we create a life in which it's safe to allow our innocence to shine. We can both hold the sparkling energy of our innocence and be discerning and wise. We can love all people and set appropriate boundaries, no longer giving second chances to toxic people who hurt us.

Today, I will explore the precious innocence within me, knowing that nothing and no one has ever impacted it in any way. I will embrace it and bring its gifts to the present.

August 23

Mental Filtering

Mental filtering is an unhelpful thought pattern that many of us use. It means that we only pay attention to certain kinds of evidence or information while disregarding the rest.

Sometimes we only notice the negative information we receive and dismiss the positive. For example, we get our hair cut short and many people tell us they love it, but all we remember and hold on to is the one person who told us they liked our long hair better.

We can also focus only on the positive information and ignore the negative. Some of us used mental filtering to justify staying in the relationship with the narcissist. We remembered only the good moments when the narcissist doled out crumbs of affection, while disregarding the times they hurt us with their words and actions.

The use of mental filtering can have unwanted consequences for us, adversely affecting our mental health and our behavior.

Becoming aware of our use of mental filtering allows us to consciously change our way of thinking, getting an accurate perspective of situations by considering all of the available information.

Today, I will reflect on whether I've ever used the unhelpful pattern of mental filtering. I will watch my thoughts, and if I notice myself using mental filtering, I will immediately pay attention to how I feel. I'll consider all the facts of the situation, including those that I initially filtered out.

August 24

Honesty

Many narcissists used honesty against us as a weapon of manipulation and control. They began the relationship telling us how honest they were, making a show of their "strong values" and assuring us they weren't like the other people who had hurt us.

Further into the relationship, the narcissist's honesty began to change into brutal honesty used to hurt and diminish us. They freely shared all that they disliked about us or thought we should fix about ourselves—which may have felt to us like everything. They showed no empathy or concern for our feelings. Instead, they were committed to telling their "truth."

When we attempted to share how their blunt words affected us, they invalidated our feelings, appalled that we would ask them to stop being honest. They reminded us that we'd known about their honesty since the beginning, a statement meant to justify every hurtful thing they'd said.

Some narcissists also disclosed encounters, casual or intimate, that they'd had with past or potential partners. This was done to cause pain and make us feel insecure. They only told us, they said, to prevent us from getting mad if we found out somewhere else. If we reacted to their disclosures, they threatened to stop telling us the truth, knowing they were triggering other insecurities within us.

Today, I will consider how the narcissist used honesty against me. I will lovingly support my adult self and my inner children affected by the narcissist's painful displays of honesty.

August 25

Image

Many of us have felt like we're on the outside looking in at all the people living "the image." They are the ones that society says have made it, possessing money, talent, and style—the right hair, clothing, cars, partners, connections, and friends.

Here is a perspective on living "the image" from a survivor of narcissistic abuse:

"The narcissist entered my life and transformed me. One day, I was a somewhat ordinary person, and several months later, I was on the inside, living 'the image.' I reshaped my body with insane workouts, purchased the right wardrobe, and lived it up, attending high-end parties and social functions. This alternate lifestyle lasted until the narcissist had drained me of everything and walked out the door.

"After surviving that loss and getting back on my feet, I realized that even though I was living 'the image,' my heart was completely shut down, and I was in pain every moment. While my time with the narcissist had some amazing highs, it also had the most painful lows I've ever been through. I'd much rather be 'ordinary' and live with my heart full of love, creativity, and passion for life as the person that I actually am."

Today, I will reflect on my ideas about living "the image." If I've ever lived it or am currently living it, I will explore any illusions I may still hold about it, and I'll consider those I've already let go of.

August 26

Cognitive Dissonance

Cognitive dissonance is the internal discomfort we experience while trying to hold two conflicting thoughts at the same time, one of which goes against our values or beliefs. We look for evidence to support the more congruent thought, while minimizing the discordant one.

The narcissist was highly skilled at creating cognitive dissonance within us, telling us they loved us profoundly one moment, then crushing us with their words and actions the next.

One survivor described an experience that clearly shows how cognitive dissonance is created.

"The narcissist proposed, and I was ecstatic about our engagement. Shortly after, we ran into one of their ex-partners. When I shared our big news, out of nowhere the narcissist declared there would be no wedding and that I'd manipulated them into proposing. I was in shock, and my heart was reeling. It was as painful to consider staying as it was to think about leaving."

This survivor was forced to hold two conflicting realities, which created tremendous cognitive dissonance within them.

The most important step in healing the effects of cognitive dissonance is maintaining No Contact with the narcissist. It's unlikely that we'll ever make sense of the narcissist's mindfuckery that created the cognitive dissonance within us, but we can work to better understand our experiences, ensuring we never fall prey to it again.

Today, I will honor and release my thoughts and feelings about the cognitive dissonance that the narcissist created within me, reaching out for support if necessary.

August 27

Men as Victims of Narcissistic Abuse

According to our outdated societal expectations, the greatest failing a man can have is to be weak, emotional, or vulnerable. Many men have internalized this stifling, sometimes deadly expectation, striving to remain strong and in control at the expense of living authentically.

Some male victims feel shame around being abused by a woman. Others feel concern about the mounting anger they carry within themselves, masking the fear and pain they've buried deep inside. Many are highly sensitive men, trying to hide behind a tough, disconnected, and painful facade.

It's important to remember that just like women, male victims have inner wounds that they didn't ask for or deserve, which made them susceptible to the narcissist's calculated charm and seduction.

You can hereby reject society's stifling expectations and create new ones, men. You have the right to create space in your life to exist. It's perfectly acceptable for you to feel every feeling within you—and honor yourselves and your pain. Cry, scream, sing, hurt, talk, or do anything else you need to that is healthy and safe for you and others.

Today, as a man in recovery from narcissistic abuse, I will release the social conditioning placed upon me, allowing my true thoughts and feelings about my experience with the narcissist to emerge. I will reach out for support to professionals or trusted people who will allow me to be myself, to work through, process, and release the feelings I hold within me.

August 28

Validation

As children, we needed validation to help us regulate our emotional state. When our thoughts and feelings were validated, we were soothed and felt like we mattered.

Many of us who didn't get the validation we needed went on to require constant validation from others to prove that we were worthy of existing. Some of us learned strategies and worked hard to ensure we were validated, for example, by caretaking others and excelling in all we did.

Validation is an important part of healing and transcending our past. When someone has hurt us, it's empowering for us to speak our truth and hear them respond with validation for our memories and feelings, remembering with us. Validation allows us to heal, repair our relationship, and move beyond the hurt.

The narcissist didn't own their abuse, making repair impossible. This left us stuck with our thoughts and feelings, constantly searching for validation and resolution.

The ability to self-validate is a powerful healing tool. It requires us to be completely present with ourselves and all that's happening within us. We can listen to our adult thoughts and feelings as well as those of our inner children, confirming that we hear and believe them and what they think, feel, and remember is valid.

Today, I will contemplate the experiences in my life when I didn't receive the validation I needed. I will dedicate time to go within and validate myself, letting all aspects of me know that what they think, feel, and remember is valid.

August 29

Expertise

There are experts on nearly any topic in existence. Often, they've received schooling or extended training in their area of expertise. Many of us defer to them for help in making informed decisions for ourselves and our lives.

Some people believe they are experts on us, professing to have our answers. They are happy to provide guidance and suggestions about what they think would be best for us. As parents, many of us are well-practiced in doing this with our children, even after they've left home.

We can listen to other people's thoughts and ideas, trying them on to see if they fit. Ultimately, though, when it comes to deciding what we want or need, what our next step is, or what works or doesn't work for us, *we* are the expert. As we do our inner work, we develop trust in ourselves and in our soul's wisdom. This trust strengthens our ability to hear our inner promptings and know what is best for us.

Discerning the answers that emerge from within us is a skill we can work to develop. By quieting our mind and body and sitting with what's happening inside of us, we create the space to hear the guidance of our soul's voice within us, leading us to the decisions and experiences that will support our truth.

Today, I will remember that stepping into the role of expert on me and my needs is an empowering way to support myself.

August 30

Taking Responsibility

The narcissist skillfully used abusive tactics to avoid responsibility for their hurtful behavior. As a result, many of us took on responsibility ourselves, for the abusive things they said and did.

After being provoked by the narcissist, we may have reacted strongly, behaving outside of our own values and integrity. The narcissist self-righteously focused on our behavior instead of their own, acting as a victim and criticizing us for our reactions.

Many of us frequently apologized to the narcissist for our words, our actions, and even for who we were. We took responsibility for things that weren't ours because we wanted to avoid the backlash that came after we attempted to hold the narcissist accountable—the disrespect, intimidation, and endless arguing about our concerns that left us feeling muddled and exhausted. Our over-responsibility relieved them of the need to take any responsibility at all for their abuse.

Some of us reverted to caretaking behaviors we'd learned in childhood, convincing ourselves that the narcissist couldn't help their abusive behaviors because of their past. We were willing to sacrifice ourselves to avoid hurting or embarrassing them by confronting their words and actions. Taking responsibility for their abuse was a heavy load to bear.

After being overly responsible in the past, we never again have to take responsibility for something that belongs to someone else.

Today, I will explore the way I handled responsibility while with the narcissist, looking for the information I need to break the patterns of the past.

August 31

Hurt People Hurt People

The popular phrase *hurt people hurt people* isn't quite as simple as it seems.

Some of us have heard this phrase, perhaps from a well-meaning therapist or friend, but it was used in a way that invalidated our feelings and experiences, making the narcissist sound like the victim. It was as though the abuse we suffered didn't count because the narcissist was just doing what hurt people do. After hearing the phrase, some of us even felt ashamed that we had anger at the narcissist, because they were hurt, too.

In truth, not all hurt people hurt people. In fact, most of them don't. Many hurt people even help people. Most people apologize and change their behavior when they realize they've hurt someone. When someone continually hurts others, they are abusive, regardless of whether they have been hurt or not.

We must be cautious of our propensity to focus on *why* hurt people hurt people while ignoring the reality of their behavior. It's not our job to figure it out for them—or even to help the hurtful person change their behavior—especially while they continue to hurt us. Our only job is to keep ourselves safe and healthy by establishing firm boundaries or implementing No Contact.

Today, regardless of what anyone else says, I will own and embrace every feeling and thought that's mine regarding my abusive relationship, whether my abuser was hurt or not.

September 1

Co-Dependency

Co-dependency is similar to an inner tornado. We appear calm, yet we have an intense cloud of needs and agendas swirling around inside of us.

Co-dependency is a complex topic with as many definitions as there are people who've tried to define it. One helpful definition is from the book *Codependent No More: How to Stop Controlling Others and Start Caring for Yourself*. The author, Melody Beattie, writes, "A codependent person is one who has let another person's behavior affect him or her, and who is obsessed with controlling that person's behavior."*

Not all narcissistic abuse survivors are co-dependent, but it's helpful to identify it when we are, since healing from co-dependency can assist us in freeing ourselves from the susceptibility to being abused.

We can explore co-dependency from different angles. From one perspective, our powerful survival instincts guided us toward co-dependent behaviors to help us get our needs met and survive the dysfunction around us. From another, co-dependency is a self-destructive behavior pattern that keeps us disconnected from ourselves and Source.

We can examine our co-dependent behaviors through the lens of our inner children. Often, they and their unmet needs are behind the co-dependent behaviors we engage in.

Today, I will use the resources in this book and any other helpful information I find to learn more about co-dependency and determine whether its concepts apply to me.

* Melody Beattie, Codependent No More: How to Stop Controlling Others and Start Caring for Yourself, Hazelden Publishing, Center City, 1986.

September 2

Co-Dependency: Behaviors

The following are common co-dependent behaviors that we may have engaged in with the narcissist:

- We sought the narcissist's **approval,** becoming who they wanted us to be to please them and avoid abandonment.
- We weren't able to set or maintain **boundaries**, giving the narcissist free reign to act as they pleased. By not setting boundaries when they were abusive, we unknowingly gave them permission to do hurtful things.
- We made ourselves constantly **available** to the narcissist, afraid that they'd stray or abandon us—and threatened by the potential loss of their "love" and security.
- We often **rescued** the narcissist from their inappropriate behaviors, making excuses for them to others and enabling their misbehavior.
- We lacked skills for healthy **communication** with the narcissist, saying yes when we meant no, and we were often unable to directly ask for what we needed.

Those self-sacrificing, co-dependent behaviors often caused anger and resentment within us as we put ourselves and our needs aside. Some of us reacted passive-aggressively as a result, perhaps expecting the narcissist to know what we needed or believing they'd figure it out if they loved us.

We can now put the focus back on ourselves, acknowledging our best efforts to get our needs met in the past and ready to find a new way that feeds and nourishes us instead of depleting us.

Today, I will lovingly explore my behaviors with the narcissist—without judgment—to identify potential co-dependent behaviors within myself.

September 3

Co-Dependency: Taking Responsibility

Embracing and owning our co-dependent behaviors with the narcissist is an important step to take as we accept full responsibility for our lives and our limiting patterns.

We looked to the narcissist to provide us with a sense of self because we hadn't yet made that connection within us. We looked to them for a place to belong since we didn't yet belong to ourselves. We worked tirelessly to make them our source of security, love, and approval since we weren't yet connected to our own Source.

Similarly, the narcissist worked to make us their source after having disowned the part of themselves that was able to connect with their own Source. They also looked to us for approval, validation, and support of their false self.

From one perspective, we were both manipulating and controlling. We tried everything possible to keep them happy and to be who they wanted us to be so they'd meet our needs. They diminished and controlled us with abuse tactics so we'd meet theirs.

We've all blamed our feelings on those around us, but true empowerment comes when we own our co-dependent patterns and choose to get our needs met in healthier ways.

Today, I will remember that Source is my source. I will work to strengthen and embrace that connection, trusting that Source will provide me with and guide me to everything necessary to meet my needs and allow me to live my best life.

September 4

Co-Dependency: Freeing Ourselves

Exploring the underlying agendas and motivations of our co-dependent behavior that we displayed with the narcissist *without discounting or minimizing our experience of being abused* is an empowering way to understand why we stayed with the narcissist and what needs we were attempting to meet.

Now, with Source's help, we can work to meet our own needs and develop our sense of self in a safe, reliable, and consistent way. And often, once we do, people who want to assist us in our efforts will show up in our lives, supporting us in ways we never imagined possible.

An important first step in freeing ourselves from co-dependency is to turn our energy, efforts, and attention inwards, lovingly observing ourselves and recognizing that it's our job to fill ourselves up.

It's hard work moving beyond the victim role and exploring our co-dependent patterns with honesty and self-compassion while we process our thoughts and feelings about having put ourselves aside for so long. It can be helpful to have the support of a healing professional trained to assist us on this journey.

When we connect with our inner world, we connect with our Source. In doing so, we begin to recognize our value and become solid in who we are, no longer willing to change or sacrifice ourselves based upon anything outside of us.

Today, I will take a moment to recognize the strength and courage it takes to look this deeply into myself.

September 5

Simplicity

Life with the narcissist was complicated.

We were consumed with finding ways to meet their needs, better ourselves, and keep things exciting so they didn't cheat on us or leave. We played detective after yet another late-night text sounded on the narcissist's phone or when they disappeared for days without any explanation. We covered for them and experienced the consequences of their addictions. We worked hard to pick ourselves up and be strong each time we were blindsided by them, and we constantly flip-flopped between living the life they wanted us to live and trying to stay true to ourselves. It was anything but simple!

After our relationship with the narcissist ended, simplicity was critical while we were raw and overwhelmed with so much going on mentally, physically, emotionally, spiritually, and financially.

Maintaining a daily practice of keeping things simple leads to a calmer mind and body, which allows us to devote more energy to healing from narcissistic abuse and living our soul's sacred potential.

Today, I will examine which areas of my life or my inner world are still complicated. I will work to simplify the ones I can so I'll have more energy for myself and my healing rather than focusing on the chaotic, disruptive things that steal my peace and drain me.

September 6

Social Media

Social media is a double-edged technology.

It's a place where we can begin to use our voice and be heard.

It's also where many of us have vented our intense, bottled-up emotions and reactions to the narcissist and some people stopped listening.

Social media can provide a needed distraction after a grueling day of recovery from narcissistic abuse.

It can also turn into a numbing addiction that takes us further away from ourselves.

After blocking the narcissist and their flying monkeys, we can use social media as a supportive tool. We can flood our feeds with educational and inspirational information from other survivors who are further along on their journey of recovery. This keeps us focused on healing and helps us stay sober and maintain No Contact.

We can also unblock the narcissist and use social media to check up on them and their new source of narcissistic supply, torturing ourselves in the process.

Being sober and aware of our intent and monitoring the way in which we're using social media is important for our self-care.

Today, I will take an honest look at my relationship with social media. I will take steps to make it a supportive tool in my life. I will consider limiting my time on it or even taking a break from it if necessary, putting my growth and healing first.

September 7

Lying

As children living in unhealthy or even dangerous situations, we quickly learned to adopt survival mechanisms, such as lying, to get our needs met and keep ourselves and others safe.

At some point, many of us figured out that it was better to tell our caretaker what they wanted to hear, or omit what they didn't, to avoid risking the frightening consequences of their anger and disapproval. We may also have lied about the dysfunction that we lived in and were ashamed of, even to people who were trying to help us.

While we experienced narcissistic abuse, we ignored the many red flags that indicated the narcissist's unacceptable behavior. We also lied to ourselves about the degree to which the abuse was affecting us. We couldn't risk losing the one person we believed would stick by us—after so much abandonment in our lives.

We maintain our survival patterns until we gain awareness of them and feel safe enough to let them go. We come to realize that when we lie, we're abandoning a part of ourselves, and eventually, we're no longer willing to do that.

Today, I will take a compassionate look at some of the lies I told myself when I experienced narcissistic abuse. As I see the truth, I will remain curious and understanding instead of judging myself. One step at a time, I will work to create a life that doesn't require survival tactics.

September 8

Inner Wisdom

As children, many of us were not encouraged to honor or rely on our own inner senses. Instead, we were taught to look outside of ourselves to those in authority.

In a sick family system, our outer reality and authority figures were often in direct opposition to our inner wisdom. We abandoned our knowing to please our caregivers and avoid abuse, abandonment, and rejection. We were, however, incredibly wise beings, still strongly connected to our inner essence and to Source.

Over the years, the pattern of distrusting ourselves and deferring to outer authorities for our answers grew. But as we begin to connect with ourselves, we come to understand that no one outside of us knows what's best for us. Supportive people can share thoughts or ideas based on their experiences, which can give us valuable additional perspectives to consider, but they cannot know our truth.

Our inner wisdom resides deep within us, where we are directly connected to our Source. When we're in harmony with this wise, dynamic energy, we can construct an inspired life that allows room for us to fully exist—and which reflects our truth.

Today, I will honor my own inner knowing and authority, allowing my incredibly intelligent wisdom to shine through me and my life like rays of golden sunshine.

September 9

Commitment

Extricating ourselves from the physical, mental, emotional, and energetic grip that the narcissist had on us was a process that took grit and commitment.

We didn't have to know exactly how to do it. We only needed to commit to doing what was necessary. When we did, a sacred dance commenced between us and Source, and we received the experiences, strength, and support we needed so we could do the hard work to free ourselves from narcissistic abuse.

"But do I have the strength to make it?" a part of us questioned as we embarked on this new journey. Indeed, we did. Our readiness to make the commitment ensured that we had everything we needed to follow through.

When we desire to make loving, supportive changes in ourselves and our life, even those that seem overwhelming, we need only declare our commitment and willingness to Source. The rest will follow as we stay tuned for each waiting step.

Today, I will focus on one change that I desire to make. I will declare my commitment to Source, conscious of my willingness to follow through with whatever is necessary. Then, I will trust that all will unfold for my highest good as I embrace this sacred partnership with Source.

September 10

Participation

After our relationship with the narcissist ended, many of us saw ourselves as a victim—a valid and truthful perspective. We were controlled, manipulated, and abused.

As we healed, our connection to ourselves and to Source grew, and our understanding of our spiritual nature deepened. We owned our inner power and began to explore the idea that we were using it to create our own reality.

Instead of continuing to see ourselves as a victim, we decided to experiment with a new perspective: Perhaps we were a participant in our relationship with the narcissist. With this shift, we gained a new understanding of why we may have chosen to engage with the narcissist the way we did—and the gifts of the experience revealed themselves.

- The narcissist molded us into someone we weren't. The gift was coming home to ourselves, discovering and owning who we are.
- The narcissist's abuse unearthed our deepest wounds, allowing us to heal the traumas that we'd hidden deep inside.
- We experienced powerlessness to such a degree that we had no choice but to take back our power to survive.
- The abuse broke down our old structures, allowing us to build a solid foundation and a beautiful new life.

From that perspective, wasn't our inner soul wisdom brilliant in choosing the narcissistic relationship, helping us deeply heal and transcend our old reality?

Today, I will explore my experience with narcissistic abuse from the perspective of being a participant, without diminishing the validity of my perspective of being a victim.

September 11

The Myth of Unconditional Love

Some of us hold unconditional love as our ideal, striving to give it and to get it. It's the love our parents were supposed to provide, though many didn't. We often receive it from our pets, but is it realistic to expect it from our intimate partner?

From one perspective, we could say that no matter how hard we try, we cannot give unconditional love because we're human. The reality is that we're all susceptible to our past patterning, busy lives, and personal needs that sometimes make us unavailable to people and unable to give our full presence and love.

Often, our inner children are still yearning for the unconditional love of a devoted caregiver. When we enter a relationship hoping or expecting our partner to provide us with the unconditional love we didn't receive in the past, we are destined for disappointment.

Instead of looking outside of ourselves for unconditional love, perhaps it's best to start with our connection to Source, which is pure, unconditional love energy. Filled with that energy, we can then learn to be our own devoted caregiver, providing ourselves with the unconditional love that we've always needed and desired.

Entering an intimate partnership filled with Source's unconditional love, as well as our own, is bringing the best of ourselves to the relationship—a loving gift to our partner.

Today, I will contemplate my own thoughts and feelings about unconditional love.

September 12

Unhelpful Thought Patterns

There are a number of unhelpful thought patterns or cognitive distortions that we may automatically default to as we try to make sense of the world around us. Once we become aware of them, we can work to change them. The following are some of the cognitive distortions identified by Dr. Aaron T. Beck, MD, creator of Cognitive Behavioral Therapy, discussed in the context of narcissistic abuse:

- **All or Nothing Thinking.** Seeing everything as black and white, with no gray. *The narcissist rejected me; therefore, I have no value.*

- **Mental Filtering.** Paying attention to select pieces of information only. *The narcissist is absolutely wonderful (while we ignore their verbal abuse, devaluation, inappropriate behavior, and boundary violations).*

- **Personalization.** Taking responsibility for something that wasn't our fault. *The narcissist cheated on me. It was my fault because I had gained weight.*

- **Minimization.** Shrinking something that impacted us to make it seem less important. *The narcissist spoke harshly to me, but only because they were in a bad mood.*

- **Emotional Reasoning.** Believing that what we feel is the truth. *I'm so in love! We're soulmates and I know that we'll be together forever.*

Today, I will explore whether I use any of these cognitive distortions as I process information, and I'll look at the impact that using them has had on me and my life.

September 13

Objectification

Narcissists often engage in objectification of their victims—partners, children, and others in their lives—viewing them as they would a shiny new sports car or article of high-end clothing designed to make them look good and ensure a steady flow of narcissistic supply.

The narcissist overlooked the fact that we were human beings with our own thoughts, beliefs, wants, needs, and inherent value. Instead, they saw us as mere objects and slowly erased our precious human qualities with their abuse, making it easier for them to manipulate us.

To prove their value to the world, and perhaps to themselves, they paraded us around on their arm as evidence of their worth. Our intelligence was also put on display, our successes further increasing their status.

At the start of a relationship with a highly-sexed narcissist, we became the object of their sexual desires, stripped of any other identity. They turned their insatiable sexual needs into our responsibility, something we accommodated willingly at first—and then out of obligation—to avoid abandonment. They were constantly focused on our bodies, regardless of impropriety of time or place. Their desire was presented as love, but it proved to be a heavy burden to carry.

Today, I will contemplate the ways in which I was objectified by the narcissist. I will also explore the truth of who I am—my thoughts, beliefs, wants, needs, and inherent value. I will celebrate those things, knowing they are precious gifts, never to be diminished or erased again.

September 14

Re-Grieving

Before beginning our healing journey, many of us tried to avoid or numb the pain of our inner wounds. We often saw the world through the eyes of our wounded inner children and reacted to triggering situations from this unhealed place. This caused chaos and frustration in our adult lives at times—as our inner children did their best to be heard.

As we grew in self-awareness, we were able to connect with our inner children and support those affected by past abuse and neglect. When speaking of their pain and betrayal, we spoke their words. When grieving, we cried their tears, which were in desperate need of release. As we embraced our inner children, they felt safe and whole. They were able to reclaim their rightful role as children rather than being the miniature adults they had been forced to become to survive. This allowed them to integrate into our system of self.

Free to live as our adult selves, we saw our inner children's traumatic experiences from a different vantage point. In the past, we had grieved *as* them. Now, we re-grieved *for* them as a parent grieves for their child. Re-grieving can be a heartbreaking yet hopeful process, indicating our progress in releasing the past and moving forward on our healing journey.

Today, if I am in the process of re-grieving, I will embrace the feelings that arise. I will breathe deeply and let them flow through me and back to Source, allowing them to be transformed into love and light.

September 15

Inner Children and the Narcissist

One survivor shared their inner children's journey through narcissistic abuse:

"Upon meeting the narcissist, my discerning seven-year-old's reaction was one of discomfort, instantly seeing through the narcissist's deceptive false front.

"Regardless, my sixteen-year-old, hungry for love and acceptance, was quickly drawn in by the narcissist, who showed great compassion as I shared my traumatic childhood experiences with them. Soon, several of my inner children opened their hearts wide to the narcissist, feeling free and believing it was safe to be vulnerable.

"When the devaluation began, everything changed. Suddenly, any mention of an inner child was met with annoyance by the narcissist, who now felt I should grow up and be the partner they required. This reinforced the deep sense of shame within me.

"As the abuse escalated, the narcissist pushed me beyond my comfort zone and constantly threatened abandonment, knowing it was my greatest fear. My inner children became alarmed. Some of them shut down completely, armoring themselves up stronger than before, unable to handle the pain and intensity of abuse.

"Finally, the relationship ended, providing me with the space to create a life in which my inner children felt safe enough to exist and heal."

Today, I will bring my full presence to the inner children that were affected by narcissistic abuse, offering them love, understanding, compassion, and support as they feel their feelings and cry the tears they've held in for so long.

September 16

Convincing

When we try to convince someone of something, we hand our power over to them in hopes that they will agree with our thoughts or beliefs. Our sense of value often depends upon their response. Attempts to convince can be driven by our fears and unmet needs.

When speaking from a place of empowerment and autonomy, knowing our own value, convincing is unnecessary. We fully own our thoughts and beliefs, and we're willing to stand alone with them.

When we try to convince ourselves of something, we may be avoiding our truth or trying to console ourselves. We attempted to convince ourselves that the narcissist loved us, a belief we questioned, to justify staying in the relationship and avoiding the pain of abandonment.

We tried to convince the narcissist that we had value. That we were worthy of their love. That we weren't crazy, lazy, selfish, or broken. That we were strong and had it all together.

We tried to convince ourselves that we were fine...totally fine. We could become who they wanted us to be. They would treat us better if we helped them heal.

Today, if I find myself trying to convince myself or anyone else of something, I will take a hard stop. I will pull my energy and power back to me and give myself what I need in that moment to return to my firm foundation of truth, detaching from others' thoughts or beliefs and embracing my own.

September 17

Baby Steps

"The journey of a thousand miles begins with one step."
— Lao Tzu

In our recovery from narcissistic abuse, we are sometimes faced with monumental tasks along the road to healing. For some of us, the first big step was leaving the relationship, something that seemed impossible, *until it didn't.*

Other seemingly insurmountable tasks we face include surviving the symptoms of aftershock, regaining our physical, emotional, and mental health, and breaking the trauma bond, all important milestones on our journey of healing and empowerment.

There may be moments when we feel paralyzed and overwhelmed as we work our way out of a painful past. At those times, baby steps are big steps. This is important to remember! Taking one small step at a time helps us stay focused and keeps us moving forward on our path.

Baby steps are big steps when we're so exhausted that we want to give up, while at the same time knowing that we can't...*and won't.*

Baby steps are big steps when change feels impossible as we face our past actions and repeating patterns.

Baby steps are big steps as we learn the vulnerable new skills of focusing inward and loving ourselves.

For today, I will remember that I don't always have to run—or even walk. I can practice self-care and take baby steps when necessary.

September 18

Random Acts of Kindness

During our journey of healing from narcissistic abuse, our lives can seem burdensome at times as we bravely walk through the pain of our past. When our soul's loving presence is overshadowed by the loud cries and pressing needs of our wounded inner children, it can be difficult to remember the Unseen Support that is always available to us.

When we are in tune with our soul's magical, uplifting, and inspiring energy, life seems like a great adventure. We wake each morning wondering what interesting things Source has on the agenda for us that day.

Participating in random acts of kindness often has the power to reconnect us with our soul and the beauty of life.

Consider the following ideas:

- Paying for the car behind us at the drive-through window of a restaurant.
- Painting rocks with uplifting sayings and placing them where they will be a delightful surprise for someone.
- Paying extra at a coffee shop and watching the next customers' faces light up with gratitude as they receive our gift.
- Whipping up our child's favorite dessert—just because.
- Assisting someone with special needs at the grocery store.
- We could even do a random act of kindness for ourselves! What would light us up today?

Today, I will commit to performing one random act of kindness and observe the effect it has upon me and others.

September 19

Living Deeply

Many of us live on the surface of our lives, afraid or unsure of how to dive in deeper and live the full human experience. Perhaps we're unaware that we are even living from this place.

Living on the surface could mean frequently moving and uprooting our foundation, entering relationships with unhealthy people, using addictions to stay numb, existing largely in the spiritual realm to avoid being fully present here, or maintaining an internal state of overwhelm.

Some of us avoid living deeply by not committing fully to anyone or anything, so we always have an "out" if needed. This survival mechanism was often our response to feeling engulfed or trapped by people and situations in our past.

Others avoid depth because we're afraid to let things get too good. After our past experiences of having the joyful, nourishing moments of our lives ruined by the chaos of toxic people or by random, unexpected life happenings, it may feel safer to forego good things entirely. This seems easier than risking the vulnerability of what we believe is the next inevitable heartbreak and loss.

These strategies helped us survive our past, but perhaps it's time to live life more fully now, allowing ourselves to connect with and bravely embrace the beauty and gifts it has to offer.

Today, I will explore how close to the surface of my life I am living. With curiosity and compassion, I will look at the ways I keep myself from living deeply.

September 20

External Validation

Our need for external validation left us vulnerable to the narcissist's manipulation as we eagerly soaked in their attention and affection, unaware that we were being lured into an abusive relationship.

Learning to validate ourselves is important—so we don't *need* it from others—though we may still desire it to some degree. We seek to be affirmed and to receive reflections of ourselves from other people's perspectives.

The narcissist's need for external validation was evidenced by the false persona they presented to the world, their need to flirt, or their propensity to insincerely flatter people. The validation they received helped them fight their own negative thoughts and feelings about themselves.

Initially, we were a powerful source of external validation for the narcissist. Once they had conquered us, however, our validation no longer fed their insatiable need, so they intensified their efforts to obtain it from others. We often took this change personally. Losing their attention while watching them shower it on others hurt us deeply and made us feel like we'd never be enough for them. In truth, no one person could be enough to fill the gaping hole within them. Their true self and Source could fill it, but that connection was broken when they adopted their false self.

Today, I will assess the strength of my need for external validation and my ability to validate myself. I will work to seek any validation that I desire from safe, genuine, loving sources.

September 21

Obedience

We learned early that the best way to be accepted and avoid abandonment was to meet the expectations of our parents, peers, and society. Many of us tried to put aside the uniqueness of our wondrous selves and adopt the "right" thoughts, behaviors, and characteristics to fit in. We soon discovered that if we couldn't shrink ourselves into the right shape, we were alone.

We carried those lessons into our adult lives, continuing our struggle to belong.

Enter the narcissist.

We were equipped with powerful survival skills that helped us discern exactly who they wanted us to be. We instantly perceived their subtle looks of disapproval or their change in demeanor, and we adjusted, fearful of losing their "love."

The narcissist's demands pushed us so far beyond any prior limits of obedience, there was no way for us to deny our awareness of what we were doing. We stopped obeying their demands when the pain of denying who we were surpassed our pain and fear of abandonment. At that moment, we threw off the old structures and began to discover a new way to exist.

Was it painful? *Yes.*

Was it scary? *Absolutely.*

Was allowing our true selves to breathe worth every second of the discomfort it took to get there? *Without question!*

Today, I will look at how I've played the good little girl or boy throughout my lifetime and to what degree I'm still using that old survival mechanism. I will explore life outside of that structure so I can make room for myself to exist exactly as I am.

September 22

Fall

"If a year was tucked inside of a clock, then autumn would be the magic hour." — Victoria Erickson

Each year, we feel its essence creeping into our end-of-summer days, even before the temperatures have begun to drop. It shows up first as a quickening within us, a knowing of what's to come. An anticipation of a slower pace and a move inward to the part of us that has been patiently waiting, filled with delighted expectation of our return.

Every fall, the trees inspire us and enliven our senses with their grand finale of magnificent color that reminds us of Source's passionate creativity.

Then, as the temperatures fall and life's tempo begins to slow, and as the crisp air heightens our senses, we nurture ourselves with the warm, nourishing comforts of the season. Fall's wild winds blow through, stirring us up and preparing us as they usher the leaves to the ground, their cycle complete. Clouds sail across the face of the Harvest Moon, creating a mystical scene that brings us inward, reconnecting us with our wild inner freedom.

Today, I will remember the magic of fall regardless of the date. I will flow with the changes that fall brings as I prepare for another inner journey, knowing there are miracles and a new life awaiting me afterwards.

September 23

Risk

Many narcissists crave dangerous adventures, such as extreme sports, aggressive driving, gambling, or risky sexual activities. When the narcissist entered our lives, we often found ourselves taking risks that were completely out of character for us. We went along with their desires—aware of, yet uncomfortable with the risks.

Perhaps we did drugs or drank alcohol to excess and then drove a car, risking other people's lives and our own. Maybe we became involved in illegal activities or joined the narcissist in unsafe sexual behaviors, putting our health in danger.

We must have compassion for ourselves as we recall our risky behavior. The stakes were high as we fought to maintain our relationship with the narcissist.

After their manipulation firmly hooked us in, the devaluation phase began. We were exhausted, confused, and addicted to them. Though they were tearing us apart, it felt like they were the only person who truly understood us and was willing to put up with us—and whom we could trust. Our worth, value, and identity were defined by them moment-to-moment. We couldn't risk losing their "love" and acceptance, so we took the risks associated with meeting their needs instead. This was less frightening than being abandoned, in the victimized state we were in.

Today, I will think about the risks I took while in relationship with the narcissist, and I will explore the reasons why. I will look at my truths and values to determine what my boundaries are moving forward.

September 24

Words

Paying attention to the words we say can often reveal our unconscious, self-sabotaging patterns. This awareness can help us avoid getting sucked back into the narcissist's vortex as we work to recover from their abuse.

We might find ourselves talking about the narcissist more frequently, perhaps even warmly, as we think of good moments in our relationship. Subtle at first, the energy behind our words builds, and some part of us has now energetically re-engaged with the narcissist. Before we know it, we break No Contact and are once again spinning around wildly in their vortex.

We may also notice ourselves using the word "we" when talking about us and the narcissist, saying things like:

We were going to get married on that day.
We had so much fun there on vacation.
We share the same philosophy on...

This can be a red flag indicating that a part of us has re-engaged—or never fully disengaged in the first place, secretly hoping or believing we're still in a relationship with them.

As we increase our self-awareness and begin to recognize these cues, we can take care of ourselves and avoid being sucked back into the narcissist's vortex, allowing us to continue without interrupting our recovery journey.

Today, I will watch my language to see if I am tiptoeing into dangerous territory.

September 25

Change

Change is something we can count on in our lives. No matter what, things will always change. This is a fact we'd like to avoid when wonderful things are happening in and around us.

During the love bombing phase of the narcissistic abuse cycle, we hoped, dreamed, and expected that those wonderful moments would last forever. When the narcissist changed, moving into the devaluation phase, our relationship was altered in ways we never imagined possible.

Change can also be something we embrace. Remembering that things will always change can give us strength to get through the difficult times—like the excruciating withdrawal symptoms we experienced after our toxic relationship ended, or the enduring effects of the trauma bond.

Often, after the most challenging changes we experience on our recovery journey, miracles happen—some great and some small. Those uplifting moments are like whispers from Source, thanking us for our continued efforts and reminding us of why we're doing this transformative inner healing work.

We can now focus on living our lives from a place of loving detachment, open to whatever changes are unfolding in the moment, trusting that we have the strength and knowledge to get ourselves through the challenging times—and the courage and wisdom to fully enjoy the beautiful times without expectations.

Today, like a tree being blown about by the winds of change, I will do my best to remain flexible, bending without breaking until the winds subside, which they always do.

September 26

Hope

Hope may have been all we had left after the painful things we endured as children. We hoped things would get better and the adults in our lives would become healthier. We hoped that someday we would be "normal" like other people. During the struggles in our lives, a persistent sense of hope kept us moving forward. We believed that better things were coming.

The moment we met the narcissist, hope became our adversary. Even though we saw red flags, we maintained the hope that things would somehow work out between us. As the abuse escalated, we desperately hoped they would once again love us like they did in the beginning—and that we would survive until they did.

After the relationship ended, the narcissist counted on our undying sense of hope to give them the power to draw us back in—all the way or just far enough so that they could get a fix of narcissistic supply from us when they needed it.

As we focus on ourselves and create a new life, we can direct our precious, boundless hope toward the things that nurture and sustain us.

Today, I will express gratitude for the hope that has gotten me through, and if I'm feeling hopeless at this moment, I will open my heart to Source, my eternal wellspring of hope.

September 27

Inner Cues

Our inner children's knowledge and sensitivity speaks through our physical body, providing us with important information about ourselves and our environment. It's our inner children who often perceive things that our distracted adult selves may not.

One survivor shared that their inner four-year-old had well-developed powers of observation and intuition, skills they had needed to survive their childhood. Within moments of encountering someone new, they could determine whether the person was safe or should be kept at a distance.

We've all had experiences with inner cues in our relationship with the narcissist, but we ignored many of the warnings, unwilling to see the truth and risk abandonment. Some examples include:

- During the love bombing stage, after the narcissist had revealed something about themselves that made us cringe inside, our shoulders instantly tensed up.
- The narcissist introduced us to their "friend" who was clearly a former lover. Our whole body felt heavy as they interacted, sensing the truth of their connection. Outwardly, we smiled. Inside, we felt nauseous.
- The narcissist delivered one of their well-timed, critical comments designed to knock us off our feet. Our inner children reeled, and our heart physically hurt as we tried to absorb the shock of the narcissist's words.

These cues are messages from our wise inner children, letting us know they are uncomfortable and there's something to pay attention to.

Today, I will explore my inner cues and assess my willingness to listen to the messages they deliver.

September 28

Mindfuckery

Narcissists gain power over us and receive large amounts of narcissistic supply by controlling what we think and how we feel.

"Let's go get ice cream," the narcissist says, lovingly extending us an invitation. Craving their affection, we happily accept.

Later, they note with disgust, "You're gaining weight." Through our hurt, we question why they invited us for ice cream.

They respond with, "You should've said you didn't want any." Mindfuckery at its finest.

Narcissists use gaslighting to project their abusive behavior back onto us. After we went through their phone and discovered their infidelity, they interrogated and berated us for invading their privacy.

They use triangulation to destabilize and disempower us, keeping us dependent upon them. "My ex sent me another sexy text telling me she wishes we were back together," the narcissist informs us, as if it's a burden to them. When we ask them to set a boundary with their ex, we're told that we're being insecure and cruel.

The narcissist initiates these mind-bending tactics once they know we're addicted to them and their supply is secure.

For today, I will remember that the narcissist's mindfuckery had nothing to do with me or my value. Instead, it was about their insecurity. I will continue to create a life that includes clear, respectful communication and connections with others. If I find myself confused or overwhelmed while interacting with someone, I will take a step back and assess the situation from the viewpoint of an observer.

September 29

Conditions

Narcissists don't have relationships. They have arrangements. Their potential partners are assessed for one thing only—their ability to meet the narcissist's need for narcissistic supply.

Many narcissists have conditions they require of their partner, which are designed to fulfill the narcissist's needs but are presented as being "for both partners." They may include things like maintaining our physical health to certain standards, allowing both partners to have contact (casual or intimate) with past partners or "friends," and agreeing to alternative sexual activities.

Destined to fail, the narcissist's conditions don't consider our humanness and changeability. In addition, their conditions are presented during the love bombing stage, a time when we're high on their "love" and will do almost anything to be with them forever.

Perhaps we hope they're just insecure and will grow out of the need for conditions as the relationship matures. (They don't.)

The narcissist must maintain a high level of control over us to ensure their needs are met. Because of their insecurities, they cannot risk living life a moment at a time or fully giving themselves to anyone or anything. Consequently, they cannot provide the loving, responsive attention and empathy that we deserve, nor can they allow the natural unfolding of a "relationship."

Today, I will evaluate the conditions that were part of my relationship with the narcissist, spoken or implied. I will take a moment to assess how those conditions affected me, honoring the feelings that arise.

September 30

Reflections

"As above, so below, as within, so without, as the universe, so the soul..." — Hermes Trismegistus

Our outer life reflects our inner world: It mirrors our internal experience as well as our beliefs about ourselves and others. These beliefs were created by our environment and the information we received about ourselves in childhood. They can be true or grossly inaccurate.

For example, we can have moments when our living space is chaotic and disorganized. Other times, it may be a calm, tranquil environment. When things are chaotic around us, we may be experiencing something chaotic within. For example, we may be processing feelings of unworthiness or overwhelm or going through inner energetic shifts that are upending our "normal" way of being. On the other hand, a tranquil home environment may reflect that our inner space has settled and we are once again able to access the calmness within us.

We can also find reflections in our relationships. The way people treat us can mirror the way we treat ourselves. It can also show us things that we believe about ourselves or others. For example, it may reveal that we believe we deserve to be treated badly or that those who love us hurt us.

Today, I will study my outer life with a non-judgmental eye to see what it is reflecting about my inner life. I will use that information to discover what I can acknowledge or release to bring me closer to the truth of who I am.

♥

October 1

Vital Energy

Our vital energy is a precious resource from our Source that fills us with light, love, joy, and courage. It fuels our creative pursuits and brings out our inner sparkle. When we're filled with this life force, the wonder of who we are emerges. Can you think of a time when you felt filled with this energy?

Narcissists aren't able to access their own vital energy because they have rejected their true selves, which is where their connection to Source lies. They maintain a false persona to try and get their needs met.

As a result, they mined our energy and inner resources to obtain the narcissistic supply they needed to function. They were exceptional at triggering reactions within us, either positive or negative, which created the supply they needed. This sapped our physical, emotional, and psychic energy, even when the reaction they elicited from us was a positive one. When they triggered a negative reaction, we may have felt worthless, broken, and disregarded.

Today, I will be conscious of my inner life force. I will pay attention to the exchanges I have with others and become aware of how much vital energy I am giving and receiving. I will monitor how I feel around people. I will practice speaking up and setting boundaries to preserve my valuable resources so I can use them to create a beautiful life.

October 2

Rigidity

We may envy people who haven't been through abuse. They seem relaxed and able to enjoy life, leaving many of us painfully aware of the rigidity and fear that accompanies us every moment.

We must have great compassion and understanding for ourselves and remember that there are valid reasons why we are more rigid in our ways than others. Trying to control our reality may have been the only way for us to find a sense of safety or sanity as we endured out-of-control situations.

After surviving narcissistic abuse, it's very normal for our inner children to be on guard. They may feel unsafe, afraid of what's coming next, or apprehensive about us making any moves.

There is hope for a gentler, more comfortable way of living. As we commit to being present with ourselves, we continue to integrate and heal. Our inner terrain changes, and we begin to feel safer, allowing a new life to emerge.

Healing is a process we must take one step at a time. Sometimes it's slow and steady while other times we move at a faster pace. It's helpful to be clear about what changes we'd like to see within ourselves so we can move forward toward our goal.

Today, I will allow myself to move at my own pace and work with myself right where I'm at. I will get a picture in my mind of my goals and ideal life. Then, I will hand my vision over, trusting Source's wisdom to lovingly guide and support my healing process.

October 3

Seasons of Healing

Our experience of healing from narcissistic abuse can be similar to the rhythm and flow of the seasons.

Winter. An icy wind brings painful changes we didn't ask for. We desperately yearn for the narcissist while being venomously angry at them...an incomprehensible paradox. The cold shame of rejection is unbearable, and we fear that we will freeze to death.

Spring. A beautiful light illuminates the darkest night we've ever known. We gather up our courage, dust ourselves off, and start anew. Hope whispers softly as we are once again able to see the beauty within and around us. We're still fragile, but we're certain we will survive.

Summer. The warmth of the sun fuels us. We find a new tempo as our strength grows within us. We recognize the miracle of Source's creation, inside and out, and it warms our heart. We are filled with gratitude and celebrate our new life.

Fall. Magnificent colors emerge from our soul and manifest in our lives, leaving us breathless. We had no idea that Source's version of us could be so beautiful. Then, the winds of change blow through to assist us in letting go of everything that is no longer aligned with our soul's vision for us.

Today, I will honor and embrace whichever season is upon me, knowing that seasons always change and new, wondrous things lie ahead of me.

October 4

Hypervigilance

If we were exposed to abuse and neglect as children, we learned to rely on ourselves after our caretakers had proven themselves untrustworthy, unsafe, and unable to meet our needs. Many of us developed the survival skill of hypervigilance, keeping us on constant alert for danger. It helped us read situations, keep ourselves safe, and work more effectively to get our needs met. Hypervigilance also gave us the feeling of having some control over our out-of-control lives. We can honor it for serving us in those important ways.

As adults, we often remain hyper-alert to potential threats that mirror the ones we experienced as children. When we are constantly anticipating danger, our ability to be present, create meaningful connections with others, and enjoy life is greatly impacted.

We've done an amazing job of surviving thus far. Now, in our own timing, can we loosen the grip of hypervigilant awareness that we've maintained, ever so slightly, while putting our trust in Source and in safe, reliable people? Can we create room within ourselves and our life to allow the grace, ease, and support that comes from being in our soul's flow?

As we continue to set boundaries and create a stable, nourishing life, our need for hypervigilance often diminishes.

Today, I will explore my relationship with hypervigilance. I will get a clear vision of the changes I'd like to make, and I will ask Source to assist me in making them.

October 5

We Cannot Think Our Way to Healing

Learning about narcissistic abuse was an empowering step in our healing process. It was helpful to discover that there are words for the hell we've been through—and that others have experienced it, too.

Some of us continued to study, attempting to "master" narcissistic abuse so we would not be deceived again. Others did so to gain power over the narcissist and expose them. We were still feeding them our energy and were not yet focusing on ourselves, which is what makes true healing possible.

No one has ever thought their way out of the effects of narcissistic abuse. Instead, we must go inside of ourselves to the wounds and deep pain that caused us to be susceptible to abuse in the first place.

It can be much more comfortable to stay in our intellect and keep our focus on the narcissist. It takes courage and fortitude to remain present enough—with ourselves and our inner children—to bring that pain to the surface and embrace it as we love and support ourselves through it.

Today, I will examine whether I'm trying to intellectualize my experience with narcissistic abuse. I will reassure my inner children that I'm here, willing to face whatever is waiting to be looked at. I know my inner wisdom will guide me, and I can ask for support when I need it. If I'm not ready yet, I can come back to this step at any time.

October 6

Limiting Beliefs

Limiting beliefs are false beliefs or opinions about ourselves or the world around us. They were formed by inaccurate information we received beginning in childhood—when we were young and impressionable. These limiting beliefs resulted in matching behavioral patterns that drew us further away from our genuine selves. These beliefs, some of which we may be unaware of, limit us from knowing and manifesting our soul's amazing potential.

Imagine a child raised by a parent suffering from anxiety. They observed their parent fearfully avoiding people and situations and witnessed their parent's overwhelm and suffering. Their parent told them over and over again to "be careful." With the information they received, they unconsciously created a belief that *the world is not a safe place.* Eventually, they began to act overly cautious in their own life to avoid potential threats.

Some common limiting beliefs include:

- *People who love me hurt me.*
- *It's not safe to be seen, heard, and known.*
- *I'm worthless unless I have something to give.*
- *My needs don't matter.*
- *I'm too...much, fat, needy, crazy, broken.*
- *Love is: chaos, shame, pain, confusion, or betrayal.*
- *I don't fit in.*

Though these beliefs may seem true to us, they aren't facts. When we unearth their roots and discover where they originated from, we can then get in touch with the truth and set ourselves free.

Today, I will think about my limiting beliefs, the ways they have affected me, and what my truth is.

October 7

Peace

Peace is something we often focus on achieving between nations and people, but the most important work we can do is to create peace within ourselves by accessing our soul's truth. When we connect with our inner peace, it radiates into the world and reflects others' potential for peace back to them. It extends an invitation for them to enter their sacred heart space where peace lives. Our wounds are also held within that space, so embracing and healing them is a part of our journey to peace.

Peace was non-existent in our relationship with the narcissist. They were unable to connect with peace because they had divorced themselves from their true self. Their abusive behavior made it impossible for us to connect with our own peace.

We can access our inner peace and live from that place in our heart through a gradual process of healing our wounds, changing our thoughts, and exploring the unhealthy patterns that we default to. Finding peace is about returning to the very fabric of our being, bringing our vision and our lives in line with our soul's truth.

Today, I will look at what's preventing me from connecting with my inner peace. I will remember that as I continue moving forward on my healing journey, I create solid, lasting changes that form a new foundation. One that supports peace.

October 8

Sarcasm

While scrolling through a dating site, I came across a prospect who listed sarcasm as one of his traits, painting this characteristic in a fun, joking light. For me, this admission was a red flag.

I paused, paying attention to the tight feeling in my stomach. *Sarcasm.* Somewhere inside of me, the word just wasn't sitting right. Though sarcasm is prevalent in our society, I realized that in my past experience, it was often sharp and cutting—and seemed to open the door for further disrespect.

The narcissist may have used sarcasm against us, delivering hurtful remarks with a smile or a laugh. "Just kidding," they'd say, trying to placate us, as they extracted the energy of our reaction and left us questioning our worth.

Perhaps we'd prefer to participate in respectful conversation that builds people up instead of tearing them down. It's completely fine for us to refuse to participate in sarcastic exchanges, either as the giver or the receiver. People might say we're too sensitive or we take things too seriously, but if we find sarcasm disrespectful, it's appropriate to set boundaries accordingly.

It is especially important to examine whether we use sarcasm against ourselves. We are amazing beings, powerful and precious beyond measure. Using self-deprecating words is an unhelpful pattern that we can change.

Today, I will explore my relationship with sarcasm. I will honor myself, knowing that I can set boundaries around sarcasm if that is something that supports who I truly am.

October 9

Grief

There is often immense grief that arises as we come to terms with the losses of narcissistic abuse.

We grieve the loss of what we believed was the greatest love we'd ever known. We loved the narcissist beyond words and felt connected to them at what seemed like a deep soul level. Later, we discovered that nothing was as it seemed because the love of our life frequently morphed into someone cruel that we didn't recognize.

We grieve for the future we imagined. We dreamed of a future with the narcissist, certain we'd be together for the rest of our lives. We were devastated to realize that the future we imagined could never be because we had fallen in love with a facade. The person we planned our future with didn't exist.

We grieve for who we used to be, forever changed after narcissistic abuse. We yearn to get back to the level of functioning we were at before narcissistic abuse. We wonder what happened to our sparkle and if we'll ever experience it again.

These are painful losses we've had to face. With loving compassion, we can allow ourselves to grieve. The sorrow may come in waves, each releasing another layer of pain within us, emptying us out. Grieving creates space for something new to emerge out of the ashes of the old.

Today, I will allow myself to grieve, compassionately embracing every wave that comes. If I need support, I will reach out for it.

October 10

Empathy

Empathy allows us to be present with others and share their experiences with them. We can draw upon past situations in which we felt similarly—to put ourselves into someone else's shoes and understand their feelings. When we receive empathetic support, we feel held, understood, and acknowledged.

The narcissist was drawn to our empathy, which ensured them a steady feed of narcissistic supply. We proved to them that we'd work hard to meet their needs and make them happy, and that we wouldn't give up easily on the relationship. With enough love and compassion, we believed we could help anyone grow and heal. We assumed that the narcissist desired to do so.

One common characteristic among narcissists is the inability to identify with others' wants, needs, thoughts, or feelings. Some narcissists feign empathy, always with a hidden agenda behind their seeming kindness and concern. Other narcissists *are* able to see things as we see them, and they use that awareness against us.

In public, appearing to show empathy can gain the narcissist external validation and respect, allowing them to fit in with others. Narcissists often pretend to empathize with us if we begin to see beyond their facade, lulling us back into the illusions of love.

Today, I will reflect on my thoughts and feelings about the narcissist's lack of empathy during our relationship. I will contrast that feeling with genuine empathy I've received in other relationships.

October 11

Perception

Where we put our energy and attention dictates how we see our reality. Different peoples' perceptions of the same situation can vary greatly, depending upon their beliefs and state of mind. None of our perceptions are right or wrong. Instead, they're all valid because they're ours.

The following examples illustrate different ways we can perceive things:

- Did the narcissist destroy us and ruin our lives, or *did they create an unparalleled opportunity for us to heal our past wounds and limiting patterns?*
- Is life a cold, cruel experience that exhausts us, or *is it an amazing experience full of learning, love, and adventure?*
- Is our Source a masculine being who judges and punishes us from afar, or *a loving, nourishing energy that supports us and with whom we co-create our life?*
- Is the world an insane, dangerous place or *a place where we can have experiences, learn more about who we are, and see miracles every single day?*

What we believe determines what we perceive, and that creates our reality. As we heal and work through our past patterns, we often find ourselves taking on different perspectives.

Today, I will explore my perceptions and use the information I gain to better understand my beliefs and thoughts about myself, others, and life.

October 12

Transforming Self-Judgment

There are different ways we can use judgment in our lives. One way is in evaluating people and situations to help us make good decisions. We can also judge whether something we say or engage in will bring us the desired outcomes.

Another type of judgment comes from our ego—and is often rooted in fear. We are our own worst critics. Judging ourselves is a reaction to past rejection or abandonment and the false beliefs we took on about ourselves as a result. When we look in the mirror and cringe at something, we're judging ourselves based upon others' criteria. Self-judgment can become a vicious cycle. The narcissist's judgment and cruelty toward us fed our already existing patterns, deepening their destructive effects.

What would happen if we became curious about ourselves instead of judging ourselves? When something makes us cringe, what are we feeling? Is there fear at the core of it? What thoughts fuel our reaction? When we explore our self-judgment, we can discover our inner truth. Then, we can give ourselves the cathartic gifts of love and acceptance.

Today, I will watch for self-judgment. I will explore the thoughts and feelings behind it and provide myself with love, reassurance, and a new perspective. I will remember that I am a one-of-a-kind work of divine creation, perfect in every way, exactly as I am.

October 13

Justifications

We think of convincing reasons to stay with the narcissist and avoid the pain of leaving. Some of our justifications can include:

- "I'm so much trouble with all of my 'issues.' I'm just glad they put up with me."
- "We're soulmates."
- "We've built a life together. I can't just throw that away."
- "They're wounded, too. They didn't mean to hurt me."
- "Others have it a lot worse."
- "Everyone says we're great together."
- "I love them more than I've ever loved anyone."

The narcissist justifies their abusive behavior in order to protect their narcissistic supply. Some of their justifications include:

- "I expect a lot from you because I want the best for you. I see your potential."
- "I always meet your needs. Why won't you meet mine?" (Often used when wanting us to engage in behavior that is unsafe, inappropriate, or uncomfortable for us.)
- "I can't help that I drink a lot. Sometimes you really stress me out."
- "I'm sorry for screaming at you like that. It's because of this time when I was a kid…"
- "I didn't want to say anything to you because you're so jealous. I might have said something that would've hurt you." (Said after a prolonged period of the silent treatment.)

Today, I will ponder the justifications that I used to remain in the abusive relationship and those that the narcissist used to rationalize their abuse.

October 14

Rekindling Our Self-Love

To know ourselves is to love ourselves. Often, we need to make a conscious effort to go within and reconnect with ourselves after being so disconnected and distant during our abusive relationship. When we do, we will find that there is much to love about us.

The following are questions we can ask ourselves to help us rekindle our self-love:

- What is our superpower?
- In what ways are we a good friend?
- What are several things we're good at?
- What stands in the way of us loving ourselves?
- What are several things we love about our body?
- What good things would others say they see in us?
- What is the most courageous thing we've ever done?
- What is one thing that people misunderstand about us?
- How do others know that we love them? Can we show ourselves that same love?

We can also use these questions as journal prompts. Writing can be a powerful way to connect with ourselves. Other things we can do to increase our self-love include taking ourselves out on a "date" somewhere special, getting a massage, making space for unstructured time during our day/week, or making time for creative passion projects.

When we rekindle our self-love, we radiate it from our heart and invite others to love themselves, too.

Today, I will contemplate the questions above and choose one new self-loving action to incorporate into my day.

October 15

Inner Children's Impact in Adult Relationships

When our inner children's insecurities are many and their cries for love strong, their inner state can disrupt or completely control our adult lives. It can affect the way we think, speak, act, and feel. As our inner children heal and integrate within us, our adult self has room to emerge, bringing with it healthier ways of being.

Some ways our inner children can impact our adult relationships include:

- They may attempt to control people or situations because of their fear of being abused or abandoned again.
- They often shut down during conflict instead of allowing us to speak our truth, feeling helpless or overpowered as they did in the past.
- Our inner children may demand our partner's time, energy, or attention, after being starved of those things for so long.
- They may send mixed signals by saying yes when they mean no, unwilling to risk abandonment by breaking their pattern of pleasing others.
- They can act passive-aggressively when they expect our partner to anticipate and meet our needs even without us asking, demanding our partner to act as the devoted parent they never had.

Deep healing happens when we fully accept our inner children, showing them love and compassion even when they're disruptive.

Today, I will remember that there are valid reasons why my inner children are emotional and reactive. I will embrace them and continue to help them heal and integrate within me, knowing that it's my responsibility to meet their needs.

October 16

Shame Triggers

The narcissist purposely triggered our past wounds, saying and doing exactly what they knew would provoke our shame. As we shrunk, overcome with pain, they grew stronger by using our reactions as narcissistic supply.

The following stories illustrate survivors' experiences with these painful triggers.

"I worked hard every day, trying to provide for and please the narcissist. Somehow, it was never enough."

"I stood at the narcissist's side as they so blatantly flirted with someone else that even the object of their flirtation appeared confused."

"While I was in a committed relationship with the narcissist, they casually mentioned that they were spending the upcoming weekend with their ex-partner to 'help them out' with some things."

"I watched my partner treat others with kindness, compassion, and respect while being ruthless with me."

"During a dinner celebrating my recent work promotion, the narcissist spent the evening critiquing my insecurities and flirting with our server. I wanted to scream, wondering when I'd ever be enough to be the object of their love and approval."

Narcissistic abuse can trigger our deepest wounds. While painful to experience, it's also a gateway for us to access and heal them.

Today, or whenever I'm ready, I will begin (or continue) the deep work of finding and healing the wounds at the root of my shame, ensuring I have all of the support I need to set myself free from the past.

October 17

Addiction

Many of us are addicted to something that helps us cope and softens life's intensity. Perhaps it's running, caffeine, gossip, wine, or romance novels—it varies from person to person. Some addictions seem less destructive and more socially acceptable than others, such as diet soda versus hard liquor. Taken to the extreme, however, any addiction has the potential to be incredibly harmful to us on many levels—capable of severing the connection with ourselves and Source.

Addiction was an integral part of our relationship with the narcissist. They went to any lengths necessary to obtain narcissistic supply, without considering the effects of their actions on others. Many were also addicted to sex, alcohol, drugs, power, or anything else that numbed the pain of separation from themselves and their Source.

We victims also had addictions. The trauma bond in our brain was perhaps the most destructive of them. As the narcissist's abuse progressed, we became intensely addicted to the chemicals released during the abuse cycle, especially the sweet relief that we experienced when the narcissist threw us another crumb of affection. We believed that the person we loved was back and that everything would be okay.

Today, I will look at what I'm addicted to. I will connect with my inner wisdom to discover what lies beneath that craving—waiting to be acknowledged. Then, I will find healthier ways to cope as I continue to heal.

October 18

Survival Mode

When we live in survival mode, we are constantly focused on protecting ourselves from perceived threats. This exhausting process leaves us with few inner resources for things like creativity, joy, connection, nurturing, and love for ourselves and others.

Always on alert, unable to let go and relax as others do, our life can seem like a series of unsafe and overwhelming moments strung together.

Is something wrong with us? *Absolutely not.*

We are responding to past trauma that left us fighting to survive. Though painful and frustrating, being in survival mode is a part of who we are, something that's important for us to understand, embrace, and honor. Once we can accept where we are, healing can begin.

We can appreciate our inner children's efforts to protect us, which has been an exhausting job for them since childhood. Though their protective measures can sometimes feel intrusive in our adult lives, it's helpful to be patient and remember what led them to adopt those behaviors. We can lovingly reassure them that *we* will now protect *them*, and we'll help them deal with their fears in a healthier, gentler way so they can feel safe and heal.

Today, I will notice with curiosity and compassion the ways I experience survival mode in my life.

October 19

Honoring Ourselves

The media floods us with images of how we could look and how wonderful our lives could be. If we'd just buy what they're peddling, we'd be more like the celebrities we see. Try as we might, we never seem to achieve that standard. It's easy to forget that the glamorized images contain people whose make-up, hair, and wardrobe were all done by professionals, not to mention the airbrushing and touch-ups that were added after. We can't match up to those images because they're not real.

We also see idealized versions of life on social media. The photos often don't represent everyday life or portray the reality of mental and physical health issues, parenting challenges, and other life stresses that we all face. As we strive to meet these standards, we get further and further away from ourselves, which is where our peace and wholeness lie.

Each of us is a magnificent, unique treasure lighting up the world in our own special way. No one else brings the wisdom, knowledge, skills, and gifts that we do. We can stop striving to imitate others and allow our own soulful beauty to emerge as we excavate our true selves.

Today, I will spend time with myself in the mirror, looking at who I am and the life I've created through a new, more accurate lens. I will find beauty in all of it.

October 20

Transparency

Living a transparent life grants us autonomy, power, and freedom. When we love and accept everything about ourselves, we don't need to hide anything. Attempts to shame us or expose our past have little effect—because with great self-compassion, we've already acknowledged, understood, accepted, healed, and moved beyond our often trauma-based behaviors and traits that didn't represent our truth.

One survivor shared their experience of fighting a two-year custody battle for their children. They were forced to be transparent about their life under the court's microscope. This deep inner exploration helped them let go of old ideas they'd held about themselves. They realized with confidence that they were a good person and a great parent. They shed the terror of losing their children and handed the situation over to Source. This brave action allowed them to stand strong for themselves and their children, even as their knees shook, and things resolved as the survivor prayed they would.

Further along on their healing journey, but still not free of their inner wounds, they entered a narcissistic relationship. It was agonizing when they realized that in exchange for the narcissist's wondrous "love," they would have to give up what they'd spent two sacred years cultivating: As they were presented with expectations far outside of their value system, they were forced to sacrifice their transparency.

Today, I will look inside at the things about myself that trigger my shame. I will gently begin working toward total acceptance of myself, asking Source to support and guide me.

October 21

Our Inner Sparkle

When our hearts are open, our needs are met, and we're enlivened by the energy of our connection with Source, we experience a phenomenon which I refer to as *our inner sparkle*. This is the energy that makes life feel like a grand adventure. When it flows through us, it lights us up inside, causing us to see the world around us with awe and wonder.

We can easily identify people who are connected to their inner sparkle. It shows in their glowing smile, the twinkle in their eyes, the warm love they radiate, and their openness, creativity, and joy.

Those of us who were in touch with our inner sparkle when we met the narcissist provided them with top-notch narcissistic supply. Some of us figured this out and used the energy of our sparkle to manipulate the narcissist into giving us more crumbs. That strategy worked for a while, until we were so energetically drained and disconnected from ourselves that we had nothing left to offer them. Then they left.

Through that experience we learned a valuable lesson: *Our inner sparkle isn't ours to give, it's ours to live, and when we keep it for ourselves, it illuminates everyone.*

Today, I will explore the idea of my inner sparkle and evaluate the depth of my connection to it. If I feel disconnected from it, I will search my childhood memories and look at photos to identify and reclaim its vibrant energy.

October 22

Power and Control

Having power is different from having power *over* someone or something.

The narcissist worked to gain full power and control *over* us. It was the only way to ensure their need for narcissistic supply would be met. This was necessary for them because no one standing in their own power would willingly hand over their energy to someone and leave themselves empty.

Having power *over* us also helped the narcissist avoid the powerlessness they felt inside. Having to obtain their power from outside of themselves left them dependent and vulnerable. Because their source could disappear at any time, the narcissist developed well-honed skills of manipulation and control to secure their supply.

We may feel powerless at times, too. Perhaps an old trauma gets triggered, and our inner children feel overpowered by someone or something. They may try to exercise control to gain back a sense of power. Because we're connected to our higher Source of power, we need only focus our attention within us to reconnect with ourselves and step back into our power.

Our ultimate power is the ability to embrace our vulnerability, fully owning and loving who we are. When we can stand in our truth and support ourselves amidst life's challenges, willing to see and feel everything in our experience, we're standing strong in our innate power.

Today, I will consider how the dynamics of power and control have played out in my life, and I will reflect on the presence of my authentic power.

October 23

Acts of Service

One way to care for ourselves and others is to perform acts of service. This could include volunteering for a community organization, cooking a meal for a friend, or watching our neighbor's child.

When we first got out of the narcissistic abuse relationship, all of our energy went toward surviving what we had just been through. Our self-care practice was critical in helping us heal. The acts of service needed at that time were those we gave to ourselves. After much hard work, we got back on our feet and found our new normal.

The experience of serving others diverts our attention from our own inner challenges for a moment, giving us an expansive new perspective. We feel more connected, we experience ourselves as part of something larger, and our self-esteem and sense of purpose grows. The gratitude of those we serve is a precious gift.

We can get creative exploring what interests us, as there is always a need for our service. *Working with the elderly? Serving food at a soup kitchen? Providing financial support for someone in need?* The possibilities are endless, and the rewards are huge.

Today, if I have the inner and outer resources to serve others, I will venture into a new experience with my sleeves rolled up and my heart open, watching for miracles.

October 24

Courage

The ability to walk through our fear and find the courage to move forward through life's challenges can be a priceless gift, revealing our deep inner strength.

We need courage often as we heal from narcissistic abuse—to continue living our lives as anxiety or depression nearly paralyzes us, to face and heal the wounds that made us susceptible to narcissistic abuse, and to begin speaking up and setting boundaries when we'd rather remain silent. Incredible courage is necessary for us to leave the narcissist and to participate in legal situations afterwards as we fight for ourselves and our children.

Kudos to each one of us for all the courageous things we've done and will do in the future. We are amazing, each in our own way!

How do we find courage? We can:

- Breathe deep and feel Source's love surrounding us, permeating our every cell.
- Tune into the energy of those who have already walked through what we're facing. That collective energy can hold and support us.
- Embrace our fear. Accept it, breathe it in, and dance with it.
- Reach out for support.
- Create a safe place for our frightened inner children. Would they enjoy going to a beach? A carnival? Playing with puppies? Reading a story? Bring in someone loving (Jesus, angels, a loved one who has passed) to keep them engaged while we do challenging things.

Today, I will look at my past experiences with courage, honoring myself for the moments when I faced difficult situations head-on.

October 25

Self-Acceptance

It's essential for us to practice self-acceptance as we extricate ourselves from the grip of narcissistic abuse. If we get seduced back into the narcissist's vortex, it's truly okay to accept that it happened and show ourselves compassion, knowing it's often part of the process.

Then, we can continue moving forward in an empowered state, knowing we did our best with the wounds, tools, and awareness we had. We can explore the experience to help us understand what we were looking for within the narcissist. Then, we can meet that need for ourselves in a healthy, loving way.

We do have the option of being harsh with ourselves. That's something we've experienced from others—and have likely done to ourselves. Usually, though, that moves us deeper into our shame and triggers feelings of helplessness and defeat.

Instead, we can own the fact that we're beloved divine creations doing the best we know. There is *never* a good reason to beat ourselves up.

Acceptance may be something we've always craved, and once we give it to ourselves, our need to seek it from others diminishes. We feel full. Then, we may find ourselves meeting new people who accept us just as we are.

Today, I will practice accepting everything about myself, even those things that aren't quite the way I want them to be. I will lovingly embrace my thoughts, emotions, actions, and especially my physical characteristics.

October 26

Distractions

The intensity of life after narcissistic abuse can be exhausting, and sometimes we just need a break.

I lived by the words of "advanced spiritual people" who said we shouldn't use anything to distract ourselves from our inner work, especially if we wanted to be like them. Then, one day, when I was completely stressed out, a friend suggested I take a break from my intense reality and watch the TV series *The Affair*.

I watched it, hesitantly, knowing that the show would likely be judged as "lower vibrational human frivolity" by those "advanced spiritual people." I was delighted to have a moment of respite that allowed me to lighten up and give my nervous system a rest.

It's okay to read a fiction book or watch a movie that doesn't teach us something. When we take a break, engaging our attention in a healthy distraction, this will often shift our energy and perspective.

Finding the balance, *our balance*, is key. We wouldn't want to numb ourselves out every moment instead of focusing on our healing. But there is a time and place to break away. It might be for a day, an hour, or ten minutes. If we look inside to our divine wisdom, we'll know what's right for us.

Today, I will give myself permission to engage in a harmless distraction that soothes me. I will do so with the intent to care for myself, not to avoid all that's happening within me.

October 27

Victim to Witness

As victims of abuse and neglect, many of us live with our hearts protected and navigate life in survival mode, still carrying our unhealed wounds within us. Owning our victimhood is a valid and necessary step on our journey of healing. It requires the courage to allow our feelings to emerge instead of burying them so we appear "normal," especially when others tell us we should "move on" or "get over it" and stop being a victim. Healing from abuse takes time, and we move past it when we're ready.

Victimhood is one stop on our journey back home to ourselves. Once we begin to heal our inner wounds and learn to love and accept ourselves unconditionally, something new emerges from within us.

We become witnesses. No longer consumed by our past, we gain a new perspective. Feeling safer in our body, we can now approach life with an open heart, grounded in love. Instead of judging people and situations, we seek understanding. It's through the eyes of our inner witness that we uncover the gifts in our traumatic experiences.

We see the pain and disconnection that consumes our abusers, and we have compassion for them while also maintaining No Contact, making our safety and self-care our highest priorities.

Today, I will consider my thoughts about the differences between being a victim and being a witness. I will assess where I stand and know that wherever I am is exactly where I'm meant to be.

October 28

Trusting Again

As children, we were supposed to be able to trust our caregivers to meet our needs and keep us safe. Many of us experienced something very different than that, which taught us that those closest to us were the least trustworthy. The narcissist triggered and deepened that distrust as their "loving" behavior gave way to the devaluation that shattered us.

After so much betrayal, how do we learn to trust again?

- By taking it *One. Step. At. A. Time.*
- By becoming devoted to ourselves.
- By identifying and meeting our own needs.
- By healing our betrayal wounds.
- By understanding that while our old ways of surviving have helped us endure the trauma we experienced, we can now choose healthier ways of responding.
- By developing all new relationships slowly. Whether with friends or lovers, we can assess their compatibility with us and see how they react in good times as well as in disappointing and frustrating times.

Once we come to know and trust ourselves, our wants and needs change. We are drawn to different people and are more discerning about who is worthy of our trust.

Today, I will respect wherever I am in the process of trusting others. I will continue to focus my energy inward with love and compassion for myself. If I do decide to begin trusting someone else, I will go at my own pace and set the boundaries I need to feel safe.

October 29

Humility

Humility is an important cornerstone to incorporate into our newly-forming solid foundation. It is a virtuous quality, ensuring that we are realistic in our evaluations of ourselves, owning our weaknesses as well as our strengths. Seeing and respecting the full spectrum of who we are allows us to do the same with others and build real connections with those around us.

The narcissist lacked humility, though they often pretended to possess this quality when it allowed them to obtain narcissistic supply more easily. When we stood in our power and owned our value, knowledge, or accomplishments, the narcissist may have told us we were being arrogant and needed to be more humble. Humility does not mean playing small or having to shrink ourselves.

We can make an honest, humble appraisal of ourselves, fully owning our challenges as well as our gifts. It's not arrogant to own our strengths, our beauty, or our capabilities. Doing so is respecting and acknowledging ourselves and our Source. Who we truly are is magnificent. We can love and own that.

Today, I will explore what the concept of humility means to me in relation to myself, others, and my Source. I will take inventory of my strengths and my challenges, fully identifying and owning them.

October 30

Devotion

As children, we thrive when our parents or caregivers are devoted to us, when they love and care for us, educate us, give us an accurate reflection of our worth, and stand beside us no matter what. Devotion allows us to feel safe enough to explore ourselves and our relationship to the world around us. Then, we can then let our creativity flow.

Many of us who experienced narcissistic abuse had never experienced devotion before. In the beginning, the narcissist's "love" and attention was intoxicating. It felt like pure devotion. Painfully, we later discovered it was only manipulation.

Source offers us mighty devotion that's always available to us. Once we realize we're worthy of it, we can allow it in and embrace it. This type of all-embracing love guides us to our highest potential—our soul's expression of who we truly are.

By experiencing Source's devotion, we learn to be devoted to ourselves. We come to love and accept who we are no matter what. When we consistently show up for ourselves, setting boundaries to ensure that our needs are met and we're safe, our life is no longer just one long battle to survive. It becomes an adventure in which we can flourish!

Today, I will think about the concept of devotion and discover what it means to me. I will quiet myself and connect with Source's energy, which is devoted to me and always present.

October 31

Soul Magic

Soul magic is an energy we feel when we're connected to Source and in our soul's flow. It defies description, yet we know it when it hits us. We feel alive, lit up from the inside, in touch with life's incredible beauty and infinite possibilities. Soul magic ignites our inner wildness, passion, strength, and innate power.

Many of us feel our soul magic come alive when we're in nature—when the sun shines its rays through towering white clouds and creates a stunning scene that makes it seem like heaven is just on the other side, or when we look up at a luminous night sky and remember our connection to our "Home." We can also experience our soul magic while relishing a song that sparks our true essence or witnessing a serendipitous moment that inspires and delights us.

Many of us felt like we were experiencing soul magic during the love bombing stage of our relationship with the narcissist. Then, when the devaluation phase began, we lost the ability to feel just about anything. Now, as we heal and deepen our connection to ourselves and our Source, we can create space in our life to invite our soul magic in often.

Today, I will work to create a life that supports and provides space for experiences of my soul magic to emerge, inspiring me and reminding me of life's joy and splendor.

November 1

Creating a Solid Foundation

Many of us lacked the guidance and support we needed in our younger years to create a solid foundation on which to build our lives. We didn't learn the skills to understand our needs or direct our lives, which left us reacting to whatever life presented us with. We often repeated the familiar survival patterns that allowed us to make it through our childhood, but which complicated our lives as adults.

After narcissistic abuse, the first step to create a solid foundation is to disengage from the narcissist. Next, finding consistent support that fits our needs will benefit us greatly. This could include establishing a relationship with a healing professional or attending support group meetings.

We may find that the process of building a solid foundation for ourselves can seem "boring" compared to the drama and excitement of narcissistic abuse. It requires our time, energy, attention, and the willingness to do healthy things for ourselves, which some of us often neglect.

Some things that will help us create a solid foundation include building a relationship with Source, taking the time to establish a connection to ourselves and our inner world, discovering and working with our inner children, identifying our wants, needs, and values, learning to set boundaries, understanding and being responsible for our financial life, and lovingly caring for our body, mind, and spirit.

Today, I will take the next step forward in building a solid foundation for myself.

November 2

Lessons

Some believe that before we entered this world, we had already set ourselves up with the life lessons and human connections that now lead to our growth and self-realization and help us accomplish what we came here to do.

Narcissists reopen our deepest wounds of the past, providing us with the opportunity to identify and heal them.

One survivor shared their perspective: "Though excruciating and destructive, my time with the narcissist taught me much about myself and my past, and it magnified every childhood survival pattern I was still using as an adult. I used that relationship to catapult myself forward into a new life.

"After my experience with narcissistic abuse, I wrestled with the desire to warn an acquaintance about their new love interest, someone who'd deeply hurt a friend of mine. While I wanted to spare someone else the pain and anguish I'd been through, I hesitated.

"A friend said to me, 'If they're meant to be with a narcissist and you interfere with that relationship, they may have to find another narcissist to live out their lessons.' I heard the potential truth in their words. I also remembered that no matter what anyone had said to me, once I was hooked, nothing could have pulled me away from the narcissist."

Today, I will explore my experiences with the narcissist through the lens of life's lessons to see if that perspective fits for me. If it does, I will explore what those lessons were for me.

November 3

Intention

Unlike working towards a goal, which involves taking specific actions, holding an intention happens within us. We embrace a new thought or desire which then affects our outer reality. For example, we can set intentions to create peace, better health, or financial abundance. We can also intend to invite loving, supportive people into our lives. When our intentions are clear, we are co-creating with Source by providing exact instructions for what we want in our lives. We then become magnetic to those things.

Setting clear intentions requires some inner exploration. We can assess where we are in relation to the characteristics and ideals we want to express in our life—and then decide where we'd like to be. We can also identify what has prevented us from embracing those things in the past, giving us the opportunity to release the emotional blocks and limiting beliefs that stand in our way.

It's important to hold an intention without having rigid expectations for how or when it manifests. If things don't turn out the way we expect, it's possible that Source may have a better plan in mind for us. Or: Perhaps we don't have the foundation in place quite yet for the change we desire.

Today, I will identify something I'd like to create in my life. I will also explore the possible reasons I haven't done so before now.

November 4

Accountability

"All I know is that my life is better when I assume that people are doing their best. It keeps me out of judgment and lets me focus on what is, and not what should or could be." — Brené Brown, PhD, MSW, *Daring Greatly*

Caring for ourselves is one of our most important responsibilities. Being accountable for our own well-being allows us to be good parents, perform well at our jobs, and live our best lives.

But what happens when past trauma affects our ability to be accountable? Or when we're being shattered by a narcissist and don't even realize what's happening?

We do the best we know with the tools, knowledge, and capacity available to us at any given moment. How ridiculous would it be to demand more of someone who is doing their best? *We can't do better than our best.* What we can do is set a goal to do better, loving ourselves and being patient as we work our way toward it.

As we support ourselves and begin to live a nourishing, vibrant life, an exciting new level of accountability opens up within us. We become accountable for bringing the miracle of our divinely given gifts to a world that so desperately needs them.

Today, I will explore what I desire to have more accountability for. Even if I don't yet know how, I will look for the first step.

November 5

Trusting Ourselves

Learning to trust ourselves again after narcissistic abuse is a process. We were lulled into the pattern of letting the narcissist define us and our reality. We often used them as a gauge to determine our value, a process that produced wildly inaccurate results.

Now, we can listen to our inner wisdom to understand who we are and what we need. Though we might be afraid of making a wrong decision as we stand strong on our developing foundation, we can keep moving forward one step at a time, reclaiming our place in the driver's seat of our life.

In the past, we did the best we could with the information we had, though others may have judged or doubted our actions. In truth, only we can know what we need. We hold that knowledge inside of us and can access it when we connect there.

If something doesn't feel right, we can trust that. If it did feel right, but in ten minutes or ten years we decide to make a different choice, that's perfectly fine. We adjust our decisions as we obtain more information from new experiences. This doesn't mean we did something wrong. It means we're growing and our perceptions are changing.

Today, I will choose to be loving and supportive toward myself, accepting that my journey of learning to trust myself may be less than graceful at times. I will not judge myself and will remember that many others have walked this road before me.

November 6

Personalization

Personalization can mean blaming ourselves or taking responsibility for something that wasn't our fault. It can also involve assuming that others' thoughts and behaviors are about us or caused by us when they have nothing to do with us. If someone doesn't call us back, we may assume they're angry at us or upset about something we've done when in reality they decided to go to a movie and left their phone at home.

Assuming that things are about us can be a trauma response. We had to attribute the abusive or neglectful treatment we got as a child to something, so many of us assumed that we caused it. That belief gave us a sense of power in an overwhelming situation.

In a dysfunctional family system, toxic caretakers often projected their own issues onto us, blaming us for things they didn't want to own about themselves—another valid reason why we personalize things as an adult.

We aren't selfish or egotistical for personalizing things. We are reacting to triggering situations with the same survival mechanisms we learned at a younger age. Understanding this allows us to refrain from judging ourselves.

Today, if I find myself personalizing something, I will examine which of my inner children feel like the situation is about them or that they're at fault. I will determine their ages and offer them what they need, whether that's love, reassurance, a listening ear, or even some fun.

November 7

Reacting vs. Responding

The narcissist's well-being depended on their ability to trigger us and get an energetic reaction. Positive or negative, it fed them the narcissistic supply they needed to survive.

Reacting is instinctive, emotion-filled, and survival based. We reacted because unhealed wounds within us were being activated, causing us to hand over our valuable resources of power, time, and energy to the narcissist.

Responding is a slower, calmer process in which we are more grounded. Before responding, we assess the situation based on our core values and determine our wisest next move before we act.

An example: The narcissist just showed us another sexy text they received from their ex.

Reaction: "What the hell?! That's not okay!!! They need to stop!!"

Response: "Being someone who still receives intimate texts from their ex-lover doesn't work for me. If you're unwilling to set a boundary with them, then I will end our relationship."

The narcissist was incredibly skilled at getting us to react, so it's important not to judge ourselves for doing so. Mastering the skill of responding instead of reacting is a process. Each time we make that shift, we empower ourselves, showing our inner children that we are capable of supporting them.

Today, I will think of a triggering situation that I reacted to. I will identify which inner child(ren) within me reacted and why. Then, I will give them the love and support they need to create healing.

November 8

Our Soul's Truth

Along my healing journey, I heard narcissistic abuse referred to as "soul rape" or "soul crushing" abuse. The word "soul" seems to convey the indescribable depth the wounds of narcissistic abuse reach within us. At first, the references to soul seemed fitting, but further experience gave me a different perspective. Consider this:

What if our soul, directly connected to Source, remained brilliant and untouched, continuing to hold the truth of who we are as we plummeted into the darkness of narcissistic abuse?

What if our soul, like a candle flame, is inextinguishable and unaffected by our human doings?

What if our soul had little room to inhabit and enliven our body when we were consumed by the dense energy of narcissistic abuse? Perhaps our soul was more *with* us and less *in* us during that time?

When I walked out of my narcissistic relationship, exhausted and empty, my inner flame felt like a dim flicker, but still it burned. I worked diligently to heal and grow, creating more inner space for my soul's vibrant energy to fill my body and express itself through me. Life became magical again. I was filled with gratitude and enjoyed a new sense of peace. I even found myself writing this book!

Exciting things become possible when we harness our soul's truth—our highest truth—to create a new life.

Today, I will examine my own thoughts and feelings about my soul's truth.

November 9

Belonging

Many of us have never had someone who was devoted to us. We didn't receive the love and support we required and deserved because our caretakers were absent or abusive. This made us feel like we didn't belong anywhere.

Along came the narcissist, larger than life. They swept us up into their vortex of chaos and illusions. We believed them when they told us they'd never felt this way about anyone else, and we held on to their words when they swore we were the love of their life. We felt complete, as if we finally had someone who loved us, a place to belong—feelings we'd yearned for our entire lives. We felt worthy from the outside in.

Once we were out of the toxic relationship and began to connect with ourselves, we learned that it wasn't the devotion of someone else we craved. It was our own love and presence that we most needed. We can now give ourselves the things we didn't get, realizing our inherent worthiness from the inside out. This allows the unhealed children within us to feel safe, and our lives become more stable and nourishing.

From this place, we enter into new relationships requiring nothing to make us complete because we belong to ourselves. Any external validation we get is icing on the cake, but we no longer need or rely on it to be okay.

Today, I will remember that belonging to myself is my truest and sweetest freedom.

November 10

Self-Esteem

Self-esteem is our internal appraisal of our worth, our confidence in who we are. Growing up with dysfunctional caretakers at a vulnerable time, when our self-concept and personality was forming, we didn't receive an accurate reflection of who we were. As a result, we began to see ourselves as worthless, an extremely inaccurate perspective.

A narcissist can quickly sense our lack of self-esteem, which makes it easy for them to build us up and seduce us into their false, self-created reality. They tell us we're wonderful and then tear us down, controlling our entire self-image with a word or a look. Eventually, the positive messages disappear, leaving us doubting whether we have any value at all.

Now, the truth: We are magnificent, extraordinary beings. Nothing that has ever happened to us on the outside has altered that. If we were abused—or did things we regret, our inherent value was not touched or altered. Our soul's glorious beauty can not be diminished.

When we connect with ourselves and Source and work to heal our wounds, our self-esteem returns. Eventually, no one else's judgments can affect it. Once we heal the wounds that damaged our self-esteem and we come to know our inherent value, we are no longer susceptible to abuse.

Today, I will acknowledge and celebrate the truth of who I am. I will take time to do an accurate assessment of myself, nurturing my growing sense of self-esteem.

November 11

Listening

As survivors of abuse, many of us have learned to fine-tune our listening skills to survive. We hear everything, spoken and unspoken.

Narcissists also listen. They study their prey, looking for weaknesses, and then use that information to get their needs met.

Some people listen with an agenda, looking for ways to change or fix us. Others listen to very little of what we say, focusing more on what they want to say next.

Being listened to by someone who is truly present with us and has no judgments or agendas is an incredible gift. Their unconditional presence offers us love, support, and a safe space to be open and vulnerable. This allows us to freely explore ourselves and our life. We feel heard, known, validated, and accepted as who we are.

The experience of being heard can teach us how to listen to ourselves. Once we can be present for ourselves, we can truly be present for others.

Today, I will remember that the most important person I can listen to is myself—because in connecting with myself through my body sensations, thoughts, feelings, and intuition, I gain all of the information I need to support myself, live my best life, and truly be there for others, too. I will ask myself the following questions: What messages does my body have for me? What are my thoughts and feelings telling me? At a spiritual level, what is my soul whispering to me?

November 12

Insanity

We've all heard the saying *the definition of insanity is doing the same thing over and over again but expecting different results.*

One example of insanity is repeatedly entering the unhealthy relationships that our past wounds left us open to, while we hoped and yearned for different results.

Another is turning our life over to people that we unconsciously hoped would care for us as our parents were supposed to (and didn't). We often lost much in the process.

When we were with the narcissist, we repeatedly gave all of ourselves to someone who continually hurt us as we waited for the next crumb of affection.

None of this makes us bad, wrong, stupid, naïve, or incompetent. On the contrary.

We developed efficient survival skills as young children, enduring impossible situations while trying to get our needs met...over and over. As adults, we're susceptible to people and situations that mimic what we're familiar with. We repeat what we've experienced until we learn another way.

Once we understand our past patterns, we can break them and find a new way.

Today, I will offer gratitude to my inner children for helping me survive. I will let go of any judgment or self-criticism about their actions, replacing it with acceptance, love, and gentleness. I will look for the gifts and knowledge I gained in all of my "insanity" experiences.

November 13

Enigma

An enigma is a person or situation that is mysterious, puzzling, and seemingly impossible to understand or explain—a fitting description for narcissistic abuse.

While we experienced narcissistic abuse, the narcissist debased and erased us at times. At other times, they said we were amazing. We wondered if we were imagining things or losing our mind.

The narcissist was careful to present a loving, passionate facade in the public eye, one that we tried hard to believe ourselves. But then we returned to our private reality, and the abuse continued.

They convinced us that what they were doing wasn't hurtful and that no one else would feel the way we did. When we were upset and wanted to discuss our feelings and concerns with them, there was somehow nothing to say. This left us in our silent prison of confusion and uncertainty while they escaped accountability.

We were being abused. It's important to acknowledge the truth of what was happening, but we need not dwell there. We can leave it behind us now as we continue moving forward on our healing journey to a beautiful new life.

Today, if I need to, I will take a moment to acknowledge the puzzling, inexplicable nature of narcissistic abuse. I will focus my attention inside my body to see if I'm still holding on to any feelings about this experience. If so, I will embrace them and allow them to flow. I will breathe deeply and release the feelings from my body, allowing their energy to be transformed back into love and light.

November 14

Humor

How many narcissists does it take to change a lightbulb? *None, they use gaslighting.*

Many victims of narcissistic abuse are survivors of a traumatic past. Many of us have felt the need to be serious, always on alert for the next crisis or threat. This state of vigilance has become our way to protect ourselves in challenging or unsafe situations.

As we begin to feel safer in the world, we can incorporate moments of humor into our lives. Laughing can be incredibly healing because it releases chemicals in our brain that strengthen or improve our health and sense of well-being.

When we laugh, we're not minimizing the seriousness or severity of our past trauma—or of the narcissistic abuse we endured. Both can coexist together. We are just taking a moment to bring ourselves some joy and lightness, a gift from our Source.

Today, I will find something to make me laugh, even if it's a corny internet joke.

November 15

Setting Our Inner Children Free

The goal of working with our inner children is to set them free from the burdens of our past, allowing them to integrate into our sense of self, becoming part of the whole rather than being separated by their unmet needs.

To free our inner children, we must first understand why they are demanding our attention and what they require to feel safe. We can then provide them with the love, support, and guidance they've craved for so long. We can meet their needs and take responsibility for the adult burdens they've carried since childhood.

As we continue to support and care for ourselves rather than abandoning ourselves as we have in the past, our inner children begin to trust that we're there and we'll keep them safe. This newfound trust gives them the freedom to let their burdens go.

We can help them create a safe place to call home within us—or in our imagination. We can also create a new role for them in our lives. They can then use their gifts to move us forward instead of fighting to survive the past.

The process of setting our inner children free gives us space to live a beautiful life with our soul and Source leading the way.

Today, I will connect with my inner children to determine the next step in setting them free from the past.

November 16

Debt

When we're angry and hurt over the devastation of the abuse we've experienced, one thing many of us consider is the debt the narcissist has created with us.

Some parts of the debt can't be repaid. It would be impossible for them to reimburse us for the time and energy we spent meeting their needs, trying to make ourselves worthy enough to earn their love, and recovering from the abuse we've suffered.

Some expenses were "indirect," such as the mental health and medical bills that resulted from the abuse.

Some of us have been devastated financially and have lost large sums of money to the narcissist. We trusted them and paid dearly for that decision.

If we beg, threaten, or demand what is owed to us when the narcissist won't settle things with integrity, we're still hooked in and feeding them our energy.

We aren't powerless. We can't control what they do, but we can choose to find resolution and free ourselves from them in a way that works for us. We can decide to resolve matters in court, settle out of court, set our concerns aside and determine a course of action when we're ready, or let what we're owed go and walk away.

Today, I will be compassionate with myself and remember that many others have been in this same situation. I will take time to go within and determine what I must do to resolve the debt incurred by the narcissist so I can let go and be free.

November 17

Fear of Choices

When we were given choices by conscientious caregivers as children, we learned our likes, dislikes, wants, and needs while developing the courage and self-confidence to effectively make difficult choices as adults.

Those of us who grew up in toxic family situations were at the mercy of our dysfunctional environment. We weren't able to practice making our own age-appropriate choices about our self-care, how we dressed, or other things that were important to us. Instead, the needs of those around us determined our choices.

When we're faced with difficult decisions as adults, we may feel overwhelmed and afraid, especially if we have no experience making the decisions that drive our lives.

When we feel insecure about making a choice, we can lovingly notice any feelings that arise and become curious about what's going on inside of us. Then, we can make our decision and do our best to trust that we can navigate any consequences that result from that choice. Consciously giving ourselves these experiences will build our confidence and increase our trust in ourselves.

Today, I will remember that my choices don't have to be perfect, that I can't do any better than my best, and that any choice I make is *perfect for me at that moment. I will also remember that I have the power to change my mind and make a different choice if I need to.*

November 18

Minimization

We were masters of minimization during the narcissistic abuse relationship. It became a habit, anchored into us during the love bombing phase when we believed we'd found our soulmate and life partner.

We experienced a blissful ecstasy we'd never known before and chose to overlook the many red flags that presented themselves. Instead, we savored the newfound excitement, "love," and devotion the narcissist seemed to be providing. It was what we'd always yearned for.

Things got darker when we entered the devaluation phase. We still embraced the facade that they had presented initially. We chose to make allowances when their behavior didn't match what we'd experienced earlier in the relationship, believing that the person we knew was still in there somewhere.

The more the intensity and harm of their abusive actions increased, the more we minimized them. Although our behavior was completely understandable in light of our past wounds, it took a toll on us as we abandoned ourselves and our knowing—and held on to an illusion instead.

Today, I will act as an observer, looking at my situation with the narcissist from the outside. Without judgment, I will recall the times I minimized their behavior and explore the reasons why. I will assess my other relationships to see if this pattern of minimization plays out anywhere else. Most importantly, I will explore whether I minimize the knowledge coming to me from Source.

November 19

Protection vs. Connection

When we experience abuse or neglect as children, our internal systems become wired for protection instead of connection. We develop thought and behavioral patterns that help to ensure our safety. Often, we gravitate toward people we need protection from because those dynamics are familiar to us.

In the love bombing phase of our abusive relationship, it seemed we were connecting at the deepest level possible. We trusted, opened ourselves completely, and loved fearlessly. Then, the devaluation phase began and we were shattered by it. The pain of losing that seeming connection was unbearable, and we quickly reverted back to our well-worn survival mechanism of protection.

Whenever the narcissist doled out another crumb of affection, we dropped our defenses again, so grateful for that moment of connection. They devalued us once more, and again we were shattered. The pattern continued, pulling us deeper into the trauma bond and away from ourselves.

After the relationship ended, we had the opportunity to heal our ingrained patterns of protection. We addressed our inner wounds and made the most important connection of all: that with ourselves. Now that we've developed a healthier sense of discernment, we choose to connect with safe people.

Today, I will explore my past relationship with protection and connection. I will set and honor my boundaries to ensure I feel safe. I will take more time to get to know others and decide if and when I'm ready for deeper connection.

November 20

Eyes Wide Shut

Many of us were born as highly sensitive people. Living in families riddled with abuse and neglect was often a confusing, unbearable experience as we saw and felt everything happening in our homes.

We may have witnessed untreated addiction, abuse, violence, and unsafe caretakers. When we questioned what was going on, our family members directly or indirectly made it clear to us that we weren't supposed to acknowledge or share what we saw with anyone inside or outside the home. As a result, we were forced to ignore what we saw, pretend it wasn't there, imagine we were seeing something else, or stop seeing altogether.

After experiencing a serious incident of abuse as a child, my vision rapidly deteriorated over a short period of time. My doctor expressed concern that such continued deterioration could result in blindness. I was trying hard not to see what was going on around me, and consequently, my eyesight suffered.

As hard as we tried to pretend that nothing was wrong, our sensitive body often did not cooperate. Instead, it physically manifested the effects of all that was happening within and around us.

Our pattern of not seeing made it easy for the narcissist to seduce us. By closing our eyes to the red flags, we opened the door for them to abuse us.

Today, I will help my inner children understand and process the things they were told not to see, assuring them that I'm with them now and they are safe.

November 21

Setting the Bar

Most of us set the bar in our relationships based on our past experiences. If we were loved and respected as children, we usually expect the same treatment in adult relationships and set our boundaries accordingly.

When we were disrespected, abused, or neglected early in our lives, we lacked the experience and the information to create and maintain healthy expectations and boundaries. If we had a bar at all, we set it low. This made us highly desirable to narcissists.

As we do our inner work and reconnect with Source, we come to understand that we are valuable beyond measure and that we deserve utmost love and respect. Based on that knowledge, we can set the bar high.

If we need to decide where to set our bar but don't yet have the awareness to understand how, we can ask ourselves how we would want someone we love to be treated—and settle for nothing less.

Today, I will explore what I was taught in the past about setting the bar in relationships. I will set new boundaries and expectations that are fitting for where I am now, based on the experience I gained from the toxic relationship and what I now know to be true about myself.

November 22

Intuition

Many believe our intuition is the voice of Source within us, guiding us through life. We all receive that guidance and information in different ways.

Clairsentience. We receive information through feelings we experience in our body.

Clairaudience. We hear Source's voice as our guidance.

Clairvoyance. We see things that will happen in the future or receive information in the form of images.

Claircognizance. We receive thoughts in our mind that seem to come from a wiser, higher Source.

When we were with the narcissist, our intuitive warnings were often drowned out by our inner children's voices, who believed they'd finally found someone who loved and cared for them.

Some of us may feel that our intuition directed us to be with the narcissist so we could gain the experiences we needed to heal our past, evolve, and spiritually advance.

Some of us realize in hindsight that we used the intuitive connection we felt with the narcissist, perhaps from a beautiful past life together, to justify staying in our current relationship.

We can explore the involvement of our intuition in our toxic relationship as we connect with a higher level of awareness. With so much going on at different levels within us, there are no right or wrong answers—only our intuitive stirrings.

Today, I will contemplate my intuition and explore whether I receive information from Source in any of the ways described above. I will also examine what role, if any, my intuition played in my relationship with the narcissist.

November 23

Anniversaries

We may remember exactly how we felt that first magical moment we laid eyes on the narcissist. Or perhaps we can still recall precisely where we were and what they said when they proposed to us, not to mention every detail of our enchanting wedding day.

After we've been discarded by the narcissist, anniversaries can knock us off our feet as we remember the beautiful moments. Anniversaries can bring us back to what seems like square one even if we've already done a significant amount of inner work.

But it isn't square one. It just feels like it.

We can honor our feelings and be present with ourselves as we grieve. We can comfort and soothe ourselves as we would a small child, and then gently move on with our day, making our self-care a priority. We can do our best not to get lost in or romanticize our relationship. Sometimes the pain is so great we can't even physically move, much less move on with our day. It's okay to rest. There is no right or wrong way to do this.

If we feel stuck, it's important to reach out for support. Healing the wounds of narcissistic abuse is deep work.

Today, I will care for myself in the best way I know, whether that is taking time to let my emotions out or reassuring myself and moving on with my day. I will reach out to my support system and do something that makes me feel nurtured.

November 24

We're Not Broken

When we were children, our caregivers may have refused to acknowledge that there were any issues in their behavior or in the family structure. Instead, our sensitive, empathic selves were seen as the problem. As the stress of dysfunction created issues in our lives, the adults around us may have tried many methods to fix us instead of focusing on the destructive problems that we were reacting to. All that attention wasn't meeting our needs. It was letting us know we weren't okay.

One survivor recounted, "As a young child, I experienced Rolfing, an extremely deep bodywork. It added trauma to my body. I was brought to alternative healers and even got my Lemurian crystals removed over the phone. (What does that even mean?) As an adult, I sought out 12-Step programs, psychologists, counselors, energy workers, and more body therapists. After I began to heal from narcissistic abuse, I realized...I'M NOT BROKEN! There never was anything to fix, only the truth of who I am to find, uncover, and cherish!"

As long as we maintain the belief that we're broken, we are easily manipulated by narcissists who use it to control us while constantly reinforcing it within us.

Today, I will work on creating a life that allows space for me to uncover the beautiful truth of who I am. I will surround myself with people who respect and accept the real me. There is no standard I must meet and nothing I have to fix. I am and have always been perfectly me.

November 25

God Moments

A God Moment is a moment in our lives when we are so fully connected with God that we are overcome with gratitude. These moments are impossible to describe with words, but they can completely change our outlook on life, ourselves, and one another. There is no one way to define a God Moment. Instead, it's an inner miracle that we simply *feel* and *know*.

God Moments happen when wonderful things are unfolding in our lives as well as when we're at our lowest and God is all we have left to hold on to. They also happen in the routine moments of our everyday lives.

The following are examples of God Moments.

Receiving messages from loved ones who have passed, leaving us with the unshakable knowledge of their well-being and love for us. This can include a bald eagle soaring high above us, a message in the clouds, or a perfectly timed flicker in the lights overhead.

Finding ourselves in a synchronistic meeting with someone that changes our entire life's direction.

Experiencing an inspirational moment in nature that envelops us in infinite love and possibility as we feel the mystical energy of creation on our skin.

When we live in God's world, there are many moments each day that captivate and transform us.

Today, I will look at the world through eyes filled with wonder, keeping my heart open to receive the God Moments.

November 26

Self-Expression

Being able to express our soul's truth is one of the most rewarding experiences we can have. Some of us do it through words, music, art, or dance—even if it's in our own living room. Others express their soul through random acts of kindness, giving gifts, and sharing encouraging, compassionate gestures with people at just the right time.

What lights you up and makes you come alive? What makes you feel so free that time disappears and you get lost in the moment?

When we go through trauma, our systems shift into survival mode, and creativity and authentic self-expression seem impossible. The part of our brain responsible for those abilities is "offline" while we fight to survive, triggered by current threats and memories of past ones.

After exiting the abusive relationship and riding the tsunami of aftershock symptoms, we begin to reclaim the energy and inner resources to create a life in which we feel safe and can discover our true self-expression, perhaps for the first time ever.

Today, I will explore what I need to give myself the gift of a safe, supported, inspired, and creative life that facilitates my self-expression.

November 27

Denial

One survivor of narcissistic abuse shared a powerful story of how they experienced denial in the narcissistic abuse relationship:

"After the toxic relationship ended, I read through my old journals, stunned to see an entry I had written when the relationship began. It read, 'They're a narcissist. I am an empath. A deadly combination.' Shortly after, they called me, saying they'd never met anyone like me. They felt I was the one they'd been waiting for their entire life. I quickly swept the powerful, accurate awareness of our 'deadly combination' aside."

We may have noticed the narcissist's pattern of substance abuse and excused it as them just wanting to relax and have a good time.

Or when the narcissist flirted with other people, we convinced ourselves *we were just being paranoid and jealous.*

Because we deeply yearned to get our unmet needs fulfilled, we denied what we were seeing and experiencing with the narcissist. At the same time, we denied our needs, wants, and the cries of our inner children that suffered from the abuse.

We often denied ourselves the sleep and healthy food we needed to function optimally in our lives, as well as alone time to recharge and clear our heads.

Today, I will not judge myself for the things I denied while I was in a relationship with the narcissist. I will remember that I was doing what I'd learned well in the past—trying to help myself survive by denying my painful reality.

November 28

Past Lives

Some survivors have used the concept of past lives or reincarnation to justify staying with the narcissist.

We excused the narcissist's abusive behavior, believing they were just stuck in a past-life memory. We thought that if we loved them enough, their true self would eventually emerge into the present, bringing all the love we yearned for with it.

We carried a fierce love for the narcissist that originated in a past life. Its strength led us to assume we'd be together forever. We were certain it would bring us through anything in this lifetime, too. Eventually, we realized that regardless of its strength, that love wasn't an indication of our future with the narcissist.

It can be agonizing to acknowledge that we're in an abusive relationship with someone who isn't going to change, no matter how many energy shifts happen or how good our past lives together were.

A past-life perspective that has been helpful for some is that we've all been the abuser and the victim in our past lives. Spiritual narcissists often use this perspective to bypass or invalidate our feelings about the abuse we encountered, and the seriousness of it. We *never* have to use it for that. Instead, we can adopt it *only* if doing so supports our healing.

Today, if the idea of past lives fits for me, I will explore what part, if any, that concept played in my experience with narcissistic abuse. If past lives don't resonate with me, I will recognize that truth, grateful to know that about myself.

November 29

Authenticity

"Authenticity is the daily practice of letting go of who we think we're supposed to be and embracing who we are." — Brené Brown, PhD, MSW, *The Gifts of Imperfection*

One survivor shared the story of embracing their authenticity:

"I worked hard to let go of the narcissists in my life and heal the inner wounds that left me open for abuse. Glimmers of a new me emerged. The process brought feelings of joy and freedom as well as fear and uncertainty. I finally had the ability to exist, which meant I'd be seen and heard, something that brought my deepest fears and grandest dreams to the surface.

"When it came time to shine my authentic self out into the world, I felt ready. There were new boundaries to set and relationships to reassess. Over time, wonderful new experiences and opportunities began to unfold. One day, I looked at a friend tentatively, unsure if it was really okay to do all the new, soul-led things that suddenly felt so right. She reassured me with a smile that indeed it was okay to be my authentic self."

Today, in awe of my life as I continue to grow into who I truly am, I will embrace the people and things that feel nurturing and life-giving to me. When I am ready, I will set new boundaries and let go of those people and things that no longer support me.

November 30

Freedom to Exist

In the beginning, the narcissist seemed to adore everything about us. Then, their behavior radically changed. Everywhere we turned, we were met with a wall—the narcissist's restrictions or expectations of us. They groomed us to conform to their ideals and meet their needs. We acquiesced to avoid our greatest fear—perhaps it was abandonment for some of us, or betrayal for others. Once the narcissist discovered our vulnerability, we were easily controlled, and the relationship became a prison.

When we lost our freedom to exist, our beauty and truth were buried. After a while, feeling restrained and frustrated by the consequences of that experience, we became resentful. Some of us acted passive-aggressively to spite the narcissist and rebel, attempting to gain back our freedom. We may have eaten an ice cream sundae or worn clothes the narcissist didn't approve of. We were still not free, though. Our choices were in reaction to the narcissist, not to support ourselves.

Outside the relationship with the narcissist, we have the freedom to be the miracle that we are—and the ability to create the life we've always dreamed of. We also have the power to tune into our soul's path, deciding for ourselves who we are and what the next right move is for us.

Today, I will celebrate my newfound freedom and consider how I can best serve myself and my life with this limitless gift. I know that wonderful things come from having the freedom to exist.

♥

December 1

Moving On

After our toxic relationship ended, some of us didn't want to move on from the narcissist. We tried hard to figure out what went wrong so we could fix it. We were consumed by pain and unable to let go.

Some of us attempted to find completion *with the narcissist*, hoping to grieve and move on like we had in other relationships. We soon discovered that grieving this loss was unlike anything we'd ever experienced before.

Some of us did the inner work required to break our addiction to the narcissist. We explored our inner wounds, felt the painful feelings, and lovingly acknowledged the wounded children within us. We found deep healing and the strength within ourselves to move on.

None of these ways of surviving abuse are wrong. We all have differing levels of readiness and capacity for change, and we move forward when it's the right time for us. There is support available to assist us in doing the profound inner work necessary to find completion and move on. We can seek professional support or hand it over to Source, along with our willingness to let go and move on.

Today, I will notice where I am in the process of moving on from my relationship with the narcissist, knowing I'm exactly where I'm meant to be. If I need to, I will explore whether I'm ready to move on at this time and identify ways to make it happen.

December 2

Daring to Love Again

"We are born in relationship, we are wounded in relationship, and we can be healed in relationship." — Harville Hendrix, PhD, & Helen LaKelly Hunt, PhD, *Getting the Love You Want: A Guide for Couples*

Am I ready to leave the safety of my new life and open myself to love again? A brave question indeed. The good news is that we no longer need to leave our lives or abandon ourselves to be accepted by other people. We can now stand firm on the solid foundation we've built, maintaining our autonomy by enforcing our boundaries and practicing self-care. From this place, we'll know the right time to allow an intimate partner into our precious and sacred life.

When venturing back into the dating world, we can dare gently one moment at a time. We aren't obliged to move any faster than we desire. Also, we can be "selfish," never losing sight of our own needs.

We must remember to go easy on ourselves. We're not only breaking old patterns but also learning and practicing new skills as we go. There's no need to expect perfection. Instead, we can have compassion and understanding for ourselves on the journey.

Today, I'll assess my readiness to love again. If I'm not ready, I'll accept and honor that. If I am, I will declare my readiness to the Universe, specifying what I'm looking for in a partner. Then, I'll let this vision go and allow the wisdom of life to unfold, knowing that when it's time, I'll love again.

December 3

New Relationships

Our values are the qualities that are important to us within ourselves, in our relationships, and in our lives. They're the ideals or principles of behavior we aren't willing to live without, such as respect, love, abundance, peace, authenticity, freedom, discipline, or collaboration.

Determining our values and setting the boundaries needed to support them is an invaluable gift to bring to a new relationship.

Initial boundaries could include not oversharing information about ourselves, moving slowly with intimacy, maintaining a focus on our own lives, paying attention to red flags and unhealthy boundaries (theirs and ours), not tolerating disrespectful behavior, and not *needing* them for anything.

In the relationship with the narcissist, we discovered our values by having lived so far outside of them. We recognized our boundaries by having them violated and then feeling the effects of being pushed well beyond them.

We can identify our values and determine the boundaries necessary to support them prior to starting a new relationship. By doing so, we make it easier to stay true to ourselves and maintain our values from the very beginning, pursuing only relationships that align with them.

Creating value-based boundaries and living our lives based on them is a process—the result of our commitment to ourselves.

Today, I will explore which values are important to me in an intimate relationship. I will consider the boundaries I need to set to uphold those values.

December 4

Teamwork

One important aspect of a healthy intimate relationship is the ability for both partners to work together as a team. Many of us who grew up in a dysfunctional family system didn't have that behavior modeled to us by our caretakers. We don't know how to do it, and some of us don't even realize it's possible.

When the narcissist seduced us, we thought we'd found a true team player who would love us forever. We soon learned that neither of those things were true. Our partner could not be part of a team, nor could they love us, because their sole focus was *and always will be* on survival—getting their need for narcissistic supply met at any cost.

Now, imagine being in a relationship with a partner who is genuinely concerned about us and our well-being. They care for us without consuming us, and we're able to work together to learn, grow, and create a strong foundation. They see our strengths and challenges as we see theirs, mutually choosing to be on this journey of life together.

Today, I will explore what teamwork looks like to me in the context of an intimate relationship. If I have no idea, I will also explore my teamwork with Source. Then, I will look for reference points in people I know, or in media that I watch, to help me identify my non-negotiable needs around teamwork with an intimate partner.

December 5

Identifying Narcissists

It's easy to spot a classic, overt narcissist with their bold, arrogant, and entitled manner. Other types of narcissists are much more difficult to identify.

When we're getting to know someone and want to discern whether they have narcissistic traits, we can look for red flag behaviors, such as:

- Telling us immediately that we're soulmates and that they've never met anyone like us before.
- Infiltrating every part of our life as the intimate relationship moves forward.
- Suggesting changes we should make about ourselves, including losing weight and changing our hair or clothing.
- Bringing up negative qualities they see in our family and friends.
- Telling us the ways in which we're better than other people...just like they are.
- Being rude to restaurant servers and others in the service industry.

The first rule of thumb in dating is to GO SLOWLY. Then, we can ensure that we're meeting our own needs and aren't abandoning ourselves or becoming dependent upon the new person.

We can also tune into our inner wisdom and body sense for our truth. One survivor listens to their four-year-old inner child to know whether someone is safe or not, a skill they had developed very early to survive the abuse they endured.

Today, I will keep my eyes wide open for red flag behaviors in new people I meet. I will listen to my feelings and thoughts and notice what's happening in my body.

December 6

Finding the Gifts

Once we've regained stability within ourselves and have begun to heal the wounds left by the narcissist, we may begin to recognize gifts in the devastating experience we've lived through. This can be a sign that we're moving out of the victim role into self-empowerment.

Below are some of the gifts that survivors have found in their experience with narcissistic abuse:

- "It brought my fears and judgments of sex to the surface to be healed."
- "I betrayed myself until it became so unbearable I knew I'd never do it again."
- "I learned to identify my needs, take care of myself, and set boundaries."
- "After paying my 'tuition,' the money I lost to the narcissist, I learned to be responsible with my finances and prioritize my interests in my business dealings."
- "All of the triggering experiences unlocked the trauma that was stored in my body so I could heal and release it."
- "I worked through my childhood issues in an adult context, seeing the roots of my dysfunctional relationship patterns more clearly."
- "I can now be fully present with others who've experienced narcissistic abuse."

The lessons and growth that come out of an experience so destructive are priceless. They bring us deep inside, giving us the opportunity to find our precious and wild true selves.

Today, like the alchemist, I will explore this raw and painful experience, find the gifts in it, and turn it into gold.

December 7

Faith

Faith is having complete trust and belief in someone or something. Having faith can seem impossible after we've been wounded by those who betrayed our faith.

As we attempted to survive the wounds of narcissistic abuse, it seemed impossible to trust or have faith in anything or anyone, especially ourselves. We felt disconnected from family, friends, and even our Source.

As we heal the wounds that the narcissist inflicted or reopened, and create a firm foundation under ourselves, we begin to realize that we are resourceful, strong, and brave. We then learn to have faith in ourselves.

Faith in ourselves is strengthened by faith in our Source. That faith doesn't come from the intellect. It involves trusting and knowing at a deep level that there is a loving energy, full of grace, present and available to us at any moment. As we connect with ourselves, we connect with our Source. Our faith rises from that connection. Then, we come to understand and embrace Source's support and the miracles it brings. We uncover the full potential of who we are and how truly inspiring the journey of life can be.

Today, I know that my faith in myself and my Source will strengthen as I practice self-love, remain connected within, and continue taking steps forward into a new life.

December 8

Manipulation

If a narcissist were to attract someone by being honest, it would sound something like this:

Hey gorgeous. After I seduce you, I'm going to deplete all of your energy and resources to meet my incessant need for narcissistic supply. I'll diminish you often so I feel powerful. In between, I'll give you random crumbs of affection to keep you hooked. When we're done, if you survive it, you won't even recognize yourself anymore. Are you in?

Obviously, honesty wouldn't work, so the narcissist uses manipulation tactics to lure us in.

A different, more empowering and healing way to look at manipulation is to focus on how we've manipulated ourselves. We told ourselves that it was fine to change who we were, that the narcissist was just trying to help us live up to our potential. We manipulated ourselves into believing that everything would be fine, in spite of the many red flags whizzing by us. We glorified the good and ignored the bad to avoid having to let go of the narcissist's "love" and affection. There are good and valid reasons we did those things. As children, many of us learned to manipulate ourselves and others to avoid abandonment and survive impossible situations.

Today, I choose to be curious and explore the ways I have manipulated myself, without judgment and with loads of love and compassion for myself. I will sit with the feelings that arise, knowing that I'm not alone and that we have all manipulated ourselves in our own way.

December 9

Paradoxes

A paradox is a statement that seems to contradict itself but is actually true. An example of a paradox is the phrase *it's the beginning of the end.*

Narcissistic abuse relationships are full of paradoxes, showing up as contradictory thoughts, behaviors, and circumstances.

The narcissist appears confident and in love with themselves, *yet inside they often feel intense shame, self-loathing, and insecurity.*

The narcissist appears to hold the power in their relationships, *yet they are at the mercy of those around them to provide them with the narcissistic supply they need to exist.*

The narcissist is incredibly vulnerable to any sign of rejection or shame from others, *yet they reject and shame their victims constantly.*

The narcissist is abusive to others, *while demanding love and respect for themselves.*

During the idealization phase of narcissistic abuse, we felt safe and secure with the narcissist, who we believed was the most loving, trustworthy, respectful partner we'd ever been with, *when in truth we were headed for possibly the most damaging and dangerous experience we'd ever have.*

At the end of the relationship, we were unsure we'd survive the pain we felt, *and the breaking open of our past wounds gave us the potential of fully coming to life.*

Today I will notice the paradoxes in my narcissistic relationship, my own and the narcissist's, identifying the conflicting truths of the situation. I will look for the healing, empowering gifts that come out of my new awareness.

December 10

Creating the Life Our Soul Intends for Us

While agonizing about whether to leave the narcissist, one survivor woke up to the thought, *I'm not the me I was designed to be.* This message from their own inner wisdom was their cue. It was time to go, a decision which allowed them to begin healing and creating the life that was meant for them.

When we stop doing what doesn't support who we are, we have the utmost privilege of discovering our truth outside of our wounds and others' perceptions of us. When we love and care for ourselves as the precious beings that we are, our soul has space to work with us.

The longer we're away from the narcissist, the more "sober" and present we get. Every day can fill us with wonder as we notice new things about ourselves, like a sense of peace we've never experienced before or a desire to try something new.

It is through our dreams and aspirations that we align with our soul's desires. What makes our soul sing? Where would we love to live? What is our dream job/career? What are our passions?

Dream big! Even if we can't imagine how it could happen, we can dream it anyway and see what manifests.

Today, I will look at the things in my life and myself that I'm ready to let go of, creating room for the beautiful life that my soul intends for me.

December 11

Surrender

"The ultimate act of power is surrender, which happens by Grace." — Krishna Das

Faced with a concerning situation that was out of our control, we've all felt powerless at times. We've obsessed about it, attempted to control it, and worked to resolve it, trying to bring about what we considered to be the best outcome. Bound to the situation and consumed by emotion, we prayed for another way.

We discovered that surrendering the entire situation to our Higher Power brought us peace, hope, and often a resolution more expansive and profound than we could've ever imagined or brought about through our own human efforts.

There is another type of surrender—a miracle—that happens only through grace: surrendering our will and our entire lives to our Source. Unable to *make* it happen, we can do our inner work, readying ourselves for surrender.

In reaching this space of surrender, we are free. We observe life without reacting to it or trying to control what's happening. We are connected to the Divine and rooted in our soul's truth and in the present moment—our grounded foundation. It is through this moment-to-moment practice of surrender that we move from fear to love, bringing our energy and power back to us.

Today, I will contemplate what surrender means to me. If it feels right for me, I will take one difficult thing I'm facing and surrender it to my Higher Power.

December 12

Inner Authority

Our journey with authority began in childhood. Our parents or guardians set boundaries for us to exist within, allowing us to safely explore ourselves and our life. In situations of abuse and neglect, we often lacked that guidance and structure. We missed out on the experiences that would have helped us build confidence and develop the inner foundation we needed to connect with and live from our inner authority.

As we grew, we had many external authority figures in our life whose guidance we internalized. The church told us how to act to end up in heaven. Teachers and gurus gave us ideals to strive for. Society taught us "the right way" to parent and to be women and men. The narcissist was only too happy to become our ultimate authority, determining who we were and how we should look, act, think, and feel.

As we heal, we realize that only we can truly know who we are or what's right for us, from within. This understanding allows us to create space in our life to develop trust in ourselves and our soul's voice. Accessing the wisdom deep inside of us gives us the confidence to live by our inner authority. Learning to trust and follow our inner guidance is a process. We learn as we go, step by step.

Today, I will contemplate whom I see as an authority figure in my life and what I'm looking for from them. I will access my inner wisdom and divine guidance to begin connecting with my unshakable inner authority.

December 13

Letting Love In

Letting love in can be a challenge for many of us after being wounded by another's "love," which was actually manipulation and abuse. We took on many false beliefs about love, including:

Love hurts.
Love is dangerous.
Love can't be trusted.
Love doesn't really exist.
Love is difficult and exhausting.
We're not worthy of receiving love.

One survivor spoke of feeling uncomfortable when someone showed them love. They smiled appreciatively, but inside, their body tensed, maintaining a protective barrier between them and the experience. They were unsure of what to do with the attention and warm sentiments coming their way.

I asked the survivor where inside of them they received love. They paused, bringing their energy and presence back into their body, where they identified their heart. Now that they had found a place within them where they could accept that loving energy, they knew what to do the next time it was offered. With practice, they experienced the gifts of receiving the powerful, nurturing energy of love.

If it's difficult to determine where in our body we allow love to enter, we can begin by creating a safe experience of love, practicing with our beloved pet or a trusted person in our life.

Today, I will explore where in my body I receive love. The next time someone offers me love, I will practice consciously allowing it in.

December 14

Stranger in the Mirror

Many survivors have shared the unforgettable feeling of looking in the mirror and not recognizing the person staring back at them after enduring narcissistic abuse. We studied our tired, empty eyes, drained of vital energy, self-esteem, hope, strength, and joy.

One survivor's family member told them, after seeing the narcissist parading them around in public, "You were so altered I didn't even know it was you." A friend later commented, after the abuse ended, "You look more like yourself again." Initially, they felt shame at hearing that, knowing they were not living up to the narcissist's expectations. Eventually, they understood that they never could, nor did they desire to.

We went to great lengths to make ourselves acceptable to the narcissist, taking even their most subtle cues of disapproval to heart in order to avoid being abandoned. However, nothing we did would have been enough to evade the eventual discard or ending of the relationship.

Now, we can discover for ourselves who we are. For perhaps the first time in our lives, we can access our own inner truth and be unapologetically ourselves!

Today, I will spend time with myself in the mirror. I will notice what I see and how I feel as I connect within. I will listen carefully to what the beautiful person in the mirror has to say.

December 15

Forgiveness

I once heard someone say they'd forgiven themselves for their abusive experiences with the narcissist. Their words confused me, and I certainly couldn't think of anything I needed to forgive myself for. I was a victim to the narcissist's abuse. This was a truth I consciously chose to embrace, forever if I needed to, rejecting the victim-shaming tendencies so prevalent in our patriarchal-influenced society.

Then, one day, I was ready for a new perspective. As I stepped into my own power, I tried on the idea that I had a level of responsibility for my involvement in the abusive situation. It fit for me, and with great self-compassion, I forgave the wounded, unhealed inner children that ignored the red flags, did things that went against my adult values, and stayed in a situation that harmed me. I understood that for them, doing what they did was literally a matter of survival.

Further along on my healing journey, without being naive or bypassing the truth of the abuse, I explored the thought that there was nothing to forgive. Perhaps I chose the experience of being so deeply wounded by the narcissist to regain access to the past wounds that I'd so carefully hidden away. This allowed me to acknowledge, heal, and release them, setting myself free to create a new reality...and write this book.

Today, I will explore and honor where I am in my journey of forgiveness. I will accept, without judgment, that I am exactly where I'm meant to be.

December 16

Court Action With the Narcissist

Going to court with the narcissist, especially when we've initiated the legal proceedings or it involves our children, may painfully reopen our deep inner wounds. Therefore, it's essential to have adequate support during the process. This could include an attorney who understands or is willing to learn about narcissistic abuse, as well as qualified healing professionals to help us process our emotions and release trauma from our body as it comes to the surface.

It's important to document, in detail, every instance of the narcissist's inappropriate behavior. It can also be helpful to refuse any undocumented communication with the narcissist, using only text, e-mail, parenting apps, or communication through a neutral third party.

Using the word "narcissist" in court often works against us, as we're not in a position to make that diagnosis. Instead, we can document and report the abusive behaviors of the narcissist.

Remaining impersonal when communication with the narcissist is required and refusing to address anything that doesn't directly involve the business at hand is critical for our own self-care.

Standing up against the narcissist in court may well be one of the most difficult things we'll ever do, but it has the potential to help us uncover our strength, find our voice, and empty ourselves of the past at a depth that little else could.

Today, I will create a strong support system around me. I will have compassion for myself, knowing I'm doing my best, and I will remember that this challenging time will not last forever.

December 17

Obligation vs. Opportunity

I have to versus I get to.

When we do things out of obligation, we feel bound to do something that we don't want to do or that isn't right for us. This often leaves us feeling depleted and frustrated. Many of us acted out of obligation when we were with the narcissist. We did things to please them that opposed our values, and we were filled with resentment afterwards for having abandoned ourselves.

When we find ourselves acting out of obligation, it's important to explore what's behind our need to do so. With the narcissist, we often did things we weren't comfortable with to avoid abandonment and prevent their intense shaming reactions. Once we understand our motivation, we can look for healthier ways to meet our needs.

There are ways we can shift feelings of obligation. We can set boundaries, no longer allowing ourselves to do things that go against our values and needs—especially those things that hurt us—prioritizing our self-care instead. We can sometimes turn an obligation into an opportunity. If we must work but dislike our current job, we can find employment that lights us up instead. When we have obligations we can't release, we may be able to reframe them as opportunities, finding the gifts in them.

Today, I will determine the things in my life that I'm doing out of obligation. I will explore what is motivating my actions. Then, I will look for loving ways to either turn them into opportunities or let them go.

December 18

Detachment

In 12-Step programs of recovery, like Al-Anon and Co-Dependents Anonymous, the word "detach" is used as a powerful acronym—*<u>d</u>on't <u>e</u>ven <u>t</u>hink <u>a</u>bout <u>c</u>hanging <u>h</u>im/<u>h</u>er*.

In a healthy intimate relationship, we connect with another person and take the time to explore them exactly as they are. We then have the necessary information to decide whether they're a fit for us, respecting our own needs and boundaries in the process.

We dove right into a relationship with the narcissist. They manipulated us with their love bombing, which moved things along quickly. We believed they were perfect for us and saw no need to give our relationship more time.

From the beginning, the narcissist tried to change nearly everything about us. It was subtle at first, but eventually left us reeling, unsure of who we were and in tremendous pain.

We empower ourselves when we recognize the ways in which we tried to change the narcissist, something we were often not even aware we were doing. Seeing our own behavior leads to true healing within us. We didn't do anything wrong by trying to change the narcissist. It led us to the wonderful thing we are doing now—looking deep inside for our own answers to set ourselves free.

Today, I will contemplate the things I wanted to change about the narcissist, acknowledging what they did that normally would have made me turn and walk (run) away. In the future, I will practice seeing things exactly as they are instead of how I want them to be.

December 19

Improving Ourselves

Society pushes us to constantly improve ourselves. We're told we must be more fit, look younger, grow smarter, and be healthier. When we were with the narcissist, we put even more effort into bettering ourselves. We worked tirelessly to meet their standards so we weren't replaced with someone new.

Finding our authentic self is the best improvement we can make–because we're the best we can be when we're fully ourselves. When we look beyond everything we're not—our past wounds, our limiting patterns, and the lies we were told about ourselves—we shine like the sun as we uncover the magnificence of who we are. And, ironically, when we live according to our truth, our body and mind often "improve," coming into alignment with an updated version of ourselves.

Close your eyes and take a few deep breaths. Just imagine that prior to your birth, in partnership with Source, you planned to look exactly as you do right now and be who you are in this moment. Consider that you made this choice for reasons you may not be aware of at this time. See everything about you as perfect. Every line and every curve is exactly as it was designed to be, to support you in accomplishing what you came here to do. Divine perfection!

Today, I will love and accept myself exactly as I am. If I can't do this for an entire day, I will try it for an hour, or even five minutes.

December 20

Time

Time is a valuable resource in our lives. During our relationship with the narcissist, we were at the mercy of their needs and desires. Their actions and expectations often showed us that our time had no value.

Our perception of time can help us understand our internal state more clearly. On days when we're in our soul's flow, time may seem to slow down, as if there is plenty of it to accomplish everything we want and need to. When we're experiencing inner chaos, turmoil, or overwhelm, time seems to fly by as if there will never be enough to finish what we must.

Our time is a precious gift. There is a finite amount of it available to us every day, and we have the right to decide how we want to spend it. We can set boundaries to ensure that our time is invested wisely, in ways that support us.

Imagine that we're eighty years old and we're looking back at our lives. Will we be content with how we've spent our time? What can we do with the rest of our time so that we'll be happy and at peace with how we've spent it?

Today, as I'm pondering thoughts about respecting my time, I will examine how I've spent it in the past. If I desire to change anything, I will go ahead and make those changes now.

December 21

Winter

For some, winter is a quiet time of year when things around us are dormant and we are guided inward to rest and revitalize. Daylight fades early, life slows down, and we have more time to spend in the stillness of our heart.

For others, winter is a difficult time of year. Many of us are affected by the lack of sunshine and isolation of being indoors, which can wreak havoc on our mental and emotional health. For survivors of narcissistic abuse, being guided inward can be a painful and scary experience as we work to survive our recent wounds and those of the past. It can be especially challenging during the holidays, when we're alone without the narcissist.

We can redefine winter as a nourishing state of being that we can access at any time. Quiet. Cozy. Soft. Gentle. Slow. Loving. Safe. Warm. A season when we put ourselves first and carve out extra time in our day to rest and be still. We can visualize it as an internal space in our imagination, full of comforting, nurturing energy that allows us to slow down safely. No matter the time of year, we can access this rejuvenating experience of winter.

What does your experience of winter look like? Does it involve snow? Candles? A warm fire dancing in the fireplace? Perhaps being wrapped in a cozy blanket while you sip hot tea? Magical energy surrounding you? You get to decide!

Today, I will determine what is nourishing to me, and I'll create a sacred, inner winter space for myself.

December 22

Intimacy

We can break down the word intimacy as "into-me-see." Intimacy becomes possible when we feel safe enough with another person to be who we truly are. In an intimate partnership, intimacy means feeling safe to be seen naked at all levels.

Unfortunately, the relationship with the narcissist did not include intimacy, though we didn't realize that at first. A narcissist is incapable of intimacy and avoids it at all costs because they have rejected and exiled their vulnerable, real selves. Instead, they created a false self for survival purposes—not believing their true self was capable of getting their needs met. As a result, they are unable to connect with their inner selves and experience intimacy.

To be intimate with someone, we must first be able to be intimate with ourselves. Then we can bring the wonderful, messy, exquisite truth of who we are to other people. Miracles happen and a new life unfolds when we become intimate with all parts of ourselves.

We are magical, wondrous beings at our core, and when we're ready, it's okay to dive in!

Today, I will take time to connect with myself in whatever way feels right. I will let the cares and distractions of the world around me go for a moment and explore my inner terrain, creating intimacy with my marvelous, multi-faceted self.

December 23

Judgment

Some people believe that we can never truly know another person's path—or the lessons and experiences they chose for their evolution. That knowledge is held between their soul and Source. From this perspective, we're judging others when we have our own ideas about how they should live their lives.

Many of us have been judged by people who have never experienced narcissistic abuse for having been seduced by the narcissist and for being unable to get over them in a timely fashion.

Without minimizing our painful experience with the narcissist, we did gain invaluable awareness from our relationship. We learned where our boundaries needed to be stronger, discovered our true selves, and created the opportunity to finally heal our past.

Were those judging us correct? Did we make a mistake and blow up our lives? Or did we have experiences that could ultimately bring us back home to ourselves?

When we look at something through the eyes of an observer, we set aside judgment and open ourselves to a more expansive view, seeing things we may have missed when we judged. We can do the same with other people—observing them and their lives instead of judging, and trusting that they're on the path that's right for them.

Today, I will explore my judgment of others from a different perspective, observing and becoming curious instead, learning all I can in the process.

December 24

Giving

Sometimes, giving can feel wonderful. Seeing the surprise on someone's face when we give them a gift or experiencing their gratitude for simply being present with them when they need support can warm our hearts.

At other times, giving can feel like a heavy obligation. We may feel resentful when we give, especially when there never seems to be enough for us. Our resentment can be an invitation to go inside and explore. How much are we giving to ourselves and receiving from others? How does that compare with what we're giving?

Many of us aren't comfortable receiving because it makes us feel vulnerable. Perhaps we learned that we couldn't trust gifts in the past because they came with a price attached. Or we believed the lies we were told about ourselves and felt unworthy of receiving them.

To get comfortable with receiving, we can start by giving to ourselves. We can also begin to allow Source to fill us with love, peace, and joy. Then, we'll always have enough to give when we choose to do so.

The narcissist gave with expectations and an agenda—to get. In the beginning, they appeared selfless. As the relationship progressed, they reduced their giving to crumbs. In response, we tried to make the relationship succeed by continually giving more—until we were empty.

Today, I will look inside at how it feels for me to give and to receive, asking Source to guide me if either is difficult.

December 25

Holidays

For some of us, holidays seemed enjoyable with the narcissist. After the relationship ended, many of us felt especially sad or vulnerable at those times.

For others, holidays with the narcissist may have been a living hell. They may have created chaos and drama to take the focus off of the holiday celebration and put it back onto them, doing cruel things to sabotage and ruin this time for us.

Almost a year after their toxic relationship ended, one survivor began to lament about not being with the narcissist at Thanksgiving. That was until they took a moment to remember how the holiday had gone. In the past, it had always been a time of rest and sacred connection. After meeting the narcissist, it turned into a shallow, hollow experience that the survivor didn't enjoy at all. In an effort to avoid abandonment, the survivor had followed along as the narcissist redefined even their holidays.

It is vital to explore and honor all of our feelings. It's also important to look at the reality of our experience and remember the actual events that took place.

Today, I will take time to reflect on how I prefer to celebrate holidays. If I am having a difficult time getting through them, I will branch out and do something new. Perhaps I will start a new tradition or reach out to someone I care about. I will also remember that not every holiday will be this uncomfortable as I heal and continue moving forward with my life.

December 26

Body Awareness

Our body is truly a miracle, created by Source to house our soul during our time on this planet. It's awe-inspiring to contemplate how everything is interconnected and orchestrated, working together in perfect harmony. How does our heart know to keep beating? How do we maintain the rhythm of our breath? The entire design is genius!

In addition to how miraculously it functions, our body remembers. It stores our physical, mental, and emotional wounds until we are ready to acknowledge, heal, and release them. Our body also holds our fragmented inner children, silenced by unbearable trauma and stuck at the moment of impact, waiting to be heard, loved, and known.

We can take a moment to breathe and scan our body from head to toe, slowly and thoughtfully. Are there aches that we normally ignore? Do some areas feel numb or isolated from the rest? What do they have to say? Are there areas of our body that we avoid? There's no right or wrong way to be. We can just observe what's happening. We can love our body and ourselves exactly as we are.

If intense feelings or sensations arise when we connect with our body, it's important to seek support—whether from a doctor, psychologist, counselor, body worker, energy worker, or even Mother Nature.

Today, I will honor my body, acknowledging the incredible gift that it is. I will practice listening to what it has to say and giving it the support it needs.

December 27

Generous Love

When our relationship with the narcissist began, we craved their bold "love." After the seduction period, we found ourselves wondering if that "love" was also being given to someone else. It stung when the narcissist shut us out and withheld it from us. It frightened us when there was less and less of it, so we worked harder to earn it.

When the narcissist held us in their "love," it was like being warmed by a blazing fire, and when they withdrew it, it was the coldest place on Earth.

Eventually, we saw the truth. What the narcissist professed as "love" was actually control. It came with an agenda and a price. The "love" they gave to us caused pain to someone else who craved and lost it—just as the "love" they gave to others during and after our relationship was withdrawn from us, causing us great pain.

Generous love is reliable, trustworthy, respectful, grounded, and soothing—and there is more than enough of it to go around. Someone who is capable of giving real love makes us feel safe and like we're part of a trusted team. When we love ourselves generously, we repel narcissists and attract healthier people into our lives.

Today, I will connect with my heart and contemplate what generous love means to me. If I'm unsure, I will ask Source to provide examples of it around in my life.

December 28

Narcissistic People Are Everywhere

As we pull ourselves out of our outdated survival patterns, heal the wounds that made us susceptible to narcissistic abuse, and set boundaries according to our needs and values, we establish beneficial lifelong skills. We will find people with varying degrees of narcissistic personality traits everywhere we go, ranging from simply being arrogant to having diagnosable narcissistic personality disorder.

Narcissistic people can be found in highly visible roles and positions. They can be movie stars, radio or television personalities, politicians, and world leaders. We can also meet them closer to home in our own community. They may be counselors, priests, school board members, non-profit employees, or grocery store sales clerks. We may also find them in our places of employment in the role of our boss or co-worker.

Once we understand a narcissist's needs, agendas, and their patterns of abuse, we become much better at interacting with them impersonally, without becoming physically, mentally, emotionally, or energetically entangled with them. When our intellect or our intuition throws up a red flag, we can maintain firm boundaries and even walk away if necessary.

We can be proud of ourselves for our efforts to create a solid foundation within ourselves, which allows us to stand strong in our interactions with narcissistic people.

Today, I will keep my eyes open for opportunities to use my awareness and self-care skills in my interactions with others. I will acknowledge the confidence I've gained, a result of my hard work and commitment to myself.

December 29

Gratitude

Being grateful has the power to transform our thoughts and feelings. When we experience gratitude, we are directly connected to our hearts and to Source. The habit and practice of gratitude can change our lives as we merge with the energy of abundance.

How do we practice gratitude?

We can start a gratitude journal, dedicating time each day to contemplate and write about five or more things we're grateful for. Is it the fluffy socks that you love to wear? Your children? Your job? Or the beautiful blue sky?

As we commit to this practice, we can observe the changes we see and feel—inside and out.

Another way to practice gratitude is to tell the people we love that we're grateful for them and why. Most importantly, we can acknowledge the gratitude we have for ourselves, recognizing the strengths and gifts that each of our inner children and our adult self bring to our life.

Today, I will begin my journey by creating my own gratitude practice and making it a special part of my day.

December 30

Healing Phases

Healing from narcissistic abuse is a process that happens over time. It's less of a linear process and more like a dance as we take steps forward and back.

In the earliest phases after the end of our relationship, we were in survival mode, sometimes unable to even meet our basic needs. Devastated, we experienced rage, numbness, and everything in between. Exhausted and even physically ill, we weren't sure if we'd make it through the pain we felt inside, but we kept going.

In the middle phases, we established a new flow in our lives. Triggers still affected us, but we had a growing sense of stability and peace as we worked to heal our inner wounds. Our anger and resentment toward the narcissist lessened and was replaced by a consistent focus on our self-care and healing. We claimed the new life that was unfolding within us, and it was easier to keep moving forward.

In the later phases, we started to see the gifts of our experience with the narcissist. We felt mostly neutral, caring about them as a human being while recognizing the destruction they brought. We were deeply committed to ourselves and able to maintain clear boundaries as our spirit soared.

Finally, one day, we knew our work with the narcissist was complete. We'd forgiven them, and most importantly, we'd forgiven ourselves. We felt gratitude for the depth of healing and transformation we had accomplished because of our experience with them, and wished them well from afar.

Today, I will keep going no matter what phase I'm in.

December 31

Celebrate

In some countries, the eve of December 31st is known as "Old Year's Night." It is celebrated by cleaning and decorating the house in preparation for bidding the old year farewell through the back door and welcoming the new year in through the front.

Today is a day to check in with ourselves and celebrate the fact that we made it through a different kind of year. We fell and we got back up. We hurt, we learned, we healed, we released, and we kept going when it seemed impossible. We had experiences that shaped us, challenged us, and taught us much about ourselves and the world around us.

If we are ever in doubt about ourselves, we only have to turn around and look behind us at everything we've walked through. We can be proud of ourselves and recognize our progress.

Today, I will review the past year while wrapping myself in pure, golden love. I will acknowledge and not judge. I will think about what I want to celebrate and what was challenging for me. I will acknowledge and be grateful for the gifts of the past year. I will honor all of it and then let it go, making room for a new year and a new adventure. I will then reflect on the blank canvas before me and decide what I'd like to create and how I will love and support myself in the new year.

Conclusion

Kudos to you for committing your time and energy to this sacred, year-long journey into yourself!

Now is a great time to look back on where you were 365 days ago. Acknowledge how far you've come and all that you've walked through on this powerful healing journey. Recognize yourself for the courage it took to be vulnerable enough to look inside for your answers, which also meant facing the pain that awaited your presence and love.

Healing is a journey that takes place over the course of our lives, filled with self-discovery and a shedding of the past. It is by choosing to take this journey that we get to create a new ending to our story, not the default ending predetermined by our past. By making the choice to heal, we change the future for ourselves and others.

I hope that *Brave Love 365* has been a nourishing, effective tool for you and that it will continue to be a resource long after the first 365 days.

For inspiration, author updates, and advance notice of my new offerings, please sign up for my mailing list on my website: **www.erikanelson.com**

Your reviews are important as they help other readers discover books they like. If you've found value in this book, please consider leaving a short review on Amazon.com. It means a lot and would be much appreciated.

Stay connected with me by joining me on social media.

Facebook: @authorerikanelson
Instagram: @authorerikanelson
Twitter: @authorerikanels
LinkedIn: Erika Nelson, MAC

Thank you for changing the world by giving yourself the gift of Brave Love.

About the Author

Erika Nelson is a mental health counselor in private practice with a focus on trauma and PTSD. She earned Bachelor of Science Degrees in Psychology and Human Development and a Master of Arts Degree in Counseling. She has several upcoming books and educational programming in development—all to assist others in healing from narcissistic abuse and toxic relationships. She is also a survivor of many things, her early history of trauma shaping her life's purpose of helping others heal from the things we don't talk about.

Through her personal and professional experience, Erika has found that our greatest pain is our most powerful medicine. She believes that each of us realizing our absolute, inherent worthiness of love would change the world, and she is committed to sharing that message through her words.

To learn more about Erika Nelson and her work, visit:

www.erikanelson.com

Acknowledgements

As they say, *it takes a village*. I am incredibly grateful for my village. It was a transformational experience writing this book and bringing it to fruition with such wonderful support.

I smiled to myself one day, realizing that in addition to discussing topics like research, evidence-based therapies, narcissists, and abuse, it was also normal in the creation of this book to discuss topics like authenticity, spirit guides, energy, soul magic, intuition, and love. I count myself blessed to have worked with this talented team.

Thank you to my editor, Jennifer Kosh of Love Matters. I'm grateful for the space of love and commitment that you held while I birthed this book into existence. Your support and encouragement as I wrote kept me going when I didn't think I could write the words *narcissistic abuse* one more time. Your grasp of the big picture and attention to the intricate details were so important to this book.

Thank you to my book designer/editor, Anna Frolik of Wonderland Publishing, for everything from the vibrant, spirited cover design to the gentle, nurturing interior pages that feel "just right." Your thoughtful final edits made everything flow. Thanks for your hard work as well as the love and magic you brought to the process.

Thank you to Tina Baeten of Baeten Counseling and Consultation Team for your uplifting encouragement, support, realness, humor, counseling expertise, and helpful feedback. You've been an inspiration since the moment I sat down in your "Introduction to Counseling" class. I'm grateful our paths have crossed and that you are part of my journey.

Thank you to my amazing, dynamic family. You are my heart. You make every day a beautiful day of learning and love. I'm so grateful for you all and for your patience with the oft barren refrigerator, dust bunnies, and dirty dishes that accumulated during the final push of this book, not to mention the many sticky notes that continuously grace the living room walls. I love you dearly!!

Thank you to my amazing, indomitable sisters Antonia, Melissa, and Lisa—who have known me since I took my first breath. I know that you'll always be there, as I will for you, and that means the world to me. I cherish our porch parties...and of course, cake. Thank you for your encouragement and excitement about my book. And Lisa, thanks for answering my many what's-the-word-I'm-looking-for calls.

Thank you to Hélène, Lizzie, Cyndee, Kate, Shannon, and Laura for being part of my foundation. It's a sacred thing having you all as dear friends for so long. Thanks for being there for a laugh, a cry, an expansive conversation, or constructive feedback on my newest idea or page of writing.

Thank you to Monica for being my mystical friend. Without you, this book would not exist. Thanks for your steadfast support as I lived out my lessons and healed from them so I could bring *Brave Love 365* into the world.

Thank you to Theresa for helping me land and find my feet after narcissistic abuse. And for your awesome feedback on this and my other books in the works. Most of all, thank you for sharing your wild and free spirit with me and for all the laughs and wonderful conversations we have!

Thank you to all the people on social media and in my life who shared their stories and offered their support and encouragement as I wrote *Brave Love 365*. Your excitement for the progress of this book and the heart-felt gratitude you expressed for my writing of it were the fuel that kept me moving forward.

Thank you to Sam for being my big-hearted, curly-haired angel and for being with me every step of the way. Thanks for laughing at and with me to keep me from taking life too seriously. Most of all, thanks for sharing your warm love with me.

Finally, thank you to Source (in all your forms!), for giving me the fortitude to keep going and for carrying me when I truly didn't possess the strength to get through all that was happening around me so many years ago. Thank you for inspiring me every day and for providing me with the energy and inspiration I need to continue bringing the words in my heart to the world.

♥

Resources

Crisis Resources

The following are supportive resources to assist you on your journey of healing from narcissistic abuse and toxic relationships. Some of these resources may resonate for you, while others may not. Please trust your own inner wisdom to guide you in choosing those that support you and in setting aside those that don't.

National Domestic Violence Hotline
Phone: (800) 799-SAFE (7233)
Text START to 88788
Chat: www.thehotline.org/get-help/

Crisis Text Line
Text HOME to 741741 to connect with a crisis counselor.

National Suicide Prevention Lifeline
Phone: Dial 988 or (800) 273-TALK (8255)
Chat: www.suicidepreventionlifeline.org/chat/

Local Options
If you're in crisis, you can also call 911 or go to the nearest hospital Emergency Room.

12-Step Programs

Al-Anon Family Groups
Support for family and friends of alcoholics
Website: al-anon.org
Phone: (888) 425-2666

Co-Dependents Anonymous
A program of recovery from co-dependency
Website: coda.org
Phone: (888) 444-2359

Adult Children of Alcoholics & Dysfunctional Families
A program for support and recovery for people who grew up in dysfunctional homes
Website: adultchildren.org
Phone: (310) 534-1815

Post-Traumatic Stress Disorder (PTSD)

National Center For PTSD
Research, education and support for PTSD and toxic stress
Website: www.ptsd.va.gov/index.asp

C-PTSD Foundation
Compassionate support, skills, and trauma-informed education for complex trauma survivors
Website: www.cptsdfoundation.org

Parenting Apps

These are several of the available parenting apps that some have found helpful. Please use them as a place to start in researching the right one for you and your family.

Our Family Wizard
Website: ourfamilywizard.com

WeParent
Website: weparent.app

2Houses
Website: 2houses.com

Books

The following books may be helpful in your recovery from narcissistic abuse.

Trauma
Complex PTSD: From Surviving to Thriving by Pete Walker, M.A.

No Bad Parts: Healing Trauma & Restoring Wholeness with the Internal Family Systems Model by Richard C. Schwartz, Ph.D.

The Body Keeps the Score: Brain, Mind, and Body in the Healing of Trauma by Bessel van der Kolk, M.D.

The Complex PTSD Workbook: A Mind-Body Approach to Regaining Emotional Control & Becoming Whole by Arielle Schwartz, Ph.D.

Waking the Tiger: Healing Trauma by Peter A. Levine, Ph.D. with Ann Frederick

What Happened to You?: Conversations on Trauma, Resilience, and Healing by Bruce D. Perry, M.D., Ph.D. and Oprah Winfrey

Co-Dependency
Codependent No More: How to Stop Controlling Others and Start Caring for Yourself by Melody Beattie

Narcissistic Abuse
Malignant Self-Love: Narcissism Revisited by Sam Vaknin

Highly Sensitive People/Empaths
Highly Sensitive Empaths: The Complete Survival Guide to Self-Discovery, Protection from Narcissists and Energy Vampires, and Developing the Empath Gift by J. Vandeweghe

(Online, www.HighlySensitiveRefuge.com is a great healing resource.)

Self-Care
The Gifts of Imperfection: Let Go of Who You Think You're Supposed to Be and Embrace Who You Are by Brené Brown, Ph.D., M.S.W.

Index

A

Abandonment 17, 37, 61, 83, 93, 101, 111, 196, 213, 214, 218, 235, 269, 275, 277, 298, 364
Abuse, Emotional 95
Abuse, Physical 58, 95, 117, 167, 178
Abuse, Psychological 83, 95, 177
Abuse Amnesia 209
Accountability 322
Acts of Service 309
Addiction 12, 169, 182, 203, 214, 260, 303
Aftershock 8, 42, 271
All-or-Nothing Thinking 266
Anger 19, 38, 143, 249
Anniversaries 180, 341
Anxiety 48, 89, 91, 129, 160, 192, 292, 310
Apologizing 45, 252
Are They Really a Narcissist? 39
Armor 230, 269
Asking for Help 148
Attachment 152
Authentic Self 20, 44, 139, 207, 226, 347, 369
Autonomy 216, 270, 306, 352
Awareness 18, 61

B

Baby Steps 271
Basic Needs 1, 10, 237
Being Alone 168
Belonging to Ourselves 108, 327
Betrayal 17, 33, 37, 74, 314
Blindsided 74

Body Awareness 376
Boundaries 22, 25, 60, 93, 114, 136, 142, 147, 155, 164, 172, 181, 187, 216, 223, 244, 256, 290, 294, 310, 316, 339, 353
Brain Chemicals 8, 12, 169, 203, 303
Brainspotting 49, 50, 167
Bullshit Standard 238, 239, 249
Burden 100, 267

C

Capacity 215
Caretaking 131, 208, 252
Change 26, 57, 279
Choices 5, 335
Circular Arguments 156
Codependency 63, 131, 175, 255, 256, 257, 258
Cognitive Dissonance 248
Commitment 263, 273
Communication 25, 55, 72, 173, 204, 217, 256
Comparing 221
Conditions 283
Confusion 91, 177, 331
Control 64, 178, 239, 246, 255, 257, 283, 288, 290, 301, 308, 377
Convincing 270
Coping Mechanisms 31, 129, 209
Costs of Narcissistic Abuse 219
Courage 242, 310
Court Proceedings 4, 25, 366
Cravings 180
Crazy 24, 45, 76, 83, 131, 143, 177
Creating a Solid Foundation 14, 153, 166, 219, 225, 264, 315, 319, 354, 378
Crisis as Opportunity 149
Criticism 116
Crumbs 56, 107, 113, 337

D

Daily Practices 200, 259
Dating 132, 136, 164, 172, 181, 224, 265, 294, 314, 327, 352, 353, 354, 355
Debt 334
Decisions 243
Denial 345
Depression 49, 89, 148, 160, 310
Detachment 29, 368
Devaluation Phase 7, 35, 66, 226, 234, 317, 336
Devotion 316, 327
Discard Phase 7, 36
Discretion 4, 366
Disengaging from the Narcissist 28, 52, 159, 351
Dissociation 31, 198
Distractions 260, 312
Divine Timing 166
Doing Nothing 42
Domestic Violence 58, 95, 117, 133
Dreams 75, 180

E

EMDR 49, 50
Embodiment 142
Emotional Reasoning 266
Emotions 73, 103, 112
Empaths 146, 164, 183, 191, 192, 193, 194, 195, 196, 215, 342
Empathy 16, 67, 296
Empowerment 181, 258, 270, 311, 325, 356, 368
Enabling 175
Energy 18, 87, 115, 119, 137, 162, 187, 223, 259, 287, 297, 307, 308, 314, 317, 326, 334
Excitement 233, 319
Exhaustion 87, 186, 213, 215, 271, 312

Expectations 150, 224, 235, 249, 339
Expertise 251
External Validation 112, 168, 170, 267, 274
Eyes Wide Shut 338

F

Facing Our Past 227
Faith 357
False Self 30, 154, 226
Fear 99, 103, 129, 173, 288, 298, 310
Feeling Lost 210
Fight, Flight, Freeze, Fawn 98, 186
Finding Our Voice 228, 260
Finding the Gifts 264, 313, 356, 380
Fixing the Narcissist 41
Flying Monkeys 159, 260
Food 1, 77, 173, 230
Forgiveness 176, 365, 380
Freedom to Exist 29, 306, 327, 348
Fun 202

G

Gaslighting 66, 177, 178, 224, 282
Gentleness 54
Getting Sucked in by the Narcissist 99, 151
Giving 374
God Box 236
God Moments 343
Grace 184
Gratitude 309, 379
Gray Rock 55
Grief 268, 295, 351
Grooming 59, 165, 348
Grounding 18, 198

Guilt 146

H

Hard Work 242
Harem 13, 23
Hate 162
Healing Phases 380
Healing Tools 18, 50, 69, 78, 97, 122, 129, 137, 143, 198, 200, 236, 250, 260, 310, 319, 376
Health Concerns 67, 219
Healthy Relationships 53, 136, 240, 353, 354, 368
Highly Sensitive Person 146, 191, 192, 193, 194, 195, 196, 215, 338, 342
Holidays 371, 375, 381
Honesty 16, 246
Honoring Ourselves 305
Hoovering 36, 144
Hope 280
Humility 315
Humor 332
Hurt People Hurt People 253
Hypervigilance 194, 212, 290, 304

I

I WILL NOT CALL List 13, 97
Idealization 7, 33, 89, 234, 359
Identifying Narcissists 355
Illusions 106, 113, 239, 305
Image 247
Improving Ourselves 369
Inappropriate Behavior 95, 147
Independence 163, 211
Inner Authority 238, 362
Inner Children 15, 26, 47, 51, 77, 107, 109, 111, 140, 141, 151, 153, 162, 173, 201, 202, 204, 205, 237, 243, 255, 265, 268, 269, 281, 301, 304, 310, 333, 355,

365, 376
Inner Cues 281
Inner Resources 24, 87, 287
Inner Sparkle 86, 119, 121, 295, 307
Inner Wisdom 71, 97, 251, 262, 323, 360, 362
Inner Work 78, 182, 291
Inner Wounds 44
Innocence 141, 244
Insanity 330
Integrity 231
Intensity 188
Intention 321
Intermittent Reinforcement 56
Intimacy 99, 120, 127, 132, 164, 224, 353, 372
Intuition 78, 166, 227, 243, 340
Isolation 35, 43, 51, 104, 161

J

Jealousy 232
Jesus 27
Journaling 200, 300, 379
Joy 86, 244, 332
Judgment 37, 92, 116, 298, 322, 323, 373
Justifications 299

L

Leaving a Toxic Relationship 133
Legal Action With the Narcissist 4, 25, 130, 134, 138, 159, 310, 334, 366
Lessons 320
Letting Go 106, 236
Limiting Beliefs 292
Listening 329
Living Above Our Lives 27
Living Deeply 273

Loss 57
Love 46, 243, 244, 265, 316, 352, 363, 377
Love Bombing 33, 34, 66, 68, 169, 317, 336
Lying 159, 261

M

Manipulation 17, 35, 56, 66, 72, 91, 111, 144, 246, 257, 274, 316, 358
Masks 207, 226
Meditation 206
Men as Victims of Narcissistic Abuse 249
Mental Filtering 245, 266
Mindfuckery 248, 282, 331
Minimization 266, 336
Miracles 82, 123, 227, 244, 279, 361, 376
Modified Contact 25, 203
Money 130, 219, 334

N

Narcissistic Abuse
    Ambient 24
    Awareness of 3, 161
    Cycle 7, 145
    Tactics 66, 156, 252, 282, 358
Narcissist and Empath Connection 183
Narcissist as Victim 145, 146, 159, 252, 253
Narcissistic
    Injury 154
    People Are Everywhere 161, 378
    Rage 38, 74
    Supply 6, 23, 28, 35, 36, 120, 156, 157, 174, 221, 226, 283, 287, 302, 303, 308, 325
    Traits 65
Narcissist's Truths 30, 81, 96, 154, 157, 308
Narcissist's Vortex 13, 14, 58, 75, 145, 151, 278

Nature 229, 317
Needing a Fallback Person 157
Needs 31, 100, 114, 170, 201, 217, 256, 345
New Beginnings 199
New Life 90, 123, 295
Nightmares 75
No Contact 13, 19, 30, 42, 79, 106, 110, 151, 153, 169, 176, 203, 248, 253
Nurturing 208

O

Obsessive Research About Narcissism 80, 291
Obsessive Thoughts 180
Obedience 275
Objectification 120, 215, 267
Obligation 100, 114, 367, 374
Our Soul's Truth 326, 328, 342, 344, 360, 361, 364, 369, 373
Our True Source 9, 135
Overgiving 240
Overwhelm 128, 237, 271, 273, 335

P

PTSD/C-PTSD 23, 31, 48, 89, 103, 152, 160, 324
Pain 10, 11, 12, 24, 28, 234, 275, 291, 302, 341
Paradoxes 359
Parenting With a Narcissist 4, 25, 138, 163
Participation 264
Passion 119, 247, 317
Past Lives 220, 340, 346
Pause 79
Peace 128, 206, 241, 293, 321, 361
People-Pleasing 213
Perception 297, 323
Perfectionism 239
Persecution 110, 220

Personalization 266, 324

Playing With Fire 214

Possessiveness 140

Presence 18, 219, 241, 296, 329

Pressure 57, 89, 185, 191, 224, 239

Projection 66

Protection 26, 168, 230, 304, 337

Power 17, 92, 270, 306, 308, 317, 361

R

Random Acts of Kindness 272

Re-Grieving 268

Reacting vs. Responding 325

Reaction vs. Curiosity 112

Reclaiming Our Own Life 170

Red Flags 53, 117, 118, 172, 261, 280, 294, 336, 338, 355

Reflections 284

Refusing to Engage 21, 52

Relapse 19, 151, 311

Release 69

Relief 234, 303

Repelling Narcissists 164

Resentment 155, 180, 256, 348, 374

Respecting Ourselves 102

Responsibility 105, 175, 252, 257

Retraumatization 212

Revenge 28, 59

Rigidity 288

Risk 277

Room to Exist 40, 170, 211, 237, 249

S

Sacrifice 218

Safety 1, 4, 11, 30, 55, 58, 133, 151, 214, 337

Sarcasm 294

Saying No 60

Seasons of Healing 82, 179, 276, 289, 371

Secrets 59, 165

Seduction 68, 171

Self-Abandonment 131, 143, 184, 185, 364

Self-Acceptance 26, 54, 108, 184, 311, 322

Self-Care 21, 26, 93, 124, 164, 186, 193, 197, 200, 206, 214, 223, 260, 294, 309, 312, 322, 341

Self-Esteem 309, 328

Self-Expression 344

Self-Love 26, 102, 108, 208, 300, 311

Self-Protection 98, 127

Self-Righteousness 92

Self-Sabotage 110, 278

Self-Trust 251, 314, 323, 335

Serenity 182

Setting the Bar 339

Sex 89, 120, 167, 224, 267, 277, 283

Shame 19, 37, 88, 103, 231, 238, 253, 302, 306, 311

Shutting Down 40, 72, 185, 301

Simplicity 259

Sleep 1, 75

Smear Campaigns 76, 123, 236

Sobriety 203, 260

Social Media 260

Soul Magic 124, 272, 317, 326

Spiritual Perspectives 264, 320, 340, 346, 365

Strength 96, 242, 310

Stockholm Syndrome 84

Stonewalling 66, 72

Strength 163, 317

Suicide/Self-Harm 11, 58, 160

Support 2, 8, 37, 43, 49, 50, 76, 104, 133, 148, 160, 212, 242, 258, 319

Surrender 63, 64, 236, 361, 366

Survival 31, 70, 98, 101, 171, 185, 186, 194, 230, 235, 239, 240, 255, 261, 273, 275, 290, 304, 324, 329, 330, 380

T

Taking Action 134, 243

Tethers 29

Thought Patterns 122, 245, 248, 266, 324, 336

Time 187, 370

Transforming Self-Judgment 298

Transparency 306

Trauma Bond 8, 12, 19, 20, 56, 84, 176, 214, 234, 271, 279, 303

Trauma Symptoms 31, 48, 89, 160

Trauma Triggers 79, 159, 197, 198

Triangulation 17, 23, 66, 221, 232, 282

Trusting 236, 314

Twelve-Step Programs 8, 63, 368

U

Unavailability 132, 152

Unconditional Love 265

Unseen Support 135

V

Validation 250

Values 22, 93, 225, 353

Victim, Being a 39, 85, 313

Victim to Witness 313

Vulnerability 74, 127, 165, 223, 308

W

Walking on Eggshells 38, 146, 234

We Cannot Think Our Way to Healing 291

We're Not Broken 24, 342

Wholeness 70,
Will 153
Willingness 10, 20, 155, 263
Winning the Inner Battle 107
Words 278
Worry 129, 236
Worthiness 121

Y

Yellow Flags 118, 172